Cost Controls
for Industry
Second Edition

Other books by the author:

PROFILE FOR PROFITABILITY: Using Cost Control and Profitability Analysis

HOW TO IMPROVE PROFITABILITY THROUGH MORE EFFECTIVE PLANNING

Cost Controls
for Industry

Second Edition

Thomas S. Dudick

Prentice-Hall, Inc, Englewood Cliffs, N.J.

Prentice-Hall International, Inc., *London*
Prentice-Hall of Australia, Pty. Ltd., *Sydney*
Prentice-Hall of Canada, Ltd., *Toronto*
Prentice-Hall of India Private Ltd., *New Delhi*
Prentice-Hall of Japan, Inc., *Tokyo*

Library of Congress Cataloging in Publication Data

Dudick, Thomas S
    Cost controls for industry.

    Includes index.
    1. Cost control.   I. Title.
HD47.5.D8 1976   658.1'552   76-2351
ISBN 0-13-181024-3

Printed in the United States of America

To my wife Ann.

About the Author

Thomas S. Dudick is a Manager in the Management Services Division of Ernst and Ernst, New York. He is a graduate of New York University with a MBA from Boston University, as well as recipient of the Ron Hutchison award from *Business Budgeting*. The Budget Executives Institute has awarded him the classification of Fellow for innovative accomplishments in the field of financial planning and control.

The author's background covers more than twenty years of firsthand experience in the installation of control and cost systems. The posts he has held are Manager for Raytheon Company, Budget Director for Allen B. DuMont Laboratories, and Supervisor for Accounting for Sylvania Electric Products.

Mr. Dudick is author of the First Edition of *Cost Controls for Industry*, published by Prentice-Hall, as well as *Profile for Profitability* and *How to Improve Profitability Through More Effective Planning*, published by John Wiley.

The author is Publicity Chairman of the Planning Executives Institute and a frequent speaker at professional societies and trade associations, in addition to serving as guest speaker at Boston University, Loyola and Harvard Business School.

Foreword

One axiom of business is that the most knowledgeable managements are also the most successful in realizing business objectives. In other words, successful management presupposes a high level of awareness and understanding of all of the forces that result in the success or failure of a new business or a product. Much has been written about the influence exerted on the product by the forces of the consumer, the competition, and the technology. But no matter how sophisticated a management may be in marketing and in product technology, unless it knows, and knows with great precision, how much the product costs to make and sell, knowledge in the other areas is largely wasted.

This book explains, first, the need for accurate cost information, and then the methods and procedures that will provide it. The importance of proper allocation of overheads to products is explained, and pitfalls or improper allocations are spelled out. The importance of completely understanding the advantages and disadvantages of various allocation methods is discussed. The book also explains in detail how a cost system, with standards and budgets, can be used to control product costs effectively. Generally, the lowest cost producer of a given product becomes and remains the most profitable. Therefore, proper application of the information offered in this book, together with a keen awareness of the kind of information needed to minimize controllable costs, can provide management with a very important competitive edge.

In addition to providing a mechanism for cost analysis and control, the information gathered provides a basis for formulating sound marketing strategies. Since, as already stated, a marketing program based on incomplete or inaccurate costs is not likely to produce maximum profits, a well-developed cost system is essential to marketing management in developing strategic plans.

Of course, not all of the subjects covered in this book can be applied completely to all production situations. While many costing methods and procedures are explained, Mr. Dudick repeatedly stresses the point that the cost system must be responsive to the needs of the operating people it is expected to serve, and tailored to the operation it is designed to control. In a highly labor intensive operation, for example, labor accountability systems should be stressed. Where direct labor is a relatively small cost a less detailed labor accountability system is required.

Since information only takes on value when it is adequately communicated, many examples of reports are included. These sample reports show the importance of always

7

providing the reader with a base of reference to make the current period figures meaningful: a budget to indicate what was expected; historical figures to indicate a trend; a standard that shows what an item should have cost. In all cases the suggested reports indicate whether operations are better or worse than expected or whether trends are good or bad—the purpose being to draw attention quickly to areas in need of attention.

This book will provide an excellent guide and reference not only for financial people, but also for all members of management interested in efficient and realistic product cost information. Together with complete and specific knowledge of the operation to be controlled, the information provided here will form a basis for developing a complete and responsive cost system for any manufacturing operation.

Herbert H. Egli
Vice President—Finance
and Controller
SCM Corporation
New York, N.Y.

Preface to the Second Edition

This new and expanded work is an encyclopedia of helpful hints on controlling costs in manufacturing companies. It is, in effect, a program of tested answers, supported by case histories of the actual experience of many companies—written in simple and direct language, with many illustrations based on actual figures.

This new edition includes a chapter dealing with the pitfalls in valuing inventories and the reasons for year-end "surprises." It outlines procedures for minimizing these year-end discrepancies. Also included is a chapter on computerizing the cost system. This chapter describes procedures in which the cost system is integrated with production control. It is generously illustrated with exhibits that spell out the particulars of the system. The section on costing rates has been expanded to provide case studies in developing costing rates for a larger range of companies with varying characteristics and sizes.

37 WAYS IN WHICH YOUR COMPANY CAN BECOME MORE PROFITABLE

1. Don't make bookkeepers out of accountants by insisting on too many overhead rates. On the other hand don't be penny-wise and pound-foolish by being overly simplistic. Read Chapter 1 for helpful ways to achieve more realistic product costing.
2. Structure your business plan so it works for you, not vice versa. Chapter 1 tells how the president of a large company used the recommended procedures as a means for developing his business plan on the "Zero-Base Budget" concept.
3. Find out how to recognize situations in which material-based overhead rates fit and don't fit in Chapter 1.
4. Analyze your overhead to find out which five or six accounts make up 75% or more of total overhead. Then find out in Chapter 2 how you fit the industry pattern.

5. Use your payroll register for a simple yet effective control of indirect labor. See Exhibits 2-1 and 2-2 in Chapter 2.

6. Don't use a broad base such as direct labor to allocate indirect expenses to production departments for determining overhead rates. Chapter 2 shows you how it's done (Exhibits 2-1 and 2-2).

7. If it takes you much longer than 30 days to put together a flexible budget you will want to read Chapter 3.

8. Develop a realistic capacity level if you find good forecasts difficult to come by. See how it's done by reading Chapter 3.

9. Don't waste time preparing scatter charts. Chapter 3 illustrates better alternatives.

10. Read Chapter 4 if you want some tips on educating operating personnel on cost behavior and budgetary controls.

11. "Package" the key support data used in developing your flexible budget for management edification. Chapter 4 illustrates the format for such a package.

12. Establish indirect labor budgets on a job-by-job basis to facilitate the "Zero-Base Budget" approach. See the format in Schedule B, Chapter 4.

13. Tie the cost center overhead rates into the flexible budget. Schedules D and E in Chapter 4 show how this is done.

14. Develop the breakeven analysis as an integral part of the flexible budget installation. Schedule F in Chapter 4 shows how it's done.

15. Don't limit yourself to a single plant-wide overhead rate just because you're not a "Fortune-500" company. Chapter 5 illustrates a simple way to provide multi-overhead rates for realistic costing.

16. Don't deprive yourself of the advantages of budget flexibility and benefits of breakeven analysis just because your company (or division) is small. Chapter 5 shows you how to do it.

17. Chapter 6 shows how to establish costing rates when the operations are partly labor paced and partly machine paced.

18. Chapter 6 provides a step-by-step overview of the construction and tie-in of the key elements needed for a complete product costing cycle.

19. For capital intensive businesses more sophisticated costing rates are required. Chapter 7 takes you through all the steps.

20. There's no mystique about handling direct labor in a machine-hour rate costing system. See Exhibit 7-5 in Chapter 7.

21. If you need more costing rates than there are cost centers, don't create new cost centers. See Exibit 7-4 in Chapter 7 for a time-saving shortcut.

22. Calculate your selling price on the return-on-investment concept. See Chapter 7.

23. Monitor productivity through measurement of physical units rather than dollars. Read Chapter 8.

24. Don't calculate selling prices for new products blindly. Make sure the new prices are consistent with other prod ts in the same family. See Chapter 9.

25. Don't expect perpetual inventory records to remain accurate "in perpetuity." Read Chapter 10 on Cycle Counting procedures.
26. Minimize those demoralizing year-end "surprises" in which book value of the inventory falls short of the physical. See Chapter 10.
27. Integrate the cost system with the production control procedures by following the steps illustrated in Chapter 11 on computerizing the cost system.
28. Use the illustrative closing transactions as a guide for booking inventory to minimize the year-end "surprises." See Chapter 11.
29. Learn two ways in which you can set up a direct costing system within the framework of a full absorption system. Chapter 12 deals with this.
30. Use a simple approach to control material costs by using the selective control technique illustrated in Chapter 13.
31. If production losses are large, Chapter 13 demonstrates some techniques for getting them under control.
32. Don't report direct labor "to death." Chapter 13 tells you how to place your priorities.
33. Know where to draw the line on those small unprofitable orders. Turn to Chapter 13.
34. Learn how two companies ride herd on actual costs to meet their projected profit goals. Read Chapter 14.
35. Hold your sales department accountable for finished goods inventories. See Chapter 15.
36. Let your operating managers have an opportunity to monitor their costs through use of precalculated tables of allowances for various levels of activity. See Exhibits 15-3 and 15-4 in Chapter 15.
37. Use graphs more effectively. See how a major newspaper unintentionally misled its readers by using incorrect scales. Chapter 16.

The poor profit performance of many companies in recent years is reflective of increasing competitiveness. It behooves managers to take a serious look at their cost controls, product costing, and cost analyses. Good understanding of costs is equally important and that is where the revised edition of *Cost Controls for Industry* plays its part.

This edition has a simplicity and ease of understanding that will be appreciated by all levels of management.

Thomas S. Dudick

Contents

9. A Cast Study in Casting a New Product Successfully *(cont'd)*

SECTION III: Inventory Accountability and Valuation

14. What Cost System Is Best for Your Purposes? *(cont'd)*

15. Sharpening Cost Responsibilities **271**

16. Highlighting Critical Financial Data Reporting Through Proper Use of Graphs **285**

17. The Ten Commandments of Systematic Cost Control **303**

Index **305**

SECTION I

New Approaches to Overhead Cost Control

1

Pinpointing Product Costs
for More Realistic Pricing

Too many financial executives serve their management's costing needs as a byproduct of normal routine accounting.

Because of our free, individualistic enterprise, the "survival of the fittest" applies to American industry in greater measure than it does to the industries of foreign countries. Survival refers not only to the company, but also to its managers, whose careers and reputations are mirrored in their ability to make a profit. Frequently, an adequate profit means only pennies per unit of product. Correspondingly, a loss of only pennies can mean failure of the company and loss of prestige for its managers.

One of the important causes of poor financial results and ultimate failure of a company as an independent entity is lack of knowledge as to the costs of its products. As a result, erroneous pricing decisions are made and seemingly unprofitable products are dropped from the line, when actually they may be profitable. Other products which appear to be highly profitable may only appear to be so because another is being penalized by the method of costing.

The author, in his experience, has found a surprising number of such examples. Several of the most common errors will be discussed in this chapter. The method of costing will be analyzed to show how costs were applied to the product, how they misstated the cost, and what remedial action was taken.

DEFICIENCIES OF THE SINGLE PLANT-WIDE OVERHEAD RATE

Although clerical errors may be at a minimum, it is still possible and, in fact, entirely probable that incorrect decisions are being made because of underlying errors in the build-up of costs. Through repetitive usage of such costs, habit patterns are formed wherein erroneous information is accepted without question.

While use of a single rate may be perfectly correct in many products where there is great similarity in relative amount of effort at various stages of production, use of a single rate can be dangerous in some situations. This would be particularly true when the manufacturing process requires use of several types of facilities having a varied incidence of overhead cost per unit of product (unit of product is frequently expressed in terms of direct labor requirements, but could be machine hours, weight, surface, or any other appropriate unit of measurement).

It is very difficult to establish rules as to how many overhead rates should be used in various situations. The nature and magnitude of the major manufacturing operations is an important determinant. The final determination is usually based on a combination of good judgment and trial and error.

The following case of a fluorescent lighting fixture manufacturer, who recognized the deficiencies in his costs (because he used a single overhead rate), may be helpful in outlining a frame of reference. The subject manufacturer noted that although two fixtures might require exactly the same amount of labor in the metal fabrication shop and in the paint shop, the amount of labor required in assembly was substantially greater for the fixture which contains four light bulbs than for the one which has only two. The reason is that four lamps call for substantially more wiring than two. Bathroom fixtures are another example. The fixture with an outlet for plugging in an electric shaver will require more wiring than a similar fixture not having such an outlet. The application of a single plant-wide overhead rate means that the fixtures which require the additional hand assembly labor will be penalized because this additional labor will absorb more than its due share of the cost of the higher overhead centers such as the fabrication and paint shop.

The addition of a louver to a fixture also results in more labor charged to that fixture. In this case the additional labor should absorb a higher rate because it was incurred principally in the press shop and paint shop. If in addition to the louver, the fixture is suspended, as contrasted to one attached flush to the ceiling, it means still more labor in the metal press shop because it is then necessary to cut and thread the pipes used for suspension. This raises the question as to whether pipe cutting and threading should take the metal press shop overhead rate or one of its own which would be based on a substantially smaller amount of depreciation, maintenance, and set-up labor. After concluding that separate overhead rates should be developed for assembly, painting, and press shop, this manufacturer decided that because of the wide range of equipment used in the press shop, it might be advisable to make a test to determine whether additional overhead rates were needed in that area. Exhibit 1-1 illustrates how the basic figures were accumulated to make this test.

Because the larger fixtures are processed on the heavier type of equipment, they are grouped into a category called "heavy presses." Another group called "light and medium presses" is shown separately in order to accumulate the costs characteristic of the smaller fixtures. The "miscellaneous" group consists of the very light type of equipment which might have been referred to as accessory equipment. This includes the threaders and cutters used for the suspension pipes.

Analysis of Metal Shop Equipment for Major Items of Overhead Cost

	Normal Complement of Operators	Monthly Cost of Major Items		Monthly Cost Per Operator	
		Monthly Depreciation	Maintenance & Rent Equivalent Cost	Depreciation	Maintenance & Rent Equivalent Cost
Heavy presses					
2 Press brakes	3	$ 368	$ 2,100	$123	$700
3 95–150 Ton presses	3	438	2,700	146	900
4 250 Ton presses	6	458	5,200	143	866
9	12	$1,664	$10,000	$139	$833
Light and medium presses					
8 50 Ton presses	8	$ 348	$ 2,600	$ 44	$325
6 Versons	4	183	1,500	46	375
9 25 Ton presses.	6	232	2,100	39	350
23	18	$ 763	$ 6,200	$ 42	$344
Miscellaneous equipment					
6 Bench presses	2	$ 28		$ 14	
6 spot welders	6	162		27	
5 Shears	5	262		52	
3 Threaders and cutoffs	2	52		26	
20	15	$ 504	$ 300	$ 35	$ 20
Total Metal Shop	45	$2,931	$16,500	$ 66	$366

Application of Above Costs to Fixtures A and B If Three Cost Centers Are Used

	No. of operators	Depreciation	Maint. & rent equivalent
Fixture A			
Heavy presses	2	$278 (2 × $139)	$1,666 (2 × $833)
Medium and light presses	½	21 (½ of $42)	172 (½ of $344)
Miscellaneous equipment	½	18 (½ of $35)	
Total	3	$317	$1,838
Fixture B			
Heavy presses	0	$ 0	$ 0
Medium and light presses	2	84 (2 × $42)	688 (2 × $344)
Miscellaneous equipment	0	0	0
Total	2	$ 84	$ 688

Application of Above Costs to Fixtures A and B If Single Cost Center Is Used

Fixture A	3	$198 (3 × $66)	$1,098 (3 × $366)
Fixture B	2	132 (2 × $66)	732 (2 × $366)

Exhibit 1-1

In order to make a test calculation of the overhead rate of each of the three groups, only the principal costs were considered. Note that one of these, depreciation, is three times as large per operator for the heavy press group as it is for the light and medium presses. Maintenance and rent equivalent costs are more than twice as large per operator for the heavy presses as in the light and medium group. The lower section of Exhibit 1-1 illustrates a test calculation to determine what the difference in fixtures A and B would be if they were costed by the three cost centers as opposed to costing on the basis of a single press shop rate.

Note in the first method that Fixture A's share of depreciation is $317, while in the second method, using a single basis of costing, the cost is $198. Fixture B's share is only $84 in the first instance but $132 in the second. Maintenance and rent equivalent costs, which have been combined in the interest of simplicity, indicate the same relationships.

The reason that Fixture A incurs the heavier charge under the three-cost-center overhead rate application method is that its manufacture requires heavier concentration on the heavy presses. Fixture B, on the other hand, requires no heavy press work, therefore its share is substantially lower.

The single overhead rate method averages out the cost so that it is spread on the basis of number of operators without any weighting given to the related overhead. In this example, the evidence appears to be stacked heavily on the side of using three separate rates rather than a single rate. In many instances such tests may not indicate conclusively the use of the more detailed method of costing, therefore the simpler method of using a single rate may be preferable. This is the type of simple test which may be used in determining the number of overhead rates needed.

WHY OPERATING EXECUTIVES COMPLAIN
ABOUT QUALITY OF ACCOUNTING INFORMATION

Operating executives with profit responsibility are frequently frustrated because of inadequate accounting information for achieving cost analysis and control. Accountants, in turn, point to the masses of data that are available—but that are not put to use. The counterclaim states that it is not a dearth of information but rather the form in which it is presented that causes anguish among the operating executives who frequently must set up their own little accounting groups.

More specifically, the complaint is that the accounting department categorizes and classifies costs for convenience in keeping its books, and expects that the operating executives should be able, without too much difficulty, to adapt this data for whatever additional information is needed.

The general managers, plant managers and other executives in the operating groups acknowledge that the financial community, government agencies and the stockholders make great demands on financial executives and force the development of highly specialized, single-purpose systems to provide for the collection of financial data. They point out that they have important data needs too—but that these are not available in the mass of figures that are being generated for purely accounting purposes. Some operating executives have cited specific examples of deficiencies, which are discussed on the next two pages.

Incorrect Product Costing

Most of the inaccuracies in product costing relate to the method of accounting for overhead, as illustrated in these four companies:

Company A: The controller of this company prided himself on the depth to which he had developed overhead rates for costing products; there were 33 production departments and an overhead rate had been provided for each of these departments, meaning that every department's overhead cost was related to its own specific direct labor. He advised all department managers in a meeting that this facilitated more accurate costing than that of many companies of this type in which a maximum of 12 overhead rates is provided.

The marketing manager, who had always been a critic of the company's overhead structure, became quite vociferous. His argument was that overhead rates should be established in this company by the nature of the process rather than by department. He cited the machining department, which has two disparate manufacturing processes. This department is a mixture of milling, drilling, reaming and boring machines. It is also made up of a fair-sized crew of weld operators who do varying amounts of welding on the products that also go through the machining operations in varying degrees. The overhead rate per unit of direct labor for welding would be a good deal lower than the rate for the machines because the overhead costs in welding are relatively low, while the machines average $55,000 to $60,000 each, require heavy maintenance costs and large floor areas.

Since some jobs going through this department require a fair amount of welding and little machining, use of a single departmental overhead rate overstates the costs of the welding jobs. That work that requires a good deal of machining and very little welding is understated because of the single rate. The solution was simply to split the department into two cost centers, each with its own overhead rate. This was finally done. The marketing manager, in recounting the incident, said: "I shouldn't be telling the controller how products should be costed—he should be telling me."

Company B: Company B has a large machining operation which is similar to Company A's except that there is no welding; this is done in a separate department. A single departmental overhead rate was adequate until the company purchased a tape-controlled machine costing $300,000 (as compared with an average of $45,000 for the existing machines in the department). The accounting department, to adjust for the addition of the new machine, revised the departmental overhead rate to include the additional costs. The previous overhead rate of 285% of direct labor now became 325%. The chief accountant of this company justified the mixing of such a high priced machine with lower cost equipment on the basis that "it all averages out at the end of the year."

What the accountant did not consider was that local machine shops were purchasing services to be performed on the tape-controlled equipment. These services were being charged out at the average departmental overhead rate of 325%. Taking into consideration the higher cost of the new machine, the additional floor space required, and the increase in maintenance costs (since two electronic technicians are needed in addition to the regular mechanical and electrical maintenance), the overhead rate of the new machine is closer to 465% than 325%. Obviously, as claimed by the plant manager, the services of the machine are being given away: "We buy a $300,000 machine and our accounting department loads it up to capacity through its giveaway pricing."

This is another real life case in which accounting routines are structured to provide financial information at the expense of adequate costing and product pricing.

Company C: This company has a specialized metal fabrication department consisting of five machines. Because of an increase in demand and a desire for cost reduction in order to become more competitive, four of these machines were equipped with automatic stops—allowing one operator to tend all four machines simultaneously instead of requiring one operator per machine. The fifth machine, because of short-run type orders, continued with a full-time direct labor operator.

The plant controller recalculated the overhead rate in this department, basing the total overhead on two direct labor operators rather than five. Because of the greatly reduced labor base with a relatively small change in overhead, the overhead rate per unit of direct labor automatically increased two-and-a-half times. This change in rate, though applicable to the four machines, was applied on a blanket basis to all the equipment, including the machine with the full-time operator in which no changes were made. Overhead costs on all products now made on that machine automatically jumped two-and-a-half times because of poor accounting. This is another example of a situation in which important costing considerations were brushed over because of concentration on non-costing considerations.

Company D: A food processing company that sold processed meat products to franchised outlets found a cost distortion in its major product, hamburger patties. The hamburger was sold raw as well as cooked, following these processing steps:

1. grinding and mixing hamburger in the mixing department
2. forming the patties
3. cooking those patties that would be sold cooked.
4. freezing.

The mixing department has its own overhead rate that is applied to all meats that are ground and mixed. The equipment on which the formed hamburger patties are cooked also has its own rate. The forming overhead rate includes the costs relative not only to the forming operation but to the freezing as well. This forming overhead is applied on the basis of the direct labor cost required to operate the forming machines. Since it takes exactly the same amount of time to form the raw patties as it does to form those that are cooked before freezing, the same amount of freezing cost is therefore applied to both the raw and the cooked product.

There is a basic deficiency in using forming as the basis for accounting for freezing costs, because the raw hamburger patties enter the freezing chambers at 30 degrees while the cooked product enters at 150 degrees. The amount of time required to freeze the cooked product is just about twice as long as for the raw product. This means that the cooked patty, instead of sharing equally in the very expensive freezer overhead, should more correctly take double the amount of freezing overhead. This is another example of a slipshod approach to development of overhead rates.

Insufficient Breakdown of Labor Costs

Most progressive companies prepare an annual business plan that seeks to embody long-term objectives and strategies in a financial plan. The president of a company manufacturing knitwear products expressed deep frustration at the lack of meaningful detail in the accounting information backing up his business plan. He complained that labor, one of the large elements of cost, was lumped into a figure called "salaries" and another called "wages." These, in turn, were shown only for the major operations— allowing no meaningful analysis to determine whether any potential for cost saving existed. The accounting department was instructed to furnish a more detailed breakdown of direct labor and indirect labor. In the indirect labor category, where labor accounted for over 80% of total overhead, his instructions where to show a headcount breakdown that identified the individual jobs in each of the departments. When this information was made available to him, he began a penetrating analysis in which questions were raised of his various departmental managers. Some examples are:

> *Direct Labor.* By having available a headcount of individual job categories within direct labor, he found that in Yarn Manufacturing 64 people were required for winding. On the accounting document that listed the individual job categories, the president wrote in longhand: "Would automatic winders pay out? In how long? A lot of people for an operation that looks as if it could be automated to a greater extent."
>
> In reviewing the direct labor for knitwear manufacturing, he noted that 118 employees were shown in the packaging department. His comment on this read: "A real opportunity for automated packaging. What progress can we make here?"
>
> *Indirect Labor.* Several categories of jobs attracted the president's attention here. These are shown below, together with his questions:

4 Elevator operators	"Cost of automating?"
9 Painters	"Could we not contract out our painting at lower cost? Seems like a lot of painters permanently on the payroll."
17 Sweepers	"Wouldn't an automatic sweeping machine reduce this?"
Departments W-2 and W-3	"Department W-2 has one supervisor for each 71 people and W-3 has one supervisor for each 33. Why this disparity? Are we undersupervised in W-2? Check this out."

The questions were distributed to the appropriate managers for investigation, with a request that the results of their review and recommendations be presented at the next management meeting. The results are summarized below:

> *Direct Labor.* The investigation into the possibility of reducing the number of employees in yarn winding showed that for one type of winding it was possible to use automated equipment that would permit one employee to operate four machines. This would eliminate 12 of the 64 employees in yarn winding. Since this change would require approximately a year, the business plan did not reflect the change until the second year.
>
> With respect to the 118 employees in the packaging department, investigation showed that 24 of these made up boxes and 94 inspected the product as they placed it in the package. The job category breakdown would have been more informative if it had been shown as:

> Box makers   24
> Inspector/packers   94

A saving of 35% could be achieved in box making through a new design which would permit boxes to be assembled without having to insert tabs into slots in each of the four corners. Redesign would take four months, so the business plan included the change in the second half of the year.

Indirect Labor. The following conclusions were arrived at in connection with indirect labor:

Automating Elevators. There is no question as to the economics of automating; there would be a payback in less than four years. However, since two of the four elevators are being used for moving material, there is some fear that material handlers, by locking the mechanism, could monopolize the elevators for long periods, leaving material handlers on other floors waiting for unreasonable lengths of time. The decision was made to automate the two passenger elevators and to continue to operate the two freight elevators manually to assure continual movement of materials on all floors.

Since the automating process could not be completed for two years, the business plan assumed no change until the third year.

Painters. Since there is enough of a certain type of painting that must be done year-round, the decision was made to retain two full-time painters year-round. All other painting would be subcontracted. This should be advantageous to the company because:

• Painting would be done only when needed—not to keep a crew of nine busy.
• Contracted painting could be done "off hours" without having to pay overtime premium.

Sweepers. The recommendation was made to purchase an automatic sweeper to clean the wide areas. This, incidentally, improved cleanliness because the vacuum action of the equipment sucked up the dust rather than agitating it. As a result, the crew of 17 sweepers was reduced to 11. The business plan took the savings into account in the current year.

Supervision in Departments W-2 and W-3. Department W-2 was found to be highly undersupervised with its ratio of 1 supervisor to each 71 employees. Although W-3 was closer to normal at a ratio of 1 to 33, 1 to 23 was considered to be a more desirable ratio for the type of work being performed in both departments. With this kind of strengthening, product quality should be expected to improve—thus reducing the number of "seconds." The additional costs of supervision and estimated savings through fewer "seconds" were taken into account in the current year's business plan.

The president made the observation, after the foregoing changes were made to the business plan, that there was obviously a serious weakness in the organization when it was necessary to have the Chief Executive Officer review costs at this level to achieve cost reduction. He questioned how many other potential savings are still going unnoticed because no one was monitoring the cost and operating controls. He criticized the accounting department for its academic approach to cost accounting but was particularly critical of the Industrial Engineering group for letting so many inefficiencies continue.

INEQUITIES IN COSTING DUE TO OVER-REFINEMENT

The assignment of a work order number to collect costs in the production of a particular product does not automatically assure that costs will be more accurately compiled. In the case of products A and B in Exhibit 1-2, costs were compiled for production of 785 of the former and 825 of the latter. Note that the cost of Product A amounted to $23.18 while the cost of Product B was $50.04—more than twice as much.

The construction of the two is exactly the same—material and labor operations are identical—the only difference being that the electrical characteristic of the final product are different because of differences in spacing of one of the elements. This difference does not, however, make the one product any more valuable than the other because both sell for the same price—$56.00.

The reason for the difference in cost is that parts which were inventoried during manufacture were not correctly identified. Obviously, since the parts for both products are exactly the same, it is difficult at inventory time to predict where the materials will finally be used. To attempt to keep an accurate check of disposition of the material would entail clerical costs which would exceed the value of the information obtained. Since cost considerations make it impractical to accurately account for usage of common parts, it would be more feasible in such a situation to accumulate the costs of Products A and B in a single work order and to calculate the average cost. When, at a certain stage of construction, actual differences in manufacture are introduced, the average cost up to the point of difference could be brought forward into separate work orders which would break out the two products from that point.

DIRECT LABOR VERSUS MACHINE HOURS
AS A BASE FOR OVERHEAD

Products which are produced by machine, and are essentially machine paced rather than operator paced, may suffer serious distortions in cost when a direct labor base, rather than machine hours, is used for application of overhead (a later chapter will demonstrate the development of machine hour rates). The reason is that in many instances when machine processing time is approximately the same for a number of

Comparison of Costs of Two Products

	Product A	Product B
Production	785	825
Material	$ 3.11	$ 9.83
Labor	5.95	9.48
	9.06	19.31
Overhead	14.12	30.73
Production Cost	$23.18	$50.04
Selling Price	$56.00	$56.00
Scrap Cost	$ 2.52	$ 4.01

Exhibit 1-2

types, there may be additional hand operations on certain of these. Use of direct labor as a base would unduly "load" machine type costs such as depreciation, maintenance, occupancy, and power on those types which had the additional hand operations. An actual case of a distortion of this kind is illustrated below:

DIRECT LABOR COST VERSUS MACHINE TIME

Product Type	Direct Labor Cost Per 100	% of Total	Machine Hours Per 100	% of Total
6AK6	$ 7.90	20%	.1260	30%
6AX8A	22.22	56	.1502	36
6GK8	9.62	24	.1378	34
	$39.74	100%	.4140	100%

BREAKDOWN OF TOTAL OVERHEAD BY THE TWO METHODS

Product Type	Based on Direct Labor Cost Per 100	Based on Machine Hours Per 100
6AK6	$15.80	$24.19
6AX8A	44.44	28.83
6GK8	19.24	26.46
	$79.48	$79.48

The section entitled "Direct Labor Cost Versus Machine Time" shows in the first column the direct labor cost per 100 for the three products. Because there are additional operations required on 6AX8A which cannot be performed by the machine, labor cost is substantially higher than for the other two. As a result of using labor as a basis for applying overhead, this product absorbs a correspondingly larger share of the overhead pool.

The machine hours required for the three products are approximately the same, indicating that all three should absorb about the same amount of depreciation, machine maintenance, power and occupancy costs.

The table, "Breakdown of Total Overhead by the Two Methods," compares the dollar amount of overhead apportioned to each of the three products. While the direct labor method penalizes one of these through an over-apportionment of machine-connected overhead, the machine hour method will tend to understate this type insofar as the labor fringe benefits on the additional labor are concerned. No method of overhead application is completely equitable, but the machine hour method comes much closer to an equitable distribution in this case than does the direct labor method.

Although one might rationalize that supply and demand, rather than cost, set the selling price for this product, it is entirely possible that many profitable products have been dropped by companies because inequitable methods of overhead distribution have distorted the true cost-selling price relationships.

MATERIAL OVERHEAD RATE

Some companies use the labor base to absorb certain items of overhead and a material base to absorb others. In connection with the latter, the base would be determined by the amount of the material used (usually dollar value). The items ordinarily included in the material overhead which is absorbed on the basis of material entering into the product are purchasing, stores, inventory control, receiving, and incoming inspection. The rate is developed by dividing the total of these material-associated costs by the total material cost. The rate is applied to the material content of the product just as the labor rate is applied to the labor content.

This type of overhead rate became popular after World War II when contracts which were cancelled by the government created problems in reimbursement for materials which were either unprocessed or only partially processed. Because little or no labor had been expended, application of a labor overhead rate would not yield a sufficient amount of recovery for material connected expenses which had been incurred.

While use of the material overhead rate serves its purpose well in costing a homogeneous group of products, serious inequities will result if two products of differing characteristics are mixed. An example would be the manufacture of low volume, high precision equipment such as oscilloscopes under the same roof with a high volume, conveyorized product, such as, perhaps, radio or television receivers.

The material-connected costs for the low volume product would be higher per unit because the high volume product would lend itself to more efficient handling. The effort expended for ordering 500 television cabinets or picture tubes a day is no greater and could possibly be less than the effort required to order cabinets or cathode ray tubes for an order of 25 oscilloscopes.

In the latter case these items would undoubtedly move into the stores area for later release over a period of several days or even weeks, while in the instance of a mechanized TV line, the cabinets and picture tubes would be placed on conveyors as soon as received and would move through the production area and then on out to the shipping area as a completed product without any intermediate handling.

Thus the material overhead rate must be used with discretion; otherwise it could penalize the high volume repetitive products and understate costs of low volume high precision products which require greater care and more handling.

CONCLUSIONS

Our highly competitive society makes it mandatory for every financial executive to regularly review his costing procedures, and to appraise them by asking himself and his subordinates the following questions:

1. What are the manufacturing processes through which the product passes?
2. Do all products spend proportionately the same amount of time in each process, or do they vary materially from one another?

3. Are my overhead rates developed in such a way as to give effect to these differences?
4. Am I using the correct activity base for application of overhead to the product?
5. Am I providing my management's cost needs only as a byproduct of routine record keeping?
6. Does my accounting system provide sufficient down-to-earth detail to facilitate effective cost analysis?

The most common errors in calculating product costs are due to improper application of overhead to the product. For this reason several chapters will deal with the subject of overhead, while several others will illustrate with case studies how different companies develop costing rates for product costing.

When the financial executive fails to take the leadership in providing good product costing, company survival forces the operating executives to take the initiative.

2

Analyzing and Monitoring Overhead
for Substantial Savings

Overhead is probably the most discussed element of cost in our modern business community. Many think of it in terms of a rate—the rate they must apply to labor or machine hours in order to recover their overhead costs. Others think of it in terms of absolute dollars—additional dollars of profit there could be, if only the magnitude of this "monster" could be reduced.

To many people, overhead is a mental image, hard to describe and difficult to measure. In achieving cost reduction, little can be accomplished by dealing in such abstractions. Better to break down this large element into its component parts and then to analyze the segments to determine a logical approach to cost reduction. That is the mission of this chapter. In the accomplishment of this mission, seven companies were analyzed to determine the relationship of overhead to material and labor costs. These overhead costs were then analyzed to determine if certain items predominate in all companies and if so, to what extent.

A simple report for monitoring the largest segment of overhead—indirect labor—is illustrated and explained. The various non-labor expenses were reviewed to determine how the majority of the companies classified them in making up their flexible budgets. This could not be done for indirect labor because all of the companies indicated that indirect labor in most of their departments contained both fixed and variable elements; the method of classifying ranged from an individual job-by-job evaluation of what was fixed and what was variable to a broad categorization wherein hourly labor was considered variable and salaried labor fixed. Finally, the chapter summarizes some suggestions relative to the allocation of overhead to the production departments for purposes of developing overhead rates.

RELATIVE AMOUNT OF OVERHEAD IN PRODUCT COST

The relative size of the three elements of cost will vary depending on the product being manufactured. In many engineering research activities one will find that product cost is made up roughly of one-third material, one-third labor, and one-third overhead. In manufacturing operations material can be as high as 70% to 80% of total product cost. This is usually the case when most of the components are purchased from an outside source. In such cases labor can be as low as 5% to 10%. When a company manufactures its own components rather than purchasing them, the material element becomes smaller and the labor becomes larger. The table below shows an actual breakdown of the three elements of cost for seven companies studied.

	COMPONENT MANUFACTURERS					EQUIP. MFRS.	
	Company M	Company RT	Company TR	Company P	Company Y	Company H	Company T
Material	27%	28%	35%	47%	59%	64%	80%
Direct Labor	21	27	25	19	5	9	6
Overhead	52	45	40	34	36	27	14
Total	100%	100%	100%	100%	100%	100%	100%

Companies M and RT shown in the preceding table manufacture a similar type of product, but RT's production is in larger volume while Company M's production is more in the order of job lots. Although Company RT is automated to a greater degree than M, its labor content is greater because the product uses a greater number of small parts which must be assembled by hand before the machine operations can be performed.

Company TR comes closest to a one-third split for the three elements of cost. Company P is more automated than its competitors. However, its labor content is greater than Company Y because the latter company is a metal stamping operation using equipment which is fully automatic. The fully automatic nature of this equipment permits a direct labor operator to tend as many as six machines at one time. Although the overhead in both Companies P and Y is slightly more than one-third, the labor content of the first is 19% and 5% in the latter. This is a good illustration of how the overhead rate can vary because of the size of the base. Company P's overhead rate would be slightly under 200% (34 divided by 19), while Company Y's rate would be slightly more than 700% (36 divided by 5).

Companies H and T are equipment manufacturers. Since many of the components are purchased rather than manuafactured, the material percentages are high (64% and 80% respectively) while the labor percentages are low (9% and 6% respectively). Note in the seven companies illustrated the wide range of fluctuations in the three elements of cost. Material varies from 27% to 80% of total product cost; direct labor from 5% to 27%; and overhead from 14% to 52%. Note that in three of the companies, overhead exceeds both material cost and labor cost. However, overhead exceeds direct labor in all seven companies.

MAKEUP OF OVERHEAD

In analyzing the makeup of overhead in a manufacturing operation, one usually finds that a few items will make up a substantial portion of the total. Using the same companies referred to previously, the overhead is broken down below to show the four major categories of cost. All others are lumped in a balancing figure.

| | COMPONENT MANUFACTURERS | | | | | EQUIP. MFRS. | |
	Co. M	Co. RT	Co. TR	Co. P	Co. Y	Co. H	Co. T
Indirect Labor	63%	69%	50%	58%	47%	65%	67%
Maintenance	8	7	7	13	17	4	3
Depreciation	5	4	6	10	10	4	3
Occupancy	5	7	4	8	9	11	9
All Other*	19	13	33	11	17	16	18
Total	100%	100%	100%	100%	100%	100%	100%

| | COMPONENT MANUFACTURERS | | | | | EQUIP. MFRS. | |
	Co. M	Co. RT	Co. TR	Co. P	Co. Y	Co. H	Co. T
*Number of items in "All Other"	24	24	30	18	23	12	24

Note that maintenance and depreciation for Companies P and Y, both of which are highly automated, are substantially greater than for the other five companies. Indirect labor includes overtime as well as fringe benefits. Note that this item (indirect labor) accounts for a substantial portion of the overhead (47% in Company Y to 69% in Company RT). Maintenance and occupancy also contain indirect labor, which would add at least 10% more to the total indirect labor.

COST BEHAVIOR

The logical first step to cost reduction is to classify the cost segments as to their behavior. Although there are numerous gradations of behavior, the major emphasis in this book will be placed on the two basic types of cost—those that remain relatively fixed with changes in volume and those that vary with volume.

Fixed Costs. A good illustration of a fixed cost is depreciation. Another is occupancy or rent-equivalent costs. Be careful to look behind the chart of account terminology in making the determination of what is fixed and what is variable. One company, following a desk-oriented approach, classified rent as a fixed cost. Upon investigation, it was found that the rental charges were based on usage rather than on a flat charge per accounting period. Therefore, a cost that appeared to be fixed was actually variable because it varied with the volume of activity. Other names given to the fixed category are "non-variable," "constant," "committed" and "managed."

Semi-variable. Costs in this category cannot be dealt with effectively; they must be separated into their fixed and variable segments. A good illustration of a semi-variable cost is maintenance. Replacement of parts that have worn out because of use represents a variable cost. However, the annual replacement of firebrick in a furnace (irrespective of volume of activity) is a fixed cost.

Variable. This category would include such items as supplies, material handling, and fringe benefits on variable labor. Variable costs are usually synonymous with direct costs.

While many like to refine terminology beyond just these two categories to give visibility to the shades of difference, it is more important to emphasize the basic behavior. The operating managers are more likely to understand and remember the ground rules of a simple approach even if it may not be technically correct in all aspects.

MONITORING INDIRECT LABOR—LARGEST ITEM OF OVERHEAD

Frequently effective controls can be developed on indirect labor on a weekly basis through a report similar to the one shown in Exhibit 2-1.

This report reflects an actual situation where two operations had been consolidated in order to reduce costs. Although the consolidation was already in effect, headcounts for indirect labor were rising rather than falling, indicating that no saving had been effected by the consolidation. In an effort to develop a weekly progress report, headcount figures by department were posted by the payroll section immediately upon completion of each week's payroll. The report was typed on a reproducible master so that each new week's information could be added to the preceding week's. Note in Exhibit 2-1 that the total headcount reached its peak during the week of April 20 when the total number was 357. It was during this period that the report was produced and issued regularly as a means of stemming the upward trend. Note that after this date the trend turned downward so that by the week ending June 29 total headcount dropped to 318—lowest count for the entire period shown. Production was stable in this period.

Concentrating on headcount alone can be misleading because of the effect of overtime on cost. Headcount can remain constant, but costs could rise as much as 20 percent because of overtime. Exhibit 2-2 shows the overtime costs for the same departments for corresponding weeks. The overtime dollars shown are all earnings over and above the earnings in a 40-hour week. Thus the figures include straight time earnings as well as half-time premium. Note that in some weeks overtime amounted to as much as $6,500. During the latter part of April when visibility had been given to these figures, the overtime costs began to decline.

It is not always possible during a hectic period of consolidation of operations to develop meaningful budgets. In the absence of a tool based on a scientific approach, other less sophisticated means, as demonstrated by Exhibits 2-1 and 2-2, can be used effectively.

EQUIPMENT MANUFACTURING DIVISION BREAKDOWN OF INDIRECT EMPLOYEES

PAYROLL FOR W/E		TOTAL	DIV. MGR.	FIELD SERVICE	SECURITY	MFG. SERV.	TRANSF. SHOP	MFG. MGR.	PROD. CONTROL	PURC- HASING	QUALITY CONTROL	COST ACCTG.	MAINT. DEPT.	PLANT ENGINEER
FEB.	16	327	5	5	3	11	7	47	127	43	15	26	36	2
	23	325	5	5	3	11	7	47	124	44	15	26	36	2
MAR.	2	332	5	5	3	11	7	47	130	44	15	27	36	2
	9	321	5	6	3	11	7	35	129	46	15	27	35	2
	16	323	5	6	2	11	7	35	134	47	15	27	32	2
	23	324	5	6	2	11	7	34	135	48	15	27	31	3
	30	327	5	6	2	11	7	35	138	47	15	27	31	3
APR.	6	365	6	15	3	11	7	62	134	45	19	27	29	2
	13	356	6	14	3	11	7	58	136	45	20	26	28	2
	20	357	6	15	3	11	7	57	137	45	20	26	28	2
	27	346	5	12	3	12	7	52	134	45	20	26	28	2
MAY	4	344	6	11	3	12	7	54	129	46	19	26	29	2
	11	347	6	11	3	13	7	55	130	46	19	23	31	2
	18	343	6	11	3	12	7	55	129	46	18	23	28	2
	25	340	6	12	3	12	6	54	130	46	18	23	28	2
JUNE	1	337	6	11	3	12	6	54	127	46	19	23	28	2
	8	332	6	12	3	12	6	55	127	40	18	23	28	1
	15	327	6	11	3	12	6	55	126	38	19	23	28	2
	22	324	6	10	3	12	6	56	127	38	19	22	23	2
	29	318	6	10	3	12	6	54	123	35	20	22	23	4

Exhibit 2-1

EQUIPMENT MANUFACTURING DIVISION OVERTIME ON INDIRECT EMPLOYEES

PAYROLL FOR W/E		TOTAL	DIV. MGR.	FIELD SERV.	SECURITY	MFG. SERVICE	TRANSF. SHOP	MFG. MGR.	PROD. CONTROL	PURC- HASING	QUALITY CONTROL	COST ACCTG.	MAINT. DEPT.	PLANT ENGINEER
FEB.	16	$6,313	$ 79	$----	$ 3	$236	$150	$310	$3,209	$1,219	$170	$205	$725	$ 1
	23	1,750	41	----	3	37	16	250	1,058	288	68	39	8	--
MAR.	2	6,574	149	----	5	231	180	419	3,433	1,022	180	251	668	31
	9	5,191	34	----	9	134	145	6	3,036	619	103	660	438	2
	16	4,985	21	----	2	193	80	4	3,391	480	142	45	597	28
	23	4,397	22	----	--	113	75	30	2,969	531	160	--	493	--
	30	5,086	19	----	2	106	68	151	3,206	798	85	201	447	19
APR.	6	4,120	21	3	1	124	59	177	2,771	324	63	528	23	15
	13	5,281	14	----	--	--	103	298	3,350	649	134	68	557	27
	20	3,861	19	----	38	--	15	251	2,578	394	223	--	349	9
	27	3,418	26	----	--	3	27	170	2,320	560	115	171	153	--
MAY	4	3,597	19	----	42	62	32	369	2,046	478	150	562	329	18
	11	3,308	15	----	--	64	16	357	1,482	501	65	89	230	--
	18	2,252	24	----	--	--	23	240	1,152	490	114	36	14	--
	25	2,045	25	----	--	47	23	183	1,268	372	113	11	25	--
JUNE	1	1,688	23	6	--	14	21	416	1,004	103	52	570	11	6
	8	3,531	18	----	--	54	21	621	1,524	195	171	140	385	--
	15	2,591	72	----	--	62	14	444	1,530	197	127	69	13	--
	22	1,755	125	----	--	--	--	395	519	79	58	283	448	--
	29	2,419	56	----	--	19	21	428	329	30	46		207	--

Exhibit 2-2

BREAKDOWN OF INDIRECT LABOR

A further analysis of indirect labor for the seven companies illustrated earlier indicates that one-third is incurred in the production departments. This would include foremen, assistant foremen, group leaders, clerks and material handlers who work directly in the production departments.

Quality control and process engineering, a significant cost in these seven companies, make up about 25% of the indirect labor, ranging from a high of 50% to a low of 15%—depending on the product. In the companies making a component which cannot be repaired if it fails in final test, quality control and process engineering costs are likely to be quite high.

Purchasing and production control (the latter includes material control, scheduling, receiving and stores) account for about 20% of total indirect labor, ranging from a high of 31% for Company H to a low of 8%. The balance of the indirect labor is made up of industrial engineering, supervision, cost accounting, and industrial relations.

THE NON-LABOR EXPENSES

Some of the more common non-labor expenses are:

Maintenance Materials. This is one of the major non-labor costs. This item includes such materials as rod, tubing, angle iron, cable, pipe, bearings, belts, gaskets, electrical fittings, lubricating oil, locks, nuts, bolts and the like. Rearrangment, unusual moves or repairs performed by outside contractors, are usually in the maintenance category, but frequently shown in a separate account for convenience of control. The majority of companies surveyed considered this expense as variable.

Occupancy. This includes the cost of maintaining buildings, ventilating systems, grounds, improvements, and boiler room repairs. This account would also include the depreciation of the building, fire insurance, boiler insurance, taxes, liability insurance, fuel and electricity used for lighting. Most companies studied treated this as a fixed cost.

Non-Capital Equipment and Tools. This would include all small tools and attachments such as grinding wheels, drills, files, pliers, hammers, soldering irons, hack saws, micrometers, reamers, and screw drivers. Some companies may also use the classification "small tools" or "expendable tools" to describe these items (considered as variable costs by most of the companies surveyed).

Operating Supplies. This would include supply items generally used in the factory. Some of these are: gloves, rope, sponges, cleaning rags, acids, aprons, kerosene, brooms, boots, pails, paint brushes (usually considered as a variable cost).

Office Supplies and Postage. Postage is shown separately in many companies where it is a large item. Included in this account would be such costs as stamps and stamped envelopes, rental and service charges on postage meters. Office supplies would include binders, books, cards, pencils, carbon paper, forms, copier supplies, blueprint paper, time cards, pencil sharpeners, clips, erasers, paper and the like. While this item could be considered as partly fixed and partly variable, it is a relatively small item in a manufacturing activity and would best be treated as a fixed cost.

Telephone and Telegraph. This includes the cost of local and long distance telephone calls, cost of installing and moving telephones, rental charges for telephone equipment, cost of telegrams, and teletype service. This could also be considered partly fixed and partly variable. If total cost is small, it should be considered as a fixed cost, otherwise rental charges could be considered as fixed and the balance variable.

Power and Light. This would cover the rental charges on equipment and power bills. Departments using ovens which must be kept up to temperature would consider this fixed. Departments using motors would consider this a variable cost.

Travel Expense. This includes the expenses of employees attending industry or educational conferences and seminars; mileage allowances made to employees for travel on company business when they use their own autos; meals, lodging, and transportation when traveling on company business. It may also include cost of moving household effects of new employees. Most of the companies interviewed treated this as a fixed cost because it was a relatively stable item.

Depreciation. Like maintenance, this is one of the major items in most manufacturing companies. It covers the charge for depreciation of equipment valued above a certain amount—depending on company policy. In some instances when tax regulations are in conflict with company policy, the depreciation figures will reflect company policy on all internal reports and statements but will be recast for purposes of making tax returns. This was treated as a fixed cost by most companies.

Amortization of Leaseholds. It covers the writeoff of improvements in a leased facility over the period of the lease. If the improvements are substantial and the initial lease agreement short in duration, the amount amortized each accounting period can be large. This was treated as a fixed cost most times.

Dues, Tuition, and Memberships. This includes subscriptions to magazines and membership dues to organizations. It would also include tuition payments when the company prescribes certain studies which it authorizes under its educational program. The majority of companies surveyed considered this a fixed cost by management decision.

Obsolescence of Raw Materials. This account is charged for the inventory value of material which is scrapped, or classified as obsolete. It would be credited when obsolete material becomes usable or when it is sold. It was considered as variable by several companies using this account.

Auto Expense. This covers the cost of operating company cars and internal trucking and would include vehicle tax and registration expense but would not include the salary of the chauffeur. Companies interviewed stated that since only a few company cars were involved, they treated this as a fixed cost.

ALLOCATION OF OVERHEAD

The allocation of services and service department overhead for developing production department (or cost center) overhead costing rates is normally accomplished on an annual basis rather than making the allocation part of the monthly accounting routine. Although there is no standard formula that can be used for all companies, the following illustrations can be used as guidelines.

Electricity	Allocation can be based on horsepower or connected load weighted by hours of use. Consult with plant electrician.
Water	Not usually a large cost unless used in a manufacturing process such as plating and painting. Discuss with plant engineer.
Gas	Portion used for heating would become part of occupancy cost allocated on a floor space basis. Portion used on equipment should be estimated or tested with flowmeter by plant engineer.
Supplies	Major items could be analyzed through study of amounts issued during a test period. Balance would be estimated by stockroom attendant.
Material-related services such as purchasing, receiving, and incoming inspection	Allocation of these items can be accomplished through use of a material based burden rate. Material-related services would be distributed on the basis of purchases or issues of material based on dollar value or weight. Works best when type of material used is reasonably similar for all products. Make sure that the larger high cost items don't distort the rate.
Purchasing, if material burden (overhead) rate is not used	In the smaller companies, purchasing can be allocated on the basis of the number of items purchased for each of the production cost centers. Bear in mind that a substantial portion of purchasing effort is devoted to procurement of expense type items.
	The purchasing function in a large operation may be broken down by buying specialty such as steel, hardware, electrical components, painting and plating material. In such a circumstance, each of the specialty functions could be charged directly to the cost center using the material.
Receiving	The receiving department might also be allocated on a basis similar to that used for purchasing.
Production and Inventory Control	This function usually includes scheduling and inventory management. Allocation to production departments (cost centers) should follow the number of item types to be scheduled and managed.
Quality Control (sometimes referred to as Quality Assurance)	Review the functional breakdown. If there is a metallurgical laboratory, this cost would properly be allocable to the cost center in which the metal is fabricated. Incoming inspection, if not part of a material burden rate, would be allocable on the basis of the type of material being inspected.

	Other quality functions should be allocated on the basis of where inspections are required within the operation.
	When a highly customized product is being produced, much of the quality control (as well as engineering) function might be directly chargeable to the job. Inclusion in the overhead rate of directly chargeable costs could result in distorted product costs.
Industrial Engineering (Manufacturing Engineering in some companies)	Allocable on the basis of the number of labor/ machine operations performed in each department. In a large company industrial engineers may be assigned to specific areas. In such instances, the allocations will be more specific.
Maintenance	Good records should be kept of maintenance costs by individual project, with departmental foremen signing off on all hours charged to the department each day. Such records would provide better controls for this major cost as well as providing a basis for allocation. If such records do not exist, the maintenance head should provide his best estimate by craft. This will not only provide a basis for allocation—it will also be a beneficial exercise for him.
Industrial Relations (Personnel)	Allocate by number of direct and indirect employees in production departments (cost centers).
Accounting	Payroll and timekeeping should be allocated by number of employees; accounts payable on same basis as purchasing; inventory accounting same as production and inventory control.
Occupancy-related costs	Includes real estate taxes, depreciation, maintenance and insurance related to the building structure, parking lot maintenance, sweeping and cleaning, lawn care, snow removal, light and heat. Occupancy costs would normally be allocated on the basis of the floor space occupied. However, bear in mind that storage and stockroom areas can account for as much as 45% of total factory floor space. In some instances, some of these areas can be identified directly with a production center. Example: the area in which sheet steel is stored would logically be allocated to the steel fabrication department.

Although there are other overhead items not included above, these represent the major portion of the cost and should provide sufficient examples for use as guidelines for allocation.

CONCLUSIONS

An important prerequisite for effective control of overhead is to know its makeup—to know the various items entering into this cost and to know their relative size. Knowing what the costs are makes it easier to forecast behavior; knowing the size of the various segments identifies the areas which warrant major attention. The author has found from his experience that the following steps represent a logical approach to better control of overhead:

1. Indirect labor usually makes up two-thirds of the overhead pool. You can install a fast and effective monitoring device right from your weekly payroll by listing the number of checks paid out by department each week. You'll have to be careful at vacation time because of extra checks, but for the most part this is a simple means of watching trends. The work can be done by a payroll clerk or timekeeper.
2. Show the overtime costs too. Bear in mind that the headcount can remain the same, but the payroll can be increased from 10 to 20 percent by the addition of overtime.
3. Don't waste time trying to control, on a departmental basis, such items as maintenance, telephone, and office supplies. Control them at the source. Let the maintenance department head account for the staff he has. Ask him for suggestions as to how maintenance costs can be cut down. The same applies to telephone. Your switchboard operator would like to be part of the team. Let her analyze the costs and point the finger at high spots so you can take action. In the same way, your stockroom attendant can tell you where the costs are going and where they can be controlled.
4. Don't play games in making up your departmental expense reports. If you can't meter the department's usage of electricity, gas, and water, don't hold them accountable for an explanation. Control the costs at the top—let your plant engineer tell you why these items are high. He'll come up with some mighty good cost-saving suggestions if you give him a chance.
5. Avoid making allocations to service departments and then reallocating to the production departments. This is needlessly circuitous, complex, and costly.
6. In making analyses for cost reduction and allocation purposes, give major emphasis to the major costs. Don't "nickel and dime" postage costs when maintenance is 15% percent of total overhead.

These recommendations are effective in spite of their simplicity. They'll reduce the number of figures which must be distributed and you'll find that the costs will get more attention when they are reported in total. *Give these half-dozen suggestions a fair trial and you won't want to go back to the old system.*

> The assignment of service department costs to production departments for development of overhead rates (costing rates) would normally be done once a year. Little will be gained by making this a monthly ritual.

3

Flexible Budgets in 30 Days:
Prime Tool
for Profit Improvement

There is little question in the mind of the modern businessman as to the benefits from use of the flexible budget concept. The problem is the inability of those responsible for making the installation to do so in a practical and expeditious manner.

One of the greatest potentials for profit improvement in the business enterprise lies in the intelligent and effective use of the flexible budget. Used sensibly, the flexible budget saves money in two ways: One, by more clearly revealing the costs and relative profit contributions of the various products or segments of the company, it paves the way toward informed decisions and action relative to pricing and product mix; and two, it serves as a budgetary control and enforcement device. The flexible budget focuses attention on weak spots in need of remedial action.

The flexible budget could be defined as a financial plan which adjusts automatically with changes in volume. It tells management:

1. what volume of activity is needed to break even
2. the gain or loss in profits due to failure to attain the planned level of activity
3. how much was spent above or below the budgeted overhead allowance based on the actual level of activity
4. the relative profitability of various products in the line

43

This is a far cry from the "fixed" or appropriation type of budget which must be revised with each change in the level of activity. The flexible budget can be used at the product cost level to control manufacturing overhead; it can be applied to below-the-line costs; and it can apply to the entire profit and loss statement to provide management with a broad control of all costs from net sales to profit.

The advantages of a flexible budget are:

1. It provides management with information critically needed in our modern competitive society—breakeven sales; profit-volume relationship; relative profit-ability of products.
2. Management can take the offensive through the marginal pricing concept. It can move confidently in an area which many companies approach by a "seat-of-the-pants" philosophy.
3. Once established, it results in a budget formula which is anchored to a firm reference point.
4. Use of the formula to determine overhead rates integrates overhead control with costing of inventories and pricing. These, too, are then tied to a firm reference point.
5. Use of a formula allows automation to be introduced into budgeting.

Some form of the flexible budget is recommended in nearly all situations because it is too easy to become complacent and allow cost excesses to accumulate. Lack of a firm reference point will obscure the extent of cost reduction needed to compensate for a drop in volume of activity. A consistent "par for the course" is just as important in management controls as it is "on the green." To get the most effective results from the flexible budget:

1. The installation and periodic revisions must be made expeditiously.
2. The operating personnel must be properly oriented as to what the flexible budget is and what it can do for them.
3. They must participate in the development of the budget.
4. The flexible budget must be simple and direct; e.g., free of "splintered" costs which are needlessly allocated to levels below which intelligent control can be exercised.
5. The variances which are developed through use of this device must be tempered with judgment.

There is a common misconception that installation must necessarily take from six months to a year, or longer. Many installations are never undertaken for this reason. Others, which take longer than 90 days, become obsolete before they are completed as a result of numerous changes brought on by our fast-moving competitive economy. Television, the most recent of our new consumer products, is a good example.

Although total sales of seven large television manufacturers increased from $450 million to $1,100 million in the first ten years of this new industry, the average factory selling price per set dropped from $280 to $120 during this same period, while profit on sales dropped from 4.7 percent to 2.4 percent. Quite naturally, the set manufacturer exerted pressure on his suppliers, one of whom, during that period, was the vacuum tube manufacturer. In addition to exerting pressure to obtain lower prices, the television manufacturer reduced the number of tubes per set through use of multipurpose tubes which performed more than one function. Fewer tubes meant fewer sockets, fewer wires, fewer points to be soldered and consequently lower labor costs. To the tube manufacturer it meant redesign of tubes to meet manufacturers' demands; this in turn meant more critical specifications when the tubes must perform more functions, it meant retooling, it meant greater scrap problems. As it turned out, more and more vacuum tubes were replaced by semi-conductors, as is evident through greater use of "solid state."

Foreign imports are another factor contributing to the fierceness of competition. Japanese products of excellent quality have been produced at labor rates that were substantially lower than those of the United States. However, surprising as it may be, even the Japanese have gone to automation to be better able to cope with the cheaper labor on the Asian mainland.

In the light of these competitive pressures, which are relentless in the paralyzing effect they have on the stability of an operation, it is obvious that any program for installation of flexible budgets for control of overhead must be accomplished expeditiously. A 30-day installation period in most companies is entirely feasible and should be an objective.

WHY SOME INSTALLATIONS TAKE SO LONG

Probably the biggest reason that installations take six months or longer is the tendency to develop the flexible budget with the expectation that it will provide management with a precise tool with which to measure deviations from budget. This attempt at a "perfectionist" approach is wasteful because manufacturing operations cannot be measured by precise mathematical formulae any more than the ups and downs of our economy can be accurately forecasted. The operating manager, knowing that a precise mathematical formula is being used to measure his performance, will be reluctant to accept this concept because he knows that there is nothing precise in the interaction of competitive pressures.

THE "BOOK" ON ORGANIZATION CHARTS

Availability of an up-to-date organization chart is usually set forth by writers on the subject as an important prerequisite for any flexible budget installation which, after all, must be patterned with areas of responsibility in mind.

The company which finds itself in need of cost controls is also in need of an organization chart. It frequently happens that transfers and changes in activities within the company may have rendered existing organization charts obsolete. What alternative, then, is there? Should the installation be stalled until the organization is formalized, or will steps be taken to move ahead without waiting? If the choice is to wait, one might well find that changes are still being made. In this waiting period many thousands of dollars may slip down the drain through lack of adequate controls.

The hourly factory employee who discovers an error in his paycheck does not need an organization chart to find the individual who will correct the error. He knows that someone is responsible for this function. If a change of responsibility has taken place, he will quickly ascertain this fact. Is there any reason, therefore, that the individual responsible for making the installation cannot do likewise when the organization is in process of change and no formal organization chart is available? Someone is responsible for signing purchase orders before material can be ordered from a supplier. Someone is responsible for manufacturing the product, for inspecting and approving the product for shipment, for receiving the materials into stock, and for shipping the finished product to the customer. This should provide the information required to draw up a rough organization chart without waiting for the formalized copy which may "take forever" before it is officially issued.

THE "BOOK" ON NEED FOR SALES FORECASTS

Books written on the subject of flexible budgets and budgetary controls take for granted the existence of a sales forecast which can be accurately broken down by number of units to be produced and the number to be sold month by month. Yet, in a survey conducted by the author recently, in which the following question was asked of key financial personnel of 28 companies: *"Do you receive sales estimates which you consider satisfactory for planning and budgeting purposes?"* 14 advised that they did not receive reliable forecasts. The remaining 14 were either satisfied with the basis of their forecasting or non-committal as to the degree of accuracy. This is easy to understand when one considers some of the factors affecting our postwar economy in which defense spending plays such a significant part. When the space exploration project was approved, for example, the estimated level of spending ranged from $22 billion to $29 billion. Another source estimated that this project would cost as much as $40 billion. Under these conditions let us examine the plight of the marketing department which must come up with sales forecasts for its company. Assuming that the company involved is not a prime contractor but one which might be a supplier to one or more prime contractors, let us enumerate the steps the marketing manager must take in evaluating the effect of a large government spending program on his company:

Step 1. The first step is to determine whether the space exploration project will cost $22, $29, $40 billions, or some other figure within this range. This becomes, obviously, a guess, because those who authorized the funds did not know themselves.

Step 2. How much of this money will be spent in the first year, the second year, and so on? How much will be spent by quarters in the first year? This is guess number 2.

Step 3. Who will the prime contractors be? How much of the funds will be awarded to them? In the first year, second year, and so on? This is guess number 3.

Step 4. The sales or marketing manager must next determine which of the prime contractors will purchase from his company and how much they will buy. This must necessarily be largely guesswork.

Step 5. Once Steps 1 through 4 have been determined and a sales volume established, it must be broken down by product line, by number of units, and by type of component if the principles of the "book" are to be followed.

Obviously, this is an impossibility. Little wonder that 14 out of 28 companies complained about lack of good sales forecasts. If the principles advanced by the "book" cannot be applied, this raises the very important question as to what basis can be used for the budget base in companies where detailed sales forcasts are not available. As in cases where organization charts are lacking, the installation cannot be delayed pending the availability of a definitive sale forcast—which may not materialize for some time in a rapidly changing industry.

The alternative, then, is to base the flexible budget on a realistic capacity level, which, in effect is another approach to arriving at a sales forecast. Once determined on this basis, the flexibility of the budget would adjust for changes in the activity level each period. Such an approach is demonstrated for two plants. The first of these is a multiproduct plant of a large company and will be identified as Plant A. The other is a highly mechanized operation making metal stampings and will be identified as Plant B.

PLANT A: PRODUCTION DEPARTMENTS

Assembly of radar tubes
Assembly of transmitting tubes
Firing department
Manual glass blowing
Automatic glass blowing
Exhaust department
Plating and spray painting
Tube development
Tube development machine shop

Under such a circumstance, where sales forecasts are lacking, the recommended approach would be to determine the range of activity in the recent past—usually the preceding 12 months. An analysis of one of the departments disclosed the following to be the activity in the preceding 12 months based on the number of direct labor employees:

	No. of Direct Labor Employees
September	25
October	26
November	26
December	30
January	32
February	38
March	40

April	38
May	35
June	37
July	32
August	37

The foreman of this department, when shown these figures during the installation, was asked to suggest a realistic range of activity for the coming year. In the example cited above, he noted that the total of 25 direct labor employees (September) was considered by him to be below the anticipated low for the coming 12 months, and 40, the high point in the preceding 12 months (March), did not represent the anticipated peak of activity in the coming year. Based on "feel," the foreman estimated his minimum number of direct labor employees for the coming year would be 36, and the maximum about 52. This, then, suggested a normal range of activity. Expenses were estimated for these two levels and the fixed and variable costs determined mathematically through the low-high method which will be discussed later.

Plant B, which consists entirely of equipment for stamping the parts used in the manufacture of radios and television sets, presented a similar problem in forecasting sales estimates because of continual changes in design; TV manufacturers are constantly changing the circuits. Forecasting of sales under these conditions becomes very unreliable and subject to change.

The equipment in Plant B is listed below by type and by number of machines. When originally acquired, the justification for purchase anticipated that certain of the equipment would be used for two shifts while other equipment would only be used on a one-shift basis. The first step, then, was to determine how many shifts each machine would be operated. This is shown in columns (2) and (3) below. These two columns, added together, show in column (4) the total potential machine hours per day. Obviously, equipment cannot be operated continuously. Time must be allowed for changing the dies, making adjustments, and repairs. Column (5) indicates this allowance in the form of a machine utilization percentage. Application of this percentage to column (4) provides a realistic capacity level in terms of machine hours per day—column (6).

PLANT B: PRODUCTION DEPARTMENTS

	No. of Presses (1)	First Shift (2)	Second Shift (3)	Mach. Hrs. Per Day (4)	% Utiliz. (5)	Adj. Mach. Hrs. Per Day (6)
Multislide Section						
#11	4	4	4	64	78%	50
#22	4	4	4	64	78	50
#28	27	27	27	432	78	337
Total	35	35	35	560		437

Large Presses					
15 Ton	5	5	2	56	75%	42
25 Ton	1	1	1	16	75	12
60 Ton	1	1		8	75	6
Total	7	7	3	80		60
Small Presses					
#0	24	24	9	264	75%	198
#01	12	12	6	144	75	108
Bliss #18	4	4	1	40	75	30
Waterbury					
Farrell	2	2		16	75	12
Total	42	42	16	464		348

Column (6) then becomes the base for the flexible budget, and is arrived at through a forecast established by projecting levels of production based on "feel." The expenses for this level are broken down into the fixed and variable portions in the manner explained in another section.

SHOULD THE BUDGET BE BASED ON ACTUAL OR STANDARD?

Because of radical product changes in many companies, existing standards can quickly become obsolete, requiring either continuous updating at great expense (which some companies prefer to avoid), or a complete revision of standards at some future time when a period of greater stability is reached—with estimates serving the purpose in the interim period. Most book approaches assume the existence of reliable standards based on a stabilized operation. Obviously, this is not always the case, and it is these instances which raise such questions as: *"If I use actual direct labor, or actual machine hours, won't the inefficient departments be rewarded through greater allowances when their efficiency deteriorates?"* The obvious answer is that use of actual labor or actual machine hours is not desirable—allowances should be based on good product only. However, lack of a proper base, which might take from six months to a year to establish, is a very poor reason for not establishing cost controls. It is far better to base a budget on *"actual"* than to await *"ideal"* conditions recommended by the book approach.

SEPARATION OF THE FIXED AND VARIABLE COSTS

The flexible budget should be established with limits which represent the normal operating range the plant can be expected to operate in during the coming year. A review of the past 12 to 15 months' level with adjustments to eliminate the unusual should furnish a clue as to the proper range. Twenty-five percent above and below "normal" or "average" is a rule-of-thumb guide used by some companies, provided this does not require additional facilities or additional shifts on the upgrade, or dropping a shift on the downgrade. In such instances, the limits of the range should be adjusted to avoid crossovers. Use of incorrect techniques for separation of fixed and variable costs can be a delaying factor in making a flexible budget installation. Because of their importance, some of these techniques will be discussed at length.

SCATTER CHARTS

While most books recommend the scatter chart method of separating fixed and variable costs, the author, in his experience, has found this method to be one of the least desirable—except in the theoretically stable operation which most books assume.

One of the disadvantages of scatter charts is that they require a voluminous amount of work which is time consuming. A plant containing 50 departments with an average of 60 items in the chart of accounts would require 3,000 scatter charts to be drawn. Allowing for time to draw up and analyze this many charts would delay the installation for weeks. This represents a tremendous clerical task which cannot be assigned to someone without some knowledge of charting and proper use of scales. Exhibits 3-1 and 3-2 illustrate what can happen if the scatter charts are prepared by an unskilled individual.

Note in Exhibit 3-1 that a straight line would be somewhat difficult to fit to the plotted points because they do not fall in a stable pattern. However, if the vertical scale values are multiplied by five and the points replotted as in Exhibit 3-2, the pattern follows a straight line and the line of variability can more easily be fitted to the points. If the scales are not properly selected, both vertically and horizontally, much trial and error charting may be necessary. This takes time, particularly when 3,000 individual charts must be drawn.

The scatter chart presents another problem in that many expenses lead activity in the factory by as much as eight weeks, while other expenses lag. The production control department, as an example, must check its inventory and place requisitions with the purchasing department long before factory activity can increase. The purchasing department, in turn, must place orders several weeks in advance. Industrial engineering must work on labor layout problems before the increased activity occurs and the personnel department must review its seniority lists and recall employees from layoff. Quality control and shipping activities, on the other hand, usually lag activity in the factory.

This lead-lag effect can produce scatter patterns which are difficult to interpret. Exhibit 3-3 illustrates an ideal situation when the expense (purchasing department used in this case) fluctuates in harmony with the volume in the factory. Most scatter charts depicted in books on the subject illustrate a pattern such as this. However, in actual practice the pattern corresponds more to the one illustrated in Exhibit 3-4. Note that the figures used for the 11 months are the same for both—adding up to a total of $111,200. Exhibit 3-3 illustrates how the fixed and variable separation would be accomplished. However, since the purchasing department activity is likely to precede factory activity, it would be at a high level when the factory level is low. When factory activity rises and purchasing has done its job, its own activity is likely to be at a reduced level, with the result that the scatter pattern would indicate an inverse relationship, as shown in Exhibit 3-4. Obviously, no fixed and variable relationship can be determined from this data. The low-high method of determining two points and

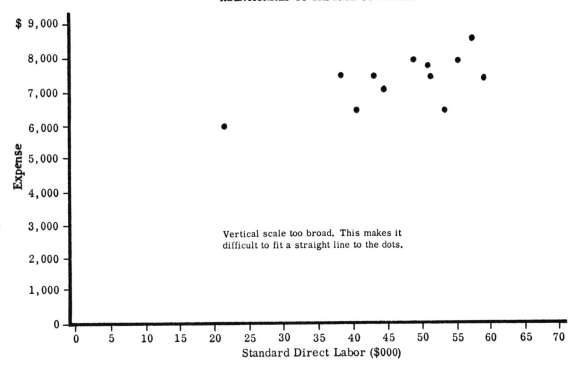

RELATIONSHIP OF EXPENSE TO VOLUME

Vertical scale too broad. This makes it difficult to fit a straight line to the dots.

Exhibit 3-1

RELATIONSHIP OF EXPENSE TO VOLUME

The same data shown in the preceding graph has been plotted to a vertical scale which was multiplied by five. Note how much more easily the line can be fitted.

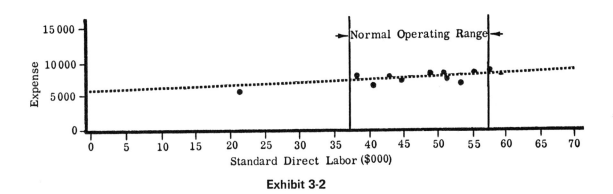

Exhibit 3-2

developing the fixed and variable relationship is a simpler variation of the scatter chart method and has many advantages over this method. The low-high method is described in the next section.

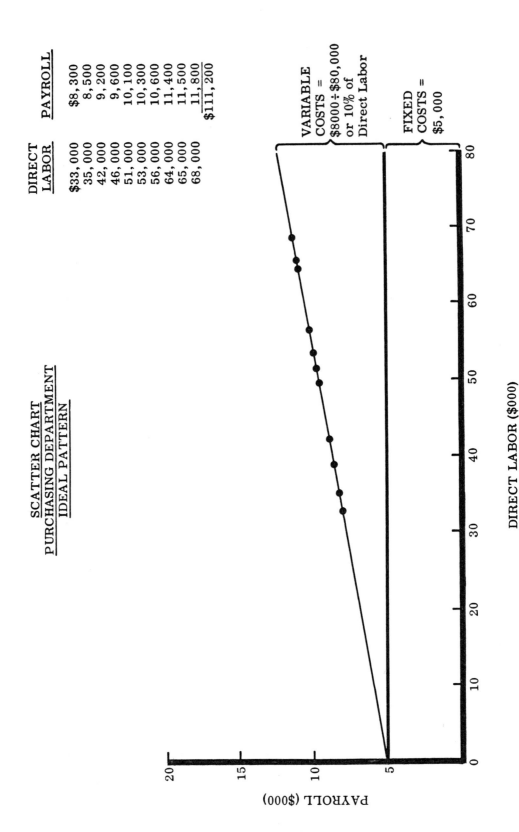

DIRECT LABOR	PAYROLL
$33,000	$8,300
35,000	8,500
42,000	9,200
46,000	9,600
51,000	10,100
53,000	10,300
56,000	10,600
64,000	11,400
65,000	11,500
68,000	11,800
	$111,200

SCATTER CHART
PURCHASING DEPARTMENT
IDEAL PATTERN

VARIABLE
COSTS =
$8000÷$80,000
or 10% of
Direct Labor

FIXED
COSTS =
$5,000

DIRECT LABOR ($000)

PAYROLL ($000)

Exhibit 3-3

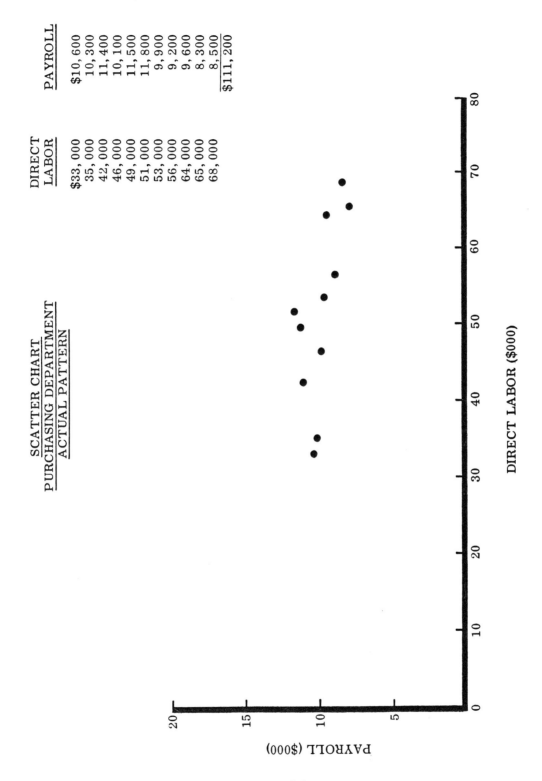

DIRECT LABOR	PAYROLL
$33,000	$10,600
35,000	10,300
42,000	11,400
46,000	10,100
49,000	11,500
51,000	11,800
53,000	9,900
56,000	9,200
64,000	9,600
65,000	8,300
68,000	8,500
	$111,200

SCATTER CHART
PURCHASING DEPARTMENT
ACTUAL PATTERN

DIRECT LABOR ($000)

PAYROLL ($000)

Exhibit 3-4

53

LOW-HIGH METHOD

This method is based on the selection of two levels of activity within the normal operating range and determining the expenses at these two levels. The difference in the two levels of activity (expressed in direct labor, machine hours, or other base) is divided into the difference in cost to arrive at a variable percentage. The application of this variable percentage to either of the activity levels will determine the variable portion of the total cost. The balance will be fixed, as shown in the example below:

COST OF OPERATING AN AUTOMOBILE

Step 1

	Low	High	Diff.
Miles driven per month	700	1,400	700
Total monthly cost	$ 94.50	$ 119.00	$ 24.50

Step 2

$24.50 divided by 700 miles (difference column) equals
variable cost per mile . . . . $.035 per mile

Step 3

Variable cost for low and high levels equals:

	Low	High
	$ 24.50	$ 49.00

Step 4

Fixed cost = total monthly cost shown in Step 1 less variable cost in Step 3

	Low	High
Total cost per Step 1	$ 94.50	$ 119.00
Less variable cost	24.50	49.00
Fixed cost	$ 70.00	$ 70.00

While the low-high method is superior to the scatter chart approach, analysis of a single experienced level has the advantage of requiring estimates of expenses for only one level. Operating managers find this method easier to understand because the fixed costs can be spelled out by item, whereas in the preceding two methods the fixed costs are lumped into one figure. The single level method will be described in the next section.

ANALYSIS OF AN EXPERIENCED LEVEL

Using the previous example of an automobile in the low-high method, let us assume that the experienced level of operations is 1,000 miles per month. Use of an experienced level has the advantage of better estimating because it represents actual fact. Through a review of actual purchases of gasoline, lubrications and oil changes, and through accruals for some of the other costs, we could estimate the fixed and variable costs for a single level of operations as shown below:

COST OF OPERATING AN AUTOMOBILE 1000 MILES PER MONTH

Variable Costs	
Gasoline	$20.00
Lubrications	1.75
Oil changes	4.25
Monthly accrual for repairs and tire replacement	9.00
Total variable costs	$35.00
Fixed Costs	
Depreciation adjusted for trade-in value	$50.00
Insurance	16.67
Registration	1.25
Monthly accrual for battery, muffler, and anti-freeze replacement	2.08
Total fixed cost	$70.00

The accrual for repairs and tire replacement takes into account the fact that the layouts for these items are made at infrequent intervals of time and the cost must be apportioned on the basis of mileage. The battery, muffler, and anti-freeze cost represents more a fixed cost than a variable cost because replacement of these items is governed more by time than by the number of miles traveled. In fact, a battery and muffler may last longer when a car is more heavily driven than when it is used only for short trips.

The chapter entitled "Installing the Flexible Budget" includes a set of schedules used in an actual flexible budget installation. The single experienced level method was used in the development of Schedules B (Personnel Requirements—Headcount) and C (Departmental Budgets).

THE STEP METHOD

This method is a highly sophisticated method which determines the expense for several capacity levels. It is not recommended for the initial installation because the setting of budget allowances for seven to ten levels of activity in the first installation is impractical and consumes far too much time. Experience should first be gained through a simpler approach, such as the low-high or single experienced level method.

IMPORTANCE OF FOLLOW-UP

While on the one hand some companies spend substantial sums of money and time for flexible budget installations based on meticulous approaches, there are others who will periodically go to the other extreme and make important management decisions through use of a "broad-brush" approach. An example would be to arbitrarily assume that hourly indirect labor, labor fringes, supplies and preventative maintenance would be variable while all other costs are fixed. This action is frequently taken to price a large bid competitively—using the marginal concept of recovering only part of the fixed costs; it may be prompted by need for breakeven information when a new acquisition is being considered, or it may be necessary to make some determination of the profit-volume relationships in a management presentation of future plans.

Whether the flexible budget has been developed in depth or by "broad-brush" treatment, follow-up as to effect on management decisions is quite important. When the assumption is made that certain costs are variable and others fixed, for purposes of bidding, for example, it should be of great importance to management to ascertain whether costs are actually behaving in the manner assumed.

Even if practical considerations preclude the possibility of dropping variable people from the payroll based on short-term fluctuations, because of a tight labor market or cost of retraining (which might exceed the savings), this fact should be known. The variances from budget in this case would tell the cost of fluctuations in production. Management might then be able to balance the cost of these variations against the cost of building inventories for the purpose of levelling out costly peaks and valleys. Perhaps prices quoted in bidding might be based on timing of the additional business in terms of seasonal activity. The business which would be taken during the low production periods might be quoted differently than that taken in peak periods.

CONCLUSIONS

There is little question in the mind of the modern businessman as to the benefits to be derived from use of a flexible budget. The problem in many companies is the inability on the part of those responsible for making the installation to do so in an expeditious manner. For some unexplained reason many financial groups, whose responsibility it would be to furnish their managements with such information, feel that the development of a flexible budget is a major undertaking. They forget that the general managers they serve must frequently turn a loss operation into the "black" in a matter of a few months. The general manager cannot approach his superiors with the excuse that competitors have dropped prices and hence the loss operation. Were he to do so, he would be quietly reminded that if competitors were able to drop prices, they must have been able to reduce costs correspondingly. And when he asks his financial group for information as to breakeven sales volume under the new conditions, or figures needed for marginal pricing, the information must be forthcoming in a matter of weeks rather than months. It would therefore behoove the financial segment of management not to justify a longer period of installation (or revision), but rather, by using the following six points as a guide, to shorten the period of time required to 30 days or less:

1. Use history as a guide but don't analyze reams and reams of historical data. Such detailed analysis is wasteful of time and accomplishes little. In fact, past

history could be misleading because of new forces which have come into play.

2. Forget the "book." The book will set forth the need for firm organization charts, the need for good sales forecasts, and the desirability of basing flexible budgets on standard rather than actual. Remember that the "book" assumes *ideal* conditions. The companies that need flexible budgets most also need organization charts, better sales forecasts, and standards.

3. Spend maximum time on major expenses. In most cases 60% of the expense accounts make up less than 20% of the cost. Don't try to split each of these into its fixed and its variable segments. Determine whether the expense is predominantly fixed or predominantly variable. Then classify it as one or the other.

4. Don't use scatter charts for separation of fixed and variable costs. This method is too time consuming and the results do not justfiy the investment of time and effort.

5. Although few variable costs follow an exact linear relationship with volume, don't try to adjust for this in the initial installation or the program will never get off the ground. Even in the installation of a flexible budget, the rule "crawl before walking" is applicable.

6. Don't spend time getting approval of each department's flexible budget as it is completed. Put the whole package together first. Then calculate the breakeven point. If your business is "cost-plus" and the breakeven point is not meaningful, then compute the overhead rates at various volume levels and let this be your guide in recommending approval of the budget.

The "perfectionist" approach to installation of the flexible budget is wasteful because manufacturing operations cannot be measured by precise mathematics any more than the ups and downs of our economy can be accurately forecasted.

4

Packaging the Flexible Budget

The documentation of many flexible budgets is limited to numerous disorganized pencilled worksheets that are available to and understood by only one individual.

In a survey of flexible budget installation in several companies, the author noted that first things were not always put first. In several instances, there was no pre-installation program for familiarizing the operating people with flexible budgets. Frequently, department managers were not consulted in the establishment of their budgets.

Because of the great importance of proper education of the operating managers, the first part of this chapter is devoted to the explanation of a technique successfully employed by the author. It consists of a series of *Budget Bulletins,* which, in simple language, explain the flexible budget concept, the determination of a breakeven point, and the application of the budget formula in determining the relative profitability of various products in the line.

It was also noted in the survey that none of the companies issued a digest of the basic information used in establishing the budget formula, probably because the basic information was not accumulated in a manner which would lend itself to easy presentation.

The author believes that this information is of sufficient value to warrant its submission to management in capsule form for review and study. A suggested format for the progressive accumulation and presentation of this information is included in this chapter. The schedules making up the "package" are explained.

It was also found that in some companies budgets were approved on a step-by-step basis so that by the time the last step of the installation was completed, all preceding steps had been approved. While, in theory, this approach seems plausible, the author will explain why he does not recommend it.

ORIENTATION OF OPERATING PERSONNEL VERY IMPORTANT

Because the average production man would find the technical aspects of flexible budgets quite uninteresting, it is important to demonstrate to him in understandable, non-technical language how the budget will work. Showmanship is as important in selling this technique as it is in selling a product—attention and interest must first be aroused. With an awakening of interest the more technical aspects can be dealt with step by step.

One method of arousing interest which can be used is the issuance of Budget Bulletins prior to the installation. Cartoons can be used effectively in the explanation of each pertinent point. Budget Bulletin 1 starts with a cartoon of a restaurant patron who is vehement in his objection to a minimum charge of $3 for a hamburger which is probably worth less than a dollar. The point made by this cartoon is that the minimum charge recognizes the concept of fixed costs. Using the illustration of an automobile, the bulletin next points out that the automobile, too, has certain costs which are fixed and certain ones which vary with mileage traveled. Assuming a fixed cost of $50 per month, and variable costs of $.03 per mile, the bulletin then shows how costs can be budgeted for varying mileages. The example is then shifted to a factory. The direct labor dollars in a factory are likened to miles traveled in a car. Using these direct labor dollars and assuming certain fixed and variable costs, an example is given of how the budget formula can be used for determining overhead costs and the effect on the cost per unit of various levels of operation.

The next bulletin, which can be issued about two weeks later, discusses the method to be used in separating fixed and variable costs (note that the terms "fixed" and "constant" are used interchangeably). It illustrates a department and lists the actual personnel after adjustment for the unusual—which might be extra help to cope with a recent emergency situation, or overtime. It discusses briefly one method of determining fixed and variable costs. Finally, it shows how the budget formula, once developed, can be used to budget the costs of the department.

With the budget formula explained, the next bulletin, Budget Bulletin 3, describes one of the major applications of the flexible budget—the development of the breakeven point. Factory managers who may be under pressure to improve their profit picture will frequently express great interest in the breakeven chart because it helps support the argument that certain minimum sales are needed to cover the fixed costs of manufacture. While all managements recognize this subconsciously, they are not likely to lend too much credence to this argument unless supporting figures are presented to them. One plant manager, who was being harassed by his division management to increase his profits, asked the author to help him develop a breakeven analysis on a rough-cut basis in order that he might have the information to study prior to his annual review which was due in a few days. After determining the breakdown of material, direct labor, overhead, and other below-the-line costs by their fixed and variable makeup, the breakeven analysis showed that actual sales were approximately 75 percent of the volume required to break even. Even though the existing sales volume indicated that losses were inevitable, the plant manager was able for the first time to take the offensive and show that more sales volume was needed in order to increase profits to any substantial degree.

The calculations used to develop the breakeven sales volume are described in this Budget Bulletin. Because volume variance is the measure of over or under absorption of fixed costs from the standard level used for developing the predetermined overhead rate, a brief explanation is in order at this point.

Question: *What is Volume Variance?*

Volume variance represents the difference between the amount of fixed costs absorbed in the product (and recovered in the sales price) and the actual amount of fixed costs incurred. The following example demonstrates this:

Figures in Thousand $	Activity level 1	Activity level 2	Activity level 3	Activity level 4	Activity level 5
Direct labor	$3,300	$3,600	$3,900	$4,200	$4,500
Overhead Absorbed					
Variable	2,310	2,520	2,730	2,940	3,150
Fixed	1,551	1,692	1,833	1,974	2,115
Total overhead absorbed	3,861	4,212	4,563	4,914	5,265
Actual Overhead*					
Variable	2,310	2,520	2,730	2,940	3,150
Fixed	1,833	1,833	1,833	1,833	1,833
Total actual overhead	4,143	4,353	4,563	4,773	4,983
Difference (Volume Variance)	(282)	(141)	–0–	141	282

*Note: Actual figures assume no variance from budgeted allowances.

Budget Bulletin 4 shows still another application of the flexible budget technique. It shows selling prices and costs for six products. The costs are broken down to show the variable costs in the fashion followed in direct costing. The variable costs are divided by the sales price to arrive at the precentage of the sales dollar which must be expended to cover variable costs. The balance, expressed as the percentage of the sales dollar left, is used as an index of profitability.

The higher the percentage, the greater the profitability of that product—other things being equal. The point is made that if such information is readily available, it is frequently possible to take steps to decrease the variable costs of a product and thus leave a greater percentage of the sales price to cover fixed costs and profits. Note throughout these bulletins that little or no stress is placed on the control feature of flexible budgets—the main emphasis is on the advantages in easier costing, determination of breakeven volume, volume variance, and knowledge regarding the relative profitability of products. While this represents only a few of the series of budget bulletins which can be issued, these are the most significant and issuance could be terminated at this point. One may well find, however, that once these bulletins have been circulated, recipients will look for future issues.

MAKING THE INSTALLATION

Step 1—The Budget Base—Schedule A

The first step in beginning the installation is to determine what the budget base should be—direct labor hours or dollars, machine hours, or any other applicable base. In this case *(see page 78)* the installation was started after the sales plan for the coming year had been approved at a level of slightly more than $6,000,000. Because most of the work was based on hand operations, direct labor was used as the base. Direct labor dollars, rather than hours, were used for accounting convenience. Because a substantial change in the manufacturing processes had been made recently, existing standards were obsolete and revision was at least six months away. Rather than lose six months to a year, it was felt that actual direct labor dollars rather than standard should be used for the initial installation. (Because of the obsolescence of the standards, actual direct labor was being used as the basis for the predetermined overhead rate used for charging overhead into production.) The sales dollars represented by the sales plan were converted to direct labor dollars, and the breakdown by production departments shown on Schedule A—Budget Base. This was, then, the base used for determining the variable percentage in the budget formula, to be explained in later discussion of Schedule C.

Step 2—Determining the Personnel Requirements—Schedule B

Indirect labor in most companies is the preponderant overhead cost. One will find in many companies that this cost makes up two-thirds of the overhead. It is with this in mind that the author, in his budget installations, has included a headcount schedule such as this one *(see page 79)*. A listing of headcount is undoubtedly one of the most basic of reports. To show the breakdown of indirect personnel by fixed and variable in a schedule such as this gives focus to an important element of cost. Determination of who should be fixed and who should be variable is not always easy. Generally, one might review management action in the past when volume has dropped or increased to determine in which areas reductions or increases in personnel have taken place. This should, however, be tempered with the questions: "Should not reductions have been made in areas which were untouched?" and "Should an increase in personnel during periods of rising volume have been made to the extent that it was made?" The individual making the installation is not usually in a position to express firm opinions on this point—his mission is to suggest and guide. The overall budget must be viewed in perspective when the breakeven point is developed and necessary action taken by a higher management level. This will be discussed later in the chapter. Once the personnel requirements are completed, the payroll cost can be calculated and we are ready for Schedule C.

Step 3—The Departmental Budget—Schedule C

The payroll cost of Schedule B is shown as accounts 10 and 24 on Schedule C *(see page 87)*. The other non-labor items of expense are then included. Only those items which are actually controllable by a department manager should be charged to him. Assessments for building and grounds maintenance, plant security, and electricity (which is usually not measurable by department without a prohibitive expenditure of

BUDGET BULLETIN

"WHAT ?! A $3.00 MINIMUM CHARGE......FOR A HAMBURGER?"

We pay minimum charge on almost every cost we incur.

Take our automobile as an example......The minimum or constant cost includes such items as depreciation, insurance, registration fees, and garage rent--all determined by passage of time without regard to the number of miles traveled.

Variable costs, which fluctuate with the miles traveled, include such costs as gasoline, oil, repairs, tires and lubrication.

Assuming that constant costs average $50 per month and variable costs $.03 per mile, let us demonstrate how easily costs can be forecasted for various mileages.

		Cost per Mile
0 miles per month at $.03 plus $50 =	$ 50	$ -
500 miles per month at $.03 plus $50 =	65	.130
1000 miles per month at $.03 plus $50 =	80	.080
1500 miles per month at $.03 plus $50 =	95	.063
2000 miles per month at $.03 plus $50 =	110	.055

If we were in the business of renting cars and wanted to project the costs of operating a fleet, note how simple it would be to multiply the mileage per car by the variable factor and add the constant cost--rather than building up all costs from the ground up.

Now let's see how a flexible budget would operate in one of our manufacturing activities using the example of a special tube plant of one of our large competitors who has had flexible budgets for ten years.

This plant has constant costs of $80,000 per month--this includes such items as depreciation, property taxes, insurance, and supervision.

Variable costs are $2.00 per Direct Labor Dollar and include such items as material handling, shipping, supplies and maintenance.

Using this formula, the cost of operating the plant at various levels is as follows:

0 Direct Labor Dollars per month at $2.00 + $80,000 =	$ 80,000
30,000 Direct Labor Dollars per month at $2.00 + $80,000 =	140,000
45,000 Direct Labor Dollars per month at $2.00 + $80,000 =	170,000
60,000 Direct Labor Dollars per month at $2.00 + $80,000 =	200,000

If each Direct Labor Dollar produces ten tubes, then the overhead cost on

300,000 tubes would be $140,000 or $.467 per tube
450,000 tubes would be $170,000 or $.378 per tube
600,000 tubes would be $200,000 or $.333 per tube

The decrease in overhead cost from $.467 to $.333 per tube results from spreading the fixed cost of $80,000 over 600,000 tubes rather than 300,000.

The flexible budget is not limited in its application to the above; our competitors use it for determining their breakeven level of sales and also to determine the relative profitability of various products in the line.

Subsequent bulletins will demonstrate these applications.

"OF COURSE I USE A
FLEXIBLE BUDGET"

BUDGET BULLETIN

Question: How would you determine the variable and constant costs in an indirect labor department which is so intermingled with both types of costs?

Step #1 would be to select a recently experienced level of activity, the results of which are fresh in mind. The current year's annual plan would also provide a good basis for a flexible budget.

Different operations have their own favorite measures of activity, such as number of tubes per month, units per day, or billings per month. Whatever the measure, it must be converted to a common denominator which will measure activity in terms of productive effort--usually direct labor.

For purposes of demonstration, let's assume that the level of activity recently experienced (or in the annual plan) runs approximately $4,350,000 per year or a total of 1,000 direct labor employees.

Step #2 involves a head count. The number of indirect labor employees required to service 1,000 direct labor employees must be determined. The indirect labor department in this case will be the Material Control Department.

In discussing the personnel requirements with the department head, we find that after elimination of 2 extra people who were needed on a temporary basis his estimate of average requirements is 20 people of whom 6 are constant and 14 variable. These break down by job as follows:

Job Classification	Total Employees	Constant	Variable
Section Head	1	1	
Secretary	1	1	
Planners	5	2	3
Material Handlers	8	1	7
Storekeepers	5	1	4
Total Head Count	20	6	14
Annual Payroll	$83,500	$31,300	$52,200

The test of a constant cost is: Will an increase of direct labor employees from 1,000 to, say 1,250, require an increase in a particular classification of indirect labor. If not, then that group can be considered to be constant.

The test of a variable cost is that it will fluctuate with direct labor. If direct labor employees should increase from 1,000 to 1,250, an indirect labor complement of 4 people would increase from 4 to 5. The reverse would, of course, also be true.

My SECRETARY is a fixed cost.

Steps 1 and 2 have dealt with indirect labor--the most significant single item of overhead and the most difficult to separate into its fixed and variable components.

Other major expenses are occupancy and depreciation, both of which are considered to be constant, and maintenance which may be considered predominantly variable.

The remaining expense other than fringe benefits, which follow labor, comprise a relatively small percentage of the total overhead so that arbitrary decisions as to variability or fixedness will not make a material difference in the final result.

Question: How can the flexible budget be used for budgetary control ?

First let us calculate the budget formula. This is accomplished as follows: Variable costs are 1.2% of direct labor; $52,200 variable cost divided by direct labor base of $4,350,000. Fixed costs of $31,300 amount to $626 per week.

Now, let us assume that the direct labor payroll for the past week was $122,000 and the payroll cost of the Material Control Department $2,250.

Multiplying the $122,000 of direct labor by the variable percentage of 1.2% gives us a variable allowance of $1,464. This, added to the $626 weekly allowance for constant costs gives us a total budget allowance of $2,090.

Since the actual costs were $2,250 and the budgeted allowance $2,090, the budget was exceeded by $160.

The next bulletin will demonstrate how the variable and fixed formula is used in determining the breakeven point.

BUDGET BULLETIN

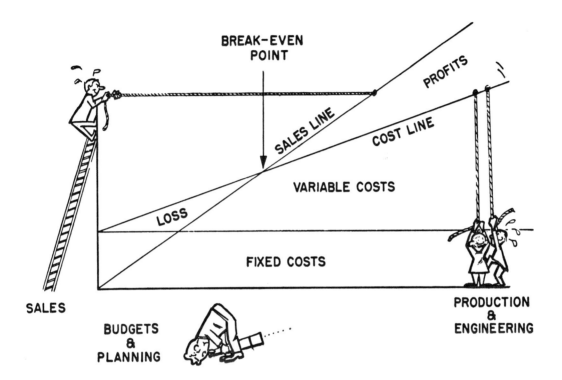

A Breakeven Chart - Note that the cost line is made up of fixed costs plus variable costs. The point at which the sales line crosses the cost line is the breakeven point - which means no profit and no loss.

The breakeven point can be lowered by:

1. Increasing sales through:

    a. selective selling
    b. raising prices (easier said than done)

2. Reducing costs through:

    a. more efficient material utilization
    b. greater labor efficiency
    c. a leaner overhead organization
    d. redesign of the product to permit lower cost production

67

Question: What is a breakeven point and how is it calculated?

The breakeven point is that amount of sales at which all fixed costs are absorbed and at which there is no profit and no loss. Steps 1 through 3 will show how the breakeven point can be calculated.

Step #1 The starting point is sales. For this illustration let's assume that the annual plan shows sales forecasted at a monthly level of $2,037,000.

Step #2 Assuming no change in inventory levels, find the variable and constant costs.

> Material and direct labor are variable because these costs fluctuate directly with the volume of production.
>
> Returns, commissions, and royalty payments are variable because their incidence is usually governed by the level of sales.
>
> Overhead will be both fixed and variable--the amount of each being determined by the flexible budget formula.
>
> Selling expenses other than commissions and service will be considered fixed for purposes of this illustration.

Step #3 List the variable and constant costs and find the percentage that variable costs are to sales:

Sales	$2,037,000	100.00%
Variable Mfg. Costs		
Material	708,600	34.8
Direct Labor	150,100	7.4
Variable Overhead	50,000	2.4
	908,700	44.6
Other Variable Costs		
Returns, Commissions, Royalties	126,300	6.2
Total Variable Cost	1,035,000	50.8
Balance left to cover Fixed Costs		49.2%
Fixed Costs		
Manufacturing	530,000	
Sales and Advertising	203,725	
Total Fixed Costs	$ 733,725	
Breakeven Sales = $733,725 ÷ 49.2%	$1,491,300	

Since variable costs require 50.8% of the sales dollar, 49.2% is left to cover fixed costs. Breakeven sales are determined by merely dividing 49.2% into the fixed cost of $733,725. The result is $1,491,300.

Question: <u>How much profit will be made on the sales levels above and below the break-even point</u>?

Since no profit will be realized on the breakeven sales of $1,491,300, we can count only on the excess over breakeven for profit recovery. Let's take the $2,037,000 sales level in Step #3--the excess over breakeven is $545,700 ($2,037,000 - 1,491,300).

The amount of profit which can be recovered, assuming that budgeted costs are met, will be 49.2% of $545,700 or $268,275. Note that a small difference will be found because the 49.2% is rounded off.

This calculation can be tested by using the analysis shown below:

Total Sales		$2,037,000
Total Variable Cost @ 50.8%	$1,035,000	
Total Fixed Cost	733,725	1,768,725
		$ 268,275

Question: <u>If Sales do not come up to breakeven, how can I estimate the loss</u>?

The loss will be 49.2% for each dollar of sales below breakeven just as the profit is 49.2% for each dollar above breakeven.

The foregoing example illustrates the dynamic nature of volume when the breakeven point is passed in either direction. The next bulletin will explain how relative profitability of various products in the line can be determined.

BUDGET BULLETIN

Question: How can I determine the relative profitability of each product type or contract in my plant?

Step #1 Assuming 6 different product types (these could be tube types, development contracts, or systems) determine the sales prices and variable costs for each as shown below:

Selling Price and Variable Plant Costs

	Product A	Product B	Product C	Product D	Product E	Product F
Sales Price	$250.00	$300.00	$200.00	$350.00	$400.00	$360.00

Total Variable Cost

	Product A	Product B	Product C	Product D	Product E	Product F
Material	$102.25	$ 89.70	$ 71.00	$129.85	$103.20	$101.88
Direct Labor	3.75	20.70	20.80	37.80	31.60	29.52
Overhead	1.25	6.90	7.00	12.60	10.40	9.72
Other Variable	15.50	18.60	12.40	21.70	24.80	22.32
Total Variable	$122.75	$135.90	$111.20	$201.95	$170.00	$163.44
Balance for Fixed Costs and Profit	$127.25	$164.10	$ 88.80	$148.05	$230.00	$196.56

Step #2 Find the percentage that variable costs are to the sales price as shown below:

Variable Costs as % of Sales Value

	Product A	Product B	Product C	Product D	Product E	Product F
Sales Price	100.0%	100.0%	100.0%	100.0%	100.0%	100.0%

Total Variable Cost

	Product A	Product B	Product C	Product D	Product E	Product F
Material	40.9%	29.9%	35.5%	37.1%	25.8%	28.3%
Direct Labor	1.5	6.9	10.4	10.8	7.9	8.2
Overhead	.5	2.3	3.5	3.6	2.6	2.7
Other Variable	6.2	6.2	6.2	6.2	6.2	6.2
Total Variable	49.1%	45.3%	55.6%	57.7%	42.5%	45.4%
Balance for Fixed Costs and Profit	50.9%	54.7%	44.4%	42.3%	57.5%	54.6%

"I ordered bacon and eggs."
"Sorry, we don't make a profit on bacon."

70

The above tabulation shows that Product E has the lowest percentage of variable costs to sales - 42.5%. This means that 57.5% of each sales dollar is left to cover fixed costs and profit.

Product D is the least profitable because its variable percentage to sales is the highest of the six - 57.7%; leaving only 42.3% of the sales dollar to cover fixed costs and profit.

Question: Granted that certain product types are more profitable than others, we can't just discontinue selling Product D and concentrate on Product E because our customers need both and expect us to supply them.

An analysis such as the foregoing is at best only a tool which must be tempered by management judgment.

While Product E is the most profitable of the entire sales mix, it may not be a large volume item. Perhaps a price reduction would result in a substantial increase in volume.

Product D, on the other hand, which is the least profitable, (variable cost 57.7% of sales) may account for a large percentage of the sales volume. It might be well to concentrate on Product D to determine if material and labor cost can be reduced through simplification of design, substitution of less expensive material, and where possible, providing more lead time to facilitate more efficient procurement of materials and better utilization of labor.

Analyses such as those presented in this bulletin will point out various alternatives and the results if such alternatives are followed.

The intangible factors which cannot always be measured in dollars and cents must also be taken into account along with the tangible.

This is where operating management steps in, weighs all the facts and makes its decision.

"With this design we cut costs by
$100 a car."

money) should not be charged to individual departments but rather to a manufacturing manager or plant manager's department. There is nothing more frustrating to a department head attempting to control his costs than variations in these assessments which far outweigh the variations in costs which he can control. To be held accountable for budget variances which include large fluctuations of costs which a manager cannot control could well result in loss of interest in the entire budget program. Schedule C for the various departments shown in the specimen flexible budget does include occupancy cost, one of the items which could be questioned as to controllability at the departmental level. In this instance, however, it was the plant manager's desire to have occupancy charges included. When the fixed and variable breakdown is determined, the fixed cost is divided by the number of days in the year to arrive at a daily figure. This figure can then be used to multiply by the appropriate number of days in the month. Some companies using the 4-4-5 calendar prefer to express the fixed cost on a per week basis. The variable costs in the service departments are divided by the total plant direct labor shown in Schedule A. In the production departments they are divided by the direct labor in the specific department. In a particular instance, when a service department performs a function exclusively for one of the production departments, it would be preferable to have its variable costs based on that production department's labor rather than the plant total. Although the flexible budget may be considered complete at this point, three additional steps are recommended. (These will be discussed as steps 4, 5, and 6.)

Step 4—Allocation of Service Department Expense to Production Departments

In the development of the flexible budget, so much information of value is assembled that calculation of overhead rates requires only a recasting of information already available. The development of and use of overhead rates tying in with the flexible budget will make for an integrated accounting system which will facilitate the determination of reasons for variations in costs.

Allocation of service department costs to production departments is a necessary prerequisite for determining overhead rates. Since overhead rates are determined by dividing the base (direct labor, in this case) into the overhead, it is necessary to distribute all overhead to the production departments for which overhead rates are to be developed. While many texts on the subject will suggest a circuitous route in the distribution, the author recommends a direct-to-production-department apportionment. An illustration of a circuitous route would be charging other service departments for purchasing services, for example. While the theory of charging each department for services rendered to it is technically correct, it is not feasible from a practical point of view. Under this theory, the personnel department would charge the accounting department a *pro rata* share for services rendered to the accounting personnel. The accounting department would charge the personnel department for services in connection with the payroll cost for making up payroll checks. The maintenance department would charge service departments for work done, which in turn might make charges to the maintenance department.

Inasmuch as all service department charges must finally be distributed to production departments for calculation of the overhead rate used for charging overhead to the product, a direct transfer of these costs to production departments is the simplest and most economical.

The method of determining the amount that should be allocated to each production department is a matter of judgment which varies from one individual to another. On the whole, if the method used has some basis in fact and is fairly consistent in application, the final result will give a good indication of overhead by production function.

Schedule D *(see page 96)* illustrates how service department costs were allocated to the production departments. Schedule E *(see page 99)* then shows the development of the overhead rates. It was determined that the Administration Department and the supervisory group in General Manufacturing would be distributed on the basis of the total number of personnel in the production departments, inasmuch as administration and over-all supervision usually follow the number of people. The Purchasing Department's distribution was based on the number of requisitions received from the various production departments during the prior year. Floor space occupied was used as the basis for the occupancy costs. Production Control, part of Industrial Engineering and Material Scheduling and Expediting were based on the number of specifications which existed in the engineering files for each production department. It was felt that the number of product types influenced activity of these departments. Incoming Inspection, Inventory Control, Stores and Receiving, and Material Handling were distributed on the basis of the dollar value of purchased material received in each production department. The portion of Industrial Engineering which was involved in job evaluation was distributed on the basis of direct labor dollars shown in Schedule A.

Step 5—Calculation of the Overhead Rate

These distributions were made for the fixed, the variable, and total overhead. Schedule E brings together the direct labor in the production departments and the overhead costs after distribution has been completed. Calculation of the overhead then becomes a matter of dividing the direct labor into the overhead.

APPROVAL OF THE BUDGET

One might reasonably ask, "Why go through all the work of putting together a flexible budget and then question whether it is acceptable—why not check it out in stages?" The reason is that a piecemeal acceptance of a budget is difficult—the total result must be viewed in proper perspective. It is conceivable that a budget might well be accepted in segments but rejected when the segments are all put together. There is a corollary advantage of putting together a budget which represents the composite thinking of the various department heads concerned. A plant or division manager will be able to ascertain the course that natural trends would take—he will get to know better the psychology of his department heads who spend the money. Their opinions as to the makeup of fixed and variable costs will be most revealing.

In one company of the author's experience a general psychology of expansion existed in the minds of many department heads because of an impending increase in volume of sales. As a result, budgets included allowance for anticipated hiring of personnel. A breakeven point was developed to show the volume of sales needed to support this budgeted addition of personnel. The indication was that the sales volume increase would be out-paced by the addition of the new personnel. This was determined by developing a breakeven point based on the existing sales volume and existing personnel and then developing a second breakeven point showing the result if the additional personnel were added. The breakeven point, then, is a valuable tool in determining the acceptability of a budget. The overhead rates generated by a budget will also assist in making a determination as to the ability of the company to meet competitive pricing.

Step 6—The Breakeven Point

Schedule F *(see page 101)* shows both graphically and statistically the development of the breakeven point. In order to carry the analysis down to the pre-tax margin, such non-manufacturing items as commissions, sales expenses and administrative costs are included. The non-controllable fixed costs shown on the graph include such items as depreciation, occupancy, and security while the controllable costs include the indirect labor, supplies, travel, and other similar items which the supervisor of a department can control directly.

The variable costs are divided by the total sales to arrive at a percentage. Subtracting this percentage from 100 percent shows the percentage of the sales dollar left to cover fixed costs (and profit). This percentage, then, divided into the fixed costs will show the volume of sales needed to break even. In the instance of the company for which this flexible budget was prepared, the management observed that the breakeven point was so close to the coming year's sales plan that a slight decrease in volume would result in a loss. It was quite obvious that the budget was unacceptable and that reductions must be made. The availability of this package which put all the pertinent facts into a capsule presentation made it possible to explore in depth. A review of Schedule B occupied the greatest amount of management attention. It was noted that the Plant Administration and General Manufacturing departments appeared to be excessively staffed. The question was raised as to why an assistant plant manager and manufacturing superintendent were needed in a plant of such small volume. Why was a full-time Fire Control and Safety Representative needed—could not this function be performed on a part-time basis by one of the industrial engineers? Why was a Chief Industrial Engineer superimposed upon a Senior Industrial Engineer, who was the department head of the industrial engineering group? Were the staff assistants really needed? Were more than 70 people needed to perform the material service functions such as scheduling, inventory control, material handling, stores and receiving? Would not a simplification and consolidation of these departments help to reduce costs? As a result of this review, 67 indirect people were dropped from the payroll and a new flexible budget developed. The savings were upwards of $400,000 per year. When this leaner organization became a reality, the revised flexible budget was used as a basis to measure any buildup in excess of the budget allowance.

The breakeven point was the force in this flexible budget which triggered badly needed management action. The breakeven point serves other purposes as well in instances where direct costing is not used. A company may determine the effect of volume on new business or on a proposal to shrink present volume to a more profitable line in order to eliminate unprofitable lines. Like all mathematical formulae, the flexible budget formula must be used with discretion and tempered with good judgment. The quickest way to discredit a tool such as this one is to apply it blindly in the hope that somehow the resulting "magic of mathematics" will provide a useful answer to a pressing problem.

HOW A FORMULA CAN MISLEAD IF NOT TEMPERED WITH JUDGMENT

A good example of blind application of a formula was illustrated in the case of one company that wanted to determine the potential profitability of making an acquisition in order to increase volume. The individual making the study, who was an administrative vice-president, directed his group to make an analysis of the fixed costs in the existing facilities which were only partially utilized. Sufficient space existed to accommodate the new business. The object was to fill the existing plant to full capacity with no additional capital expenditure beyond that involved in the acquisition.

The existing volume was based on a production level of approximately 20,000 units per year. The study was to show the fixed costs per unit at the present volume, at 30,000, 40,000 and 50,000 units per year. Upon completion of the study, a recommendation was made by the vice-president to approve the acquisition because the increased volume would result in a substantial reduction in fixed costs per unit. A summary of these costs became the focal point of his recommendation:

Production	Fixed Cost Per Unit
20,000	$14.00
30,000	9.33
40,000	7.00
50,000	5.60

Because the company had only recently gone into this line of business and because there was some question as to the large savings indicated in the figures, the officials to whom this recommendation was made requested that a more detailed survey be made by another source—just as a double-check.

An investigation into the makeup of the present sales disclosed that the present sales volume was split about 75% to the replacement market and 25% to a single large manufacturer. The replacement sales were being made through manufacturers' agents who charged a 5% commission. The liaison with the large manufacturer of equipment which used the component was made by one of the officials without the aid of a sales organization. Thus no sales organization was needed beyond those functions which a billing department could perform. No sales expense of consequence was required in selling to the manufacturer; on the other hand the selling price was lower and specifications for manufacture were somewhat tighter than for the replacement market. Frequently, components which did not meet the requirements of the manufacturer would easily meet the requirements of the replacement market.

A similar review of the company being considered for acquisition revealed that its sales were about 20% to the replacement market and 80% to equipment manufacturers. Current sales were made up by 19 such manufacturers. The replacement sales were being made through manufacturers' agents, but the sales to the equipment manufacturers required a sales organization which had varied in size from 12 to 18 people in the past year—the total cost, including travel of salesmen, amounting to $175,000. This factor had been taken into account in the original study but it had been pointed out that the lower fixed cost per unit would more than offset the additional cost.

Because specification requirements to equipment manufacturers are customarily tighter than to the replacement market, the manufacturing superintendent was interviewed as to what his additional costs due to rejects would be. He estimated that the present 5% reject rate could easily rise to 10%. The current rate was not at all representative because a substantial number of units rejected for equipment use were being channeled into the replacement market. With a marked increase in sales to equipment manufacturers and only a small increase to the replacement market, the number of non-saleable rejects would increase substantially. This factor coupled with lower selling prices to the manufacturers would almost wipe out the savings in fixed cost due to the increased volume of 50,000 units.

Further conversations with the manufacturing and industrial relations people determined that production of 50,000 units would require two and a half shifts of work rather than the single shift currently being operated. A factor which had not been taken into account is that most of the work was performed by women and that, although machine capacity was available, women were reluctant to work on the second and third shifts because companies in the area were advertising for women to work on the first shift. The manufacturing superintendent indicated that it was highly improbable that a volume of 50,000 units could be attained under the circumstances. His estimate as to the optimum capacity before the law of diminishing returns set in was no more than 35,000 units. This would require a full first shift and a partial second shift. The second shift would be used to perform bottleneck machine operations and men could be utilized for this function.

Under these circumstances it was quite apparent that blind acceptance of lowered unit costs without considering the other more important though less tangible factors, could result in an erroneous decision. The management, in this case, decided against the acquisition but did increase the capacity of the partially utilized plant by bringing into it a product requiring similar manufacturing operations which were now being performed in an overcrowded plant.

While modern costing techniques can aid management immeasurably, this example illustrates the importance of looking beyond the statistical schedules and probing into the areas where the intangibles defy all attempts at easy analysis. There is little likelihood that any "push button" technique will ever be devised that will permit important business decisions to be made from behind a desk.

CONCLUSIONS

There are three basic ingredients to a successful installation:

1. The departmental managers must understand and accept the concept and they must be a party to making up their departmental expense budgets.
2. The installation must be simple, yet complete.
3. The finished product must meet the test of acceptability from a financial point of view.

To gain the acceptance of the department managers who will be measured by the budget, it is necessary that they clearly understand how the budget works and how it can be used to benefit the company. Not only must the department managers clearly understand the concept—but it is imperative that the key financial executives also understand. This may seem like a play on the obvious, but it is a fact that a surprisingly large number of financial people do not understand the workings of a flexible budget and its use as a management tool. As a result, they cannot lend active support to the program—thus jeopardizing its success.

In many installations the basic figures used in developing the budget exist only on workpapers which are filed away. Frequently the buildup of the information is so complex that effective presentation is impossible. The author recommends a technique for formal presentation of the basic data in a "package" similar to the one contained in this chapter and illustrated in Schedules A through F. A package such as this should be distributed to key members of management for relaxed review at a time of their own choosing. This will not only serve as an educational tool for those whose knowledge on the subject is limited, but it will also provide a complete picture of the operation from a new and different perspective.

An installation which incorporates these three ingredients will be of immeasurable value to management—not only in the control of actual costs—but in the important analytical value of knowing the profit volume relationship and having a clearer insight into the relative profitability of the company's products.

INDEX

Schedule A

Direct labor level with a breakdown by cost center to facilitate calculation of cost center overhead rates.

BUDGET BASE—DIRECT LABOR DOLLARS

Department	Direct Labor Dollars
A	$ 232,892
B	384,771
C	244,857
D	332,108
E	201,953
F	217,297
TOTAL	$1,613,878

PERSONNEL REQUIREMENTS—HEAD COUNT

A job-by-job evaluation of the number of people needed to attain the production volume indicated by Schedule A with a breakdown by those jobs considered as constant and those considered to vary with the activity level.

PLANT ADMINISTRATION—DEPT. 6810

	Total	*Constant*	*Variable*
Plant Manager	1	1	—
Assistant Plant Manager	1	1	—
Coordinator	1	1	—
Chief Industrial Engineer	1	1	—
Budgets and Procedures Assistant	1	1	—
Staff Assistant	2	2	—
Fire Control and Safety Representative	1	1	—
Executive Secretary	1	1	—
Stenographer	1	1	—
Total Headcount	10	10	—
Total Payroll	$87,274	$87,274	—

PURCHASING—DEPT. 6819

	Total	*Constant*	*Variable*
Department Head	1	1	—
Buyers	3	1	2
Follow-Up Man	2	2	—
Buyer's Clerk	3	1	2
Typist A	3	1	2
Total Headcount	12	6	6
Total Payroll	$46,935	$26,119	$20,816

GENERAL MANUFACTURING—DEPT. 6849

	Total	Constant	Variable
Manufacturing Superintendent	1	1	—
Department Head	1	1	—
Mechanical Engineer	1	1	—
Production Mechanic	1	1	—
Total Headcount	4	4	—
Total Payroll	$31,700	$31,700	—

PRODUCTION CONTROL—DEPT. 6851

	Total	Constant	Variable
Production Control Manager	1	1	—
Superintendent	1	1	—
Order Control Department Head	1	1	—
Order Service Specialist	1	—	1
Order Review Specialist	1	1	—
Coil Material Analyst	1	—	1
Material Control Specialist	1	1	—
Staff Assistant	2	—	2
Supervisor—Evening Shift	1	—	1
Secretary	1	—	1
Scheduler Asst. "A"—Section Leader	1	—	1
Scheduler Asst. "B"	1	1	—
Scheduler Asst. "C"	1	1	—
Dispatcher (Work Center)	5	3	2
Return Material Coordinator	1	—	1
Expediter (Inside)	7	2	5
Storekeeper—Dispatcher	1	—	1
Clerks (Days)	3	2	1
Clerks (Evenings)	5	—	5
Total Headcount	36	14	22
Total Payroll	$152,516	$70,302	$82,214

INDUSTRIAL ENGINEERING—DEPT. 6852

	Total	Constant	Variable
Department Head (Sr. Industrial Engineer)	1	1	—
Cost Estimating Section			
Department Head (Cost Estimating)	1	1	—
Cost Estimators—Monthly Payroll	5	5	—
Cost Estimators—Office Payroll	9	6	3
Clerical—Office Payroll	8	7	1
Industrial Engineering Section			
Industrial Engineers—Monthly Payroll	7	7	—
Industrial Engineers—Office Payroll	4	2	2
Clerical—Office Payroll	2	1	1
Total Headcount	37	30	7
Total Payroll	$170,844	$146,245	$24,599

INCOMING INSPECTION—DEPT. 6862

	Total	Constant	Variable
Section Head	1	1	—
Instructor	.1	.1	—
Mechanical Inspectors	10	8	2
Total Headcount	11.1	9.1	2
Total Payroll	$46,834	$38,400	$8,434

MATERIAL SCHEDULING AND EXPEDITING—DEPT. 6891

	Total	Constant	Variable
Scheduler Assistant "A"	2	1	1
Project Clerk "A"	1	—	1
Project Clerk "B"	1	—	1
Scheduler Assistant "B"	2	2	—
Dispatcher (Shop Work Center)	1	—	1
Shop Order Status Clerk	1	—	1
Total Headcount	8	3	5
Total Payroll	$29,347	$12,793	$16,554

INVENTORY CONTROL—DEPT. 6892

	Total	Constant	Variable
Department Head—Stores	1	1	—
Supervisor—Inventory Control	1	1	—
Material Records Clerk	3	1	2
Project Clerk "B"	1	—	1
Inventory Control Clerk	4	3	1
Production Control Clerk	1	1	—
Senior Pricing Clerk	2	—	2
Total Headcount	13	7	6
Total Payroll	$44,066	$28,767	$15,299

STORES, RECEIVING, AND MATERIAL HANDLING—DEPT. 6893

	Total	*Constant*	*Variable*
Storeskeeper Specialist (Group Leader)	1	1	—
Receiver—Packer—Shipper	3	2	1
Storeskeeper	6	—	6
Material Handler	2	2	—
Storeskeeper Receiver	3	2	1
Storeskeeper—Dispatcher Specialist	1	1	—
Storeskeeper Specialist	1	1	—
Total Headcount	17	9	8
Total Payroll	$59,250	$32,614	$26,636

PRODUCTION DEPT. A

	Total	*Constant*	*Variable*
Department Head	1	1	—
Foreman	2	2	—
Senior Clerk	1	1	—
Clerk	1	—	1
Group Leaders	.8	.8	—
Tool Crib Attendant	1	1	—
Material Handler	1	1	—
Total Headcount	7.8	6.8	1
Total Payroll	$39,466	$36,326	$3,140

PRODUCTION DEPT. B

	Total	Constant	Variable
Department Head	1	1	—
Foremen	4	3	1
Section Supervisors	2	2	—
Group Leaders	7	7	—
Instructors	9	—	9
Secretary	1	1	—
Clerks	2	2	—
Utility	3	2	1
Total Headcount	29	18	11
Total Payroll	$107,556	$70,965	$36,591

PRODUCTION DEPT. C

	Total	Constant	Variable
Department Head	1	1	—
Foremen	2	2	—
Assistant Foreman	1	1	—
Secretary	1	1	—
Intermediate Clerk	1	1	—
Group Leaders	8	8	—
Instructors	7	2	5
Storekeepers	2	1	1
General Utility	5	2	3
Total Headcount	28	19	9
Total Payroll	$104,398	$73,767	$30,631

84

PRODUCTION DEPT. D

	Total	Constant	Variable
Department Head	1	1	—
Office Clerk A	1	1	—
Foremen	4	2	2
Scheduler	1	1	—
Group Leader	4	2	2
Instructors	2	—	2
Mold Cleaner and Pan Glazer	1	—	1
Sandblaster and Degreaser	.5	—	.5
Material Handler	1	—	1
Total Headcount	15.5	7	8.5
Total Payroll	$42,388	$17,920	$24,468

PRODUCTION DEPT. E

	Total	Constant	Variable
Foremen	2	2	—
Senior Clerk	1	1	—
Material Handlers	2	2	—
Group Leaders	1.5	—	1.5
Total Headcount	6.5	5	1.5
Total Payroll	$30,516	$24,374	$6,142

PRODUCTION DEPT. F

	Total	Constant	Variable
Department Head	1	1	—
Foremen	3	3	—
Section Heads	4	3	1
Stenographers	2	2	—
Group Leaders	1.5	1	.5
Instructors	.5	.4	.1
Test Equipment Maintenance	3	2	1
Expediter	1	1	—
Total	16	13.4	2.6
Additions			
Foremen	1	1	—
Stenographer	1	1	—
Section Head	1	1	—
Total Headcount	19	16.4	2.6
Total Payroll	$53,634	$41,988	$11,646

Schedule C

A summary of total overhead by department broken down by account and reflecting the portion of each account which remains constant and the portion which varies with volume.

PLANT ADMINISTRATION—DEPT. 6810

Account	Total	Constant	Variable	Constant Per Day	Variable % of D.L.
10—Indirect Labor	$ 87,274	$ 87,274	—	$357.68	—
29—Labor Fringe Benefits Applied	11,770	11,770	—	48.21	—
32—Office Supplies & Printed Matter	600	600	—	2.46	—
34—Tools, Equip., Furn. (Non-Capital)	200	200	—	.82	—
46—Rearrangement	600	600	—	2.46	—
52—Rent—Equipment	50	50	—	.21	—
73—Travel & Meals	5,000	5,000	—	20.50	—
74—Employee Procurement	1,250	1,250	—	5.12	—
75—Dues—Publications—Miscellaneous	1,250	1,250	—	5.12	—
81—Maintenance Shop Service	120	120	—	.49	—
83—Occupancy Distribution	2,200	2,200	—	9.03	—
84—Telephone Distribution	1,600	1,600	—	6.56	—
Total Expenses Before Credits	$111,914	$111,914	—	$458.66	—
Less 50% to Engineering	55,957	55,957	—	229.33	—
Net Charge to Production	$ 55,957	$ 55,957	—	$229.33	—

Account	Total	Constant	Variable	Constant Per Day	Variable % of D.L.
10—Indirect Labor	$46,362	$25,783	$20,579	$105.62	1.27
24—Absentee & Severance Pay	573	336	237	1.39	.01
29—Labor Fringe Benefits Applied	6,320	3,520	2,800	14.42	.17
32—Office Supplies & Printed Matter	1,800	1,640	160	6.73	.01
34—Tools, Equip., Furn. (Non-Capital)	600	600	—	2.46	—
52—Rent—Equipment	240	240	—	.99	—
65—Transportation—Materials	14,400	8,640	5,760	35.42	.36
73—Travel & Meals	600	400	200	1.64	.01
75—Dues—Publications—Miscellaneous	120	120	—	.49	—
81—Maintenance Shop Service	120	120	—	.49	—
83—Occupancy Distribution	1,700	1,700	—	6.97	—
84—Telephone Distribution	9,600	7,680	1,920	31.49	.12
Total Expenses Before Credits	$82,435	$50,779	$31,656	$208.11	1.95
Less 25% to Engineering	20,609	12,695	7,914	52.03	.49
Net Charge to Production	$61,826	$38,084	$23,742	$156.08	1.46

GENERAL MANUFACTURING—DEPT. 6849

Account	Total	Constant	Variable	Constant Per Day	Variable % of D.L.
10—Indirect Labor	$ 31,700	$ 31,700	—	$129.95	—
29—Labor Fringe Benefits Applied	4,280	4,280	—	17.57	—
31—Operating Supplies	400	150	$ 250	.60	.01
32—Office Supplies & Printed Matter	60	60	—	.25	—
34—Tools, Equip., Furn. (Non-Capital)	1,200	1,200	—	4.92	—
46—Rearrangement (Job Orders)	9,000	9,000	—	36.83	—
54—Insurance	2,400	2,400	—	9.82	—
73—Travel & Meals	325	325	—	1.34	—
76—Depreciation—Normal	27,000	27,000	—	110.59	—
81—Maintenance Shop Service	5,760	4,000	1,760	16.37	.11
83—Occupancy Distribution	480	480	—	1.96	—
84—Telephone Distribution	225	225	—	.92	—
86—Security & Guard Service	27,000	27,000	—	110.60	—
89—Other Internal Services	53,640	53,640	—	220.00	—
Total Expenses Before Credits	$163,470	$161,460	$2,010	$661.72	.12

PRODUCTION CONTROL—DEPT. 6851

Account	Total	Constant	Variable	Constant Per Day	Variable % of D.L.
10—Indirect Labor	$150,178	$69,482	$80,696	$284.30	4.99
24—Absentee & Severance Pay	2,338	820	1,518	3.37	.09
29—Labor Fringe Benefits Applied	20,590	9,491	11,099	38.85	.69
31—Operating Supplies	130	104	26	.45	—
32—Office Supplies & Printed Matter	4,940	4,030	910	16.60	.06
34—Tools, Equip., Furn. (Non-Capital)	650	—	650	—	.04
52—Rent—Equipment	195	195	—	.80	—
72—Outside Services—Other	6,500	4,550	1,950	18.75	.12
73—Travel & Meals	650	650	—	2.80	—
81—Maintenance Shop Service	650	520	130	2.25	.01
83—Occupancy Distribution	4,870	4,870	—	19.95	—
84—Telephone Distribution	3,250	2,600	650	10.70	.04
Total Expenses Before Credits	$194,941	$97,312	$97,629	$398.82	6.04

INDUSTRIAL ENGINEERING—DEPT. 6852

Account	Total	Constant	Variable	Constant Per Day	Variable % of D.L.
10—Indirect Labor	$168,839	$144,855	$23,984	$593.67	1.48
24—Absentee & Severance Pay	2,005	1,390	615	5.69	.04
29—Labor Fringe Benefits Applied	23,020	19,700	3,320	80.74	.20
31—Operating Supplies	2,030	500	1,530	2.05	.09
32—Office Supplies & Printed Matter	7,350	5,000	2,350	20.50	.15
34—Tools, Equip., Furn. (Non-Capital)	5,000	2,500	2,500	10.25	.16
52—Rent—Equipment	300	100	200	.41	.01
68—General Engineering	1,200	200	1,000	.82	.06
71—Outside Services—Professional	4,300	4,000	300	16.40	.02
72—Outside Services—Other	3,180	1,000	2,180	4.10	.14
73—Travel & Meals	750	—	750	—	.05
74—Employee Procurement	1,500	—	1,500	—	.09
75—Dues—Publications—Miscellaneous	110	50	60	.20	.01
81—Maintenance Shop Service	1,900	200	1,700	.82	.11
83—Occupancy Distribution	3,000	3,000	—	12.30	—
84—Telephone Distribution	1,690	1,690	—	6.93	—
89—Other Internal Services	500	100	400	.41	.02
Total Expenses Before Credits	$226,674	$184,285	$42,389	$755.29	2.63

INCOMING INSPECTION—DEPT. 6862

Account	Total	Constant	Variable	Constant Per Day	Variable % of D.L.
10—Indirect Labor	$46,834	$38,400	$8,434	$157.25	.520
29—Labor Fringe Benefits Applied	6,335	5,822	513	23.82	.030
32—Office Supplies & Printed Matter	260	185	75	.76	.005
34—Tools, Equip., Furn. (Non-Capital)	670	610	60	2.51	.004
73—Travel & Meals	145	120	25	.49	.002
81—Maintenance Shop Service	181	144	37	.59	.002
83—Occupancy Distribution	3,060	3,060	—	12.55	—
84—Telephone Distribution	212	180	32	.74	.002
89—Other Internal Services	600	480	120	1.97	.008
Total Expenses Before Credits	$58,297	$49,001	$9,296	$200.68	.573

Account	Total	Constant	Variable	Constant Per Day	Variable % of D.L.
10—Indirect Labor	$28,613	$12,473	$16,140	$51.10	1.00
24—Absentee & Severance Pay	734	320	414	1.31	.03
29—Labor Fringe Benefits Applied	3,960	1,729	2,231	7.08	.14
32—Office Supplies & Printed Matter	660	300	360	1.23	.02
84—Telephone Distribution	220	110	110	.45	.01
Total Expenses Before Credits	$34,187	$14,932	$19,255	$61.17	1.20

INVENTORY CONTROL—DEPT. 6892

Account	Total	Constant	Variable	Constant Per Day	Variable % of D.L.
10—Indirect Labor	$43,255	$28,337	$14,918	$116.13	.93
24—Absentee & Severance Pay	811	430	381	1.75	.02
29—Labor Fringe Benefits Applied	5,950	3,875	2,075	15.90	.13
32—Office Supplies & Printed Matter	1,800	1,000	800	4.10	.05
83—Occupancy Distribution	3,270	3,270	—	13.40	—
84—Telephone Distribution	660	400	260	1.64	.02
Total Expenses Before Credits	$55,746	$37,312	$18,434	$152.92	1.15

STORES, RECEIVING & MATERIAL HANDLING—DEPT. 6893

Account	Total	Constant	Variable	Constant Per Day	Variable % of D.L.
10—Indirect Labor	$59,250	$32,614	$26,636	$133.66	1.65
29—Labor Fringe Benefits Applied	8,000	4,400	3,600	18.00	.22
31—Operating Supplies	6,250	4,000	2,250	16.40	.14
32—Office Supplies & Printed Matter	675	425	250	1.74	.02
81—Maintenance Shop Service	600	450	150	1.84	.01
83—Occupancy Distribution	16,400	16,400	—	67.21	—
84—Telephone Distribution	300	200	100	.82	.01
Total Expenses Before Credits	$91,475	$58,489	$32,986	$239.67	2.05

PRODUCTION DEPT. A

Account	Total	Constant	Variable	Constant Per Day	Variable % of D.L.
10—Indirect Labor	$39,466	$36,326	$ 3,140	$148.87	1.3500
18—Downtime	14,009	—	14,009	—	6.0200
25—Absentee & Severance Pay	125	125	—	.51	—
29—Labor Fringe Benefits Applied	38,676	4,921	33,755	20.17	14.5000
31—Operating Supplies	1,868	1,668	200	6.84	.0009
32—Office Supplies & Printed Matter	300	300	—	1.23	—
34—Tools, Equip., Furn. (Non-Capital)	13,500	11,000	2,500	45.09	1.0800
52—Rent—Equipment	216	216	—	.88	—
72—Outside Services—Other	2,136	2,136	—	8.76	—
73—Travel & Meals	25	—	25	—	.0001
75—Dues—Publications—Miscellaneous	144	—	144	—	.0006
81—Maintenance Shop Service	6,000	4,000	2,000	16.40	.8600
83—Occupancy Distribution	14,820	14,820	—	60.74	—
84—Telephone Distribution	312	312	—	1.28	—
89—Other Internal Services	17,000	17,000	—	69.66	—
Total Expenses Before Credits	$148,597	$92,824	$55,773	$380.43	23.8116

PRODUCTION DEPT. B

Account	Total	Constant	Variable	Constant Per Day	Variable % of D.L.
10—Indirect Labor	$107,556	$70,965	$ 36,591	$290.84	9.510
18—Downtime	28,546	—	28,546	—	7.420
25—Absentee & Severance Pay	2,001	2,001	—	8.20	—
29—Labor Fringe Benefits Applied	70,588	9,850	60,738	40.37	15.780
31—Operating Supplies	480	180	300	.75	.008
32—Office Supplies & Printed Matter	900	400	500	1.64	.013
34—Tools, Equip., Furn. (Non-Capital)	4,800	1,500	3,300	6.15	.090
72—Outside Services—Other	350	200	150	.82	.004
73—Travel & Meals	300	300	—	1.23	—
81—Maintenance Shop Service	6,500	3,500	3,000	14.35	.080
83—Occupancy Distribution	10,400	10,400	—	42.62	—
84—Telephone Distribution	360	360	—	1.50	—
Total Expenses Before Credits	$232,781	$99,656	$133,125	$408.47	32.905

PRODUCTION DEPT. C

Account	Total	Constant	Variable	Constant Per Day	Variable % of D.L.
10—Indirect Labor	$104,398	$ 73,767	$30,631	$302.32	12.5100
18—Downtime	15,837	—	15,837	—	6.4500
25—Absentee & Severance Pay	891	891	—	3.65	—
29—Labor Fringe Benefits Applied	49,408	10,079	39,329	41.31	16.0600
31—Operating Supplies	976	700	276	2.87	.0011
32—Office Supplies & Printed Matter	741	741	—	3.04	—
34—Tools, Equip., Furn. (Non-Capital)	5,357	4,357	1,000	17.86	.4100
52—Rent—Equipment	121	121	—	.50	—
72—Outside Services—Other	150	150	—	.61	—
73—Travel & Meals	487	—	487	—	.0020
75—Dues—Publications—Miscellaneous	244	244	—	1.00	—
81—Maintenance Shop Service	4,100	3,100	1,000	12.70	.4100
83—Occupancy Distribution	16,880	16,880	—	69.18	—
84—Telephone Distribution	487	487	—	2.00	—
Total Expenses Before Credits	$200,077	$111,517	$88,560	$457.04	35.8431

PRODUCTION DEPT. D

Account	Total	Constant	Variable	Constant Per Day	Variable % of D.L.
10—Indirect Labor	$ 42,388	$17,920	$ 24,468	$ 73.44	7.3600
18—Downtime	19,929	—	19,929	—	6.0000
25—Absentee & Severance Pay	752	752	—	3.09	—
29—Labor Fringe Benefits Applied	53,350	2,522	50,828	10.34	15.3000
31—Operating Supplies	14,000	10,000	4,000	40.98	1.2000
32—Office Supplies & Printed Matter	700	600	100	2.46	.0003
34—Tools, Equip., Furn. (Non-Capital)	9,200	7,200	2,000	29.52	.6000
52—Rent—Equipment	180	180	—	.74	—
73—Travel & Meals	180	100	80	.41	.0002
75—Dues—Publications—Miscellaneous	200	120	80	.49	.0002
81—Maintenance Shop Service	8,000	5,000	3,000	20.49	.9000
83—Occupancy Distribution	19,390	19,390	—	79.47	—
84—Telephone Distribution	370	370	—	1.52	—
Total Expenses Before Credits	$168,639	$64,154	$104,485	$262.95	31.3607

PRODUCTION DEPT. E

Account	Total	Constant	Variable	Constant Per Day	Variable % of D.L.
10—Indirect Labor	$30,516	$24,374	$ 6,142	$ 99.89	3.0400
18—Downtime	13,354	—	13,354	—	6.6300
25—Absentee & Severance Pay	59	59	—	.25	—
29—Labor Fringe Benefits Applied	33,194	3,298	29,896	13.51	14.8500
31—Operating Supplies	330	330	—	1.35	—
32—Office Supplies & Printed Matter	300	300	—	1.23	—
34—Tools, Equip., Furn. (Non-Capital)	3,050	1,200	1,850	4.92	.9200
52—Rent—Equipment	60	60	—	.0003	—
72—Outside Services—Other	50	—	50	—	.0002
73—Travel & Meals	160	60	100	.0003	.0004
81—Maintenance Shop Service	3,200	1,500	1,700	6.15	.8500
83—Occupancy Distribution	9,300	9,300	—	38.13	—
84—Telephone Distribution	300	300	—	1.23	—
Total Expenses Before Credits	$93,873	$40,781	$53,092	$166.66	26.2906

94

PRODUCTION DEPT. F

Account	Total	Constant	Variable	Constant Per Day	Variable % of D.L.
10—Indirect Labor	$ 53,634	$41,988	$11,646	$172.09	5.360
18—Downtime	15,640	—	15,640	—	7.190
25—Absentee & Severance Pay	636	636	—	2.61	—
29—Labor Fringe Benefits Applied	38,774	5,753	33,021	23.60	15.190
31—Operating Supplies	447	100	347	.41	.002
32—Office Supplies & Printed Matter	2,000	1,100	900	4.51	.410
34—Tools, Equip., Furn. (Non-Capital)	7,800	6,000	1,800	24.58	.820
45—Repairs (Job Orders)	1,020	1,020	—	4.18	—
52—Rent—Equipment	100	100	—	.41	—
73—Travel & Meals	290	290	—	1.19	—
75—Dues—Publications—Miscellaneous	816	816	—	3.35	—
81—Maintenance Shop Service	4,975	4,100	875	16.79	.400
83—Occupancy Distribution	10,432	10,432	—	42.74	—
84—Telephone Distribution	482	482	—	1.97	—
89—Other Internal Services	8,500	7,500	1,000	30.73	.460
Total Expenses Before Credits	$145,546	$80,317	$65,229	$329.16	29.832

Schedule D

Allocation of service department costs to the productive cost centers for calculation of overhead rates.

Constant and Variable Costs are allocated separately to facilitate a breakdown of the overhead rate by its constant and variable components.

ALLOCATION OF CONSTANT COSTS

SERVICE DEPARTMENTS	Total	6810	6819	6849	6851	6852	6862	6891	6892	6893	Total After Distribution	Basis of Allocation
6810—Administration	$ 55,957	$(55,957)									—	A
6819—Purchasing	38,084		$(38,084)								—	B
6849—General Manufacturing	161,460			$(161,460)							—	A, C, F
6851—Production Control	97,312				$(97,312)						—	D
6852—Industrial Engineering	184,285					$(184,285)					—	D, G
6862—Incoming Inspection	49,001						$(49,001)				—	E
6891—Material Scheduling and Expediting	14,932							$(14,932)			—	D
6892—Inventory Control	37,312								$(37,312)		—	E
6893—Stores, Receiving, and Material Handling	58,489									$(58,489)	—	E
Total—Service Departments	$ 696,832	$(55,957)	$(38,084)	$(161,460)	$(97,312)	$(184,285)	$(49,001)	$(14,932)	$(37,312)	$(58,489)	—	
PRODUCTION DEPARTMENTS												
Department—A	92,824	5,595	7,998	16,538	16,543	29,440	7,350	2,540	5,696	8,775	193,299	
—B	99,656	13,989	3,809	37,070	17,516	38,830	8,330	2,700	6,340	9,889	238,129	
—C	111,517	11,751	13,329	38,516	24,328	36,561	21,071	3,740	15,849	25,200	301,862	
—D	64,154	10,071	7,997	34,957	15,570	34,250	4,900	2,376	3,731	5,850	183,856	
—E	40,781	7,835	2,285	17,897	7,785	18,570	7,350	1,200	5,696	8,775	118,174	
—F	80,317	6,716	2,666	16,482	15,570	26,634		2,376			150,761	
Total—Production Departments	$ 489,249	$ 55,957	$ 38,084	$ 161,460	$ 97,312	$ 184,285	$ 49,001	$ 14,932	$ 37,312	$ 58,489	$1,186,081	
Total—Production and Service Departments	$1,186,081	—	—	—	—	—	—	—	—	—	$1,186,081	

BASIS OF ALLOCATION

A—Headcount
B—Requisitions Placed
C—Floor Space
D—Number of Specs. in Department
E—Value of Purchased Material
F—Analysis
G—Direct Labor Dollars

ALLOCATION OF VARIABLE COSTS

SERVICE DEPARTMENTS	Total	6810	6819	6849	6851	6852	6862	6891	6892	6893	Total After Distribution	Basis of Allocation
6810—Administration	$ —	$ —									—	A
6819—Purchasing	23,742		$(23,742)								—	B
6849—General Manufacturing	2,010			$(2,010)							—	C
6851—Production Control	97,629				$(97,629)						—	D
6852—Industrial Engineering	42,389					$(42,389)					—	D, G
6862—Incoming Inspection	9,296						$(9,296)				—	E
6891—Material Scheduling and Expediting	19,255							$(19,255)			—	D
6892—Inventory Control	18,434								$(18,434)		—	E
6893—Stores, Receiving, and Material Handling	32,986									$(32,986)	—	E
Total—Service Departments	$245,741	$ —	$(23,742)	$(2,010)	$(97,629)	$(42,389)	$(9,296)	$(19,255)	$(18,434)	$(32,986)		

PRODUCTION DEPARTMENTS	Total	6810	6819	6849	6851	6852	6862	6891	6892	6893	Total After Distribution	
Department—A	55,773		4,980	322	16,600	6,690	1,390	3,280	2,760	4,940	96,735	
—B	133,125		2,374	502	17,629	9,160	1,580	3,470	3,140	5,600	176,580	
—C	88,560		8,390	422	24,400	8,030	4,006	4,820	7,930	14,210	160,768	
—D	104,485		4,980	402	15,600	8,074	930	3,080	1,844	3,296	142,691	
—E	53,092		1,358	161	7,800	4,420	1,390	1,525	2,760	4,940	77,446	
—F	65,229		1,660	201	15,600	6,015	—	3,080	—	—	91,785	
Total—Production Departments	$500,264	$ —	$ 23,742	$ 2,010	$ 97,629	$ 42,389	$ 9,296	$ 19,255	$ 18,434	$ 32,986	$746,005	
Total—Production and Service Departments	$746,005	—	—	—	—	—	—	—	—	—	$746,005	

BASIS OF ALLOCATION

A—Headcount
B—Requisitions Placed
C—Floor Space
D—Number of Specs. in Department
E—Value of Purchased Material
F—Analysis
G—Direct Labor Dollars

Schedule E

Cost Center overhead shown in Schedule D divided by the cost center direct labor base shown in Schedule A.

The availability of a separate rate for variable overhead facilitates calculation of the relative profitability of various products in the line.

Calculation of Overhead Rate for Total Costs

Department	Direct Labor From Schedule A	Total Overhead From Schedule D	Overhead Rate
A	$ 232,892	$ 290,034	124%
B	384,771	414,709	108
C	244,857	462,630	189
D	332,108	326,547	98
E	201,953	195,620	98
F	217,297	242,546	112
Total	$1,613,878	$1,932,086	120%

Calculation of Overhead Rate for Constant Costs

Department	Direct Labor From Schedule A	Constant Overhead From Schedule D	Overhead Rate
A	$ 232,892	$ 193,299	83%
B	384,771	238,129	62
C	244,857	301,862	123
D	332,108	183,856	55
E	201,953	118,174	59
F	217,297	150,761	70
Total	$1,613,878	$1,186,081	74%

Calculation of Overhead Rate for Variable Costs

Department	Direct Labor From Schedule A	Variable Overhead From Schedule D	Overhead Rate
A	$ 232,892	$ 96,735	41%
B	384,771	176,580	46
C	244,857	160,768	66
D	332,108	142,691	43
E	201,953	77,446	39
F	217,297	91,785	42
Total	$1,613,878	$ 746,005	46%

Schedule F

A quick calculation based on recent mix to show statistically and pictorially the breakeven volume.

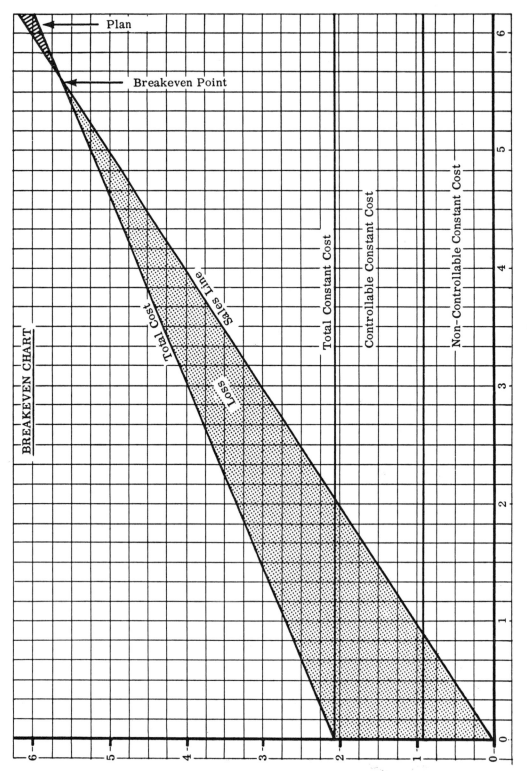

BREAKEVEN CHART

Plan

Breakeven Point

Sales Line

Total Cost

Loss

Total Constant Cost

Controllable Constant Cost

Non-Controllable Constant Cost

TOTAL COST - MILLIONS $

SALES - MILLIONS $

Sales	$6,095,000	100.00%
Variable Manufacturing Costs		
Material	$1,560,000	
Less: Parts Production	272,000	
Material Excluding Manufactured Parts	$1,288,000	21.13%
Direct Labor	1,613,878	26.48
Variable Overhead	746,005	12.24
Total Manufacturing Variable Costs	$3,647,883	59.85%
Other Variable Costs		
Packing and Shipping	$ 57,000	.94%
Tooling—Interdivisional Sales	100,000	1.64
Tooling—Outside Sales	10,000	.16
Commissions	23,500	.39
Total Other Variable Costs	$ 190,500	3.13%
Total Variable Costs	$3,838,383	62.98%
Constant Manufacturing Costs		
Plant Administration	$ 55,957	
Purchasing	38,084	
Production Department—A	92,824	
—B	99,656	
—C	111,517	
—D	64,154	
—E	40,781	
General Manufacturing	161,460	
Production Control	97,312	
Industrial Engineering	184,285	
Production Department—F	80,317	
Incoming Inspection	49,001	
Material Scheduling and Expediting	14,932	
Inventory Control	37,312	
Stores, Receiving, and Material Handling	58,489	
Total Manufacturing Constant Costs	$1,186,081	

Other Constant Costs

Sales Expense	$ 211,500
General and Administrative Expense	416,000
Environmental Testing and Production Engineering	260,000
Total Other Constant Costs	$ 887,500

Total Constant Cost	$2,073,581
Percentage of Sales Dollars Left After Variable Costs	
Breakeven Sales—$2,073,581 ÷ 37.02%	$5,601,245

Note: Warranty costs are included under *Variable Manufacturing Costs.*

Credibility of the flexible budget can be assured only through logical presentation of formalized step-by-step schedules available to key managers.

SECTION II

How to Develop Product Manufacturing Rates for Better Costing

5

Implementing Departmental Machine-Hour Rates in Small and Medium Size Companies

> Direct labor and overhead cost assignment to products is just as important to the small company (or, small division) as it is to its giant counterpart. However, it's not enough to average costs for the entire activity for a plantwide rate—meaningful analysis must be based on Departmental Machine-Hour Rates in this company.

Detailed record keeping and sophisticated cost systems are for the most part limited to large companies whose operations are substantial enough to sustain a fairly complex organizational structure. For the smaller company, like Fabricators, Ltd., the problem is how to obtain meaningful cost analyses without the investment in staff and equipment characteristic of its larger competitor.

This task, while not impossible, is difficult. The small company's cost systems must necessarily be simpler than the large company's, but they must not be so oversimplified as to lead to misleading results.

Allocations of direct and overhead costs must take into account differences within the manufacturing process; few operations are simple enough to permit averaging of costs for the entire activity. Fixed and variable costs must be segregated to permit calculation of breakeven points, profit/volume relationships, and individual products' marginal profit contributions. Failure to observe these simple rules can lead to erroneous conclusions about the cost and hence the profitability of products.

COST DIFFERENCES

The effects of failure to recognize cost differences can be illustrated by the case of a small metal stamping company which used three types of equipment to fabricate small metal parts: multislides, punch presses, and automatics. To estimate the overhead and direct labor cost of production the company used an average costing rate of $6 per machine hour. This rate was calculated by rounding the sum of $3.32, which represented the plantwide rate for overhead, and $2.70, which represented the hourly rate of pay for machine operators.

DIRECT LABOR

Use of the overall rate of $2.70 for direct labor in calculating costs per machine hour for all three types of equipment led to deceptive results in costing the products made on these machines.

In the case of the automatics, which the company had perfected through innovations of its own, no direct labor operators at all were required. The machines were loaded and the necessary adjustments were made by the set-up men in the department, who were classified as overhead. Inclusion of direct labor cost in the machine-hour rate made this department appear to be less profitable than the other two when its production was costed and compared with the competitive selling prices.

Even in the other departments the use of an overall direct labor rate was not justified. For certain types of parts it was possible to use devices which, while not completely automatic, did not require the operator's full-time attention. The operator then could tend two or more machines simultaneously. Thus, instead of $2.70 per machine hour, the direct labor cost would have been $1.35 if the operator tended two machines or $.90 if he tended three.

OVERHEAD

The use of an average plantwide overhead rate was equally fallacious. To show why—and to illustrate how overhead costs might be allocated in a small company—let us review the way in which the total overhead cost pool was assigned after the company had realized its costing deficiencies. Every small company must, of course, make its own cost allocations on the basis of its own judgment. This company's methods, however, illustrate the type of analysis required.

The eventual allocation of overhead to the three types of equipment used in the metal stamping company—and its segregation into fixed and variable costs—are shown in Exhibit 5-1. This overhead breakdown became the basis for determining departmental overhead rates per machine hour. The various categories of overhead cost were broken down and allocated in the following manner:

OFFICE COSTS

Office Salaries. Office salaries as an overhead cost included the general manager, the office manager, an engineer, a production control supervisor, the purchasing agent, and several clerks. The salaries of the general manager, office manager, and a payroll clerk were distributed among the three production areas on the basis of the number of workers in each area. This decision was based on the observation that the distribution of these persons' efforts was affected by the relative number of employees to be supervised and serviced in the three production centers.

The distribution of salaries of the other overhead office personnel to the three production centers was based on the number of product types being produced in the three centers. This basis appeared to be the most reasonable because purchasing, scheduling, and engineering were affected more by number of products than by number of units produced.

Office Expenses. Rather than code and classify such expenses as telephone, stationery, and subscriptions to periodicals by individual category, clerical effort was minimized by classifying as office expenses all invoices other than those representing direct and indirect factory materials.

There was no sacrifice of control because these invoices were so few in number that the office manager could review and approve each one personally. (Travel expenses, which were approved by the general manager, were also included in office expenses.) After payment the invoices were filed by vendor name. Since the vendor supplying each item or service was known, if there was interest in a particular type of expense, the expense could be analyzed simply by perusing the invoice file without the need for detailed coding and summarization in sub-ledgers.

Expenses for stationery used for payroll and personnel records were allocated among the production centers on the basis of the number of workers employed since the volume of such paperwork required was related directly to the size of the work force. Usage of stationery for production records, purchasing, and blueprint supplies, on the other hand, was affected more by the number of product types than by the number of units of product; hence, these expenses were allocated on this basis.

Other office expenses were similarly analyzed. Most of them were allocated to the production centers on the basis of the number of products rather than employees.

Foremen and Set-up Men. Each of the three machine groups had its own foreman, who was responsible for the operations of the machines in his department. Thus, each department was charged with its foreman's salary.

The set-up men removed the dies from equipment after a job was run and installed dies for the next job. They also made the needed adjustments in the course of each run when the parts began to get "out of spec." During long runs they occasionally had to remove dies for sharpening or for replacement of worn and broken punches. The costs of the set-up men, like those of the foremen, were identified and charged to the department they serviced.

Maintenance Salaries. Most of the cost classified as maintenance salaries represented the time spent by toolmakers in the repair and sharpening of dies. (The portion of their time devoted to construction of new dies was not included because such costs were generally recovered through direct billings to customers.) Toolmaker costs were assigned to the production departments on the basis of services rendered.

Maintenance costs also included the salaries of the mechanics who repaired the building and equipment. Equipment maintenance costs were allocated on the same basis as toolmaker costs. The portion of maintenance costs devoted to keeping the building in good repair was allocated to the production departments on the basis of the floor space they occupied.

Depreciation. Depreciation of the equipment in each of the three product centers, calculated by the straight-line method, was determined by analyzing the equipment records and breaking them down by type. Each production center was charged directly with the depreciation of its own equipment.

Supplies. The cost category of supplies, which might more accurately be termed indirect materials, included such indirect materials used in production as expendable tools, solvents used for degreasing, cleaning rags, oil, and repair parts used in equipment maintenance. Since requisitions were used to withdraw these items from stock, a breakdown of requisitions from the three centers was readily determinable. Thus, this cost could be assigned on the basis of actual usage by the production departments.

Electricity. The bulk of the electric power consumed was used in the operation of equipment. Distribution of this cost was based on the horsepower ratings of the motors, factored by estimated hours of usage of the various machines. This estimate was prepared by the electrician in the maintenance group.

Occupancy Costs. Occupancy costs included such items as rent, heat, fire insurance, public liability insurance, and cleaning services. Some part of the electric power used might have been more correctly chargeable as occupancy cost, but this amount was felt to be so small that, in the interest of simplicity, it was included in the total pool of electric power costs. All costs classified as occupancy were allocated on the basis of the floor space occupied by the three production departments.

Employee Fringe Benefits. Fringe benefits included such items as the company's share of social security payments, state and Federal unemployment insurance, hospitalization insurance, pensions, and group insurance. These costs were allocated on the same basis as the costs of the labor on which they were incurred.

FALLACY OF PLANTWIDE RATE

Once overhead costs had been allocated in the manner just described, with the results shown in Exhibit 5-1, it became obvious that for two of the three types of equipment used in the company, overhead costs per machine hour were quite different from the plantwide average rate of $3.32. This analysis, based on figures taken from Exhibit 5-1, is shown in Exhibit 5-2.

FIXED VS. VARIABLE

Overhead costs were further broken down into fixed and variable categories for use in evaluating the relative profitability of the various products in the line. This breakdown is shown in Exhibit 5-3.

ASSIGNMENT OF OVERHEAD TO MACHINE GROUPS

	Total	Multi-slides	Punch Presses	Auto-matics
Office salaries	$20,020	8,529	8,383	3,108
Office expenses	7,553	2,595	3,251	1,707
Foremen & set-up men	10,663	4,403	4,034	2,226
Maintenance salaries	14,100	7,580	4,180	2,340
Depreciation	12,112	5,847	5,330	935
Occupancy costs	6,150	1,845	2,768	1,537
Supplies	3,455	1,589	1,194	672
Electricity	1,300	650	507	143
Employee fringe benefits	12,500	4,500	6,375	1,625
Total Overhead	$87,853	37,538	36,022	14,293

RECAP OF FIXED AND VARIABLE COSTS

	Total	Multi-slides	Punch Presses	Auto-matics
Fixed	$60,066	24,164	25,105	10,797
Variable	27,787	13,374	10,917	3,496
Total Overhead	$87,853	37,538	36,022	14,293

Exhibit 5-1

DEPARTMENTAL OVERHEAD COSTS

	Machine-Hours	Overhead Cost	Overhead Per Machine-Hour
Multislides	8,740	$37,538	$4.29
Punch presses	10,200	36,022	3.53
Automatics	7,560	14,293	1.89
Total	26,500	$87,853	$3.32

Exhibit 5-2

BREAKDOWN OF OVERHEAD RATES BY FIXED AND VARIABLE

	Total	Variable	Fixed
Multislides	$4.29	1.53	2.76
Punch presses	3.53	1.07	2.46
Automatics	1.89	.46	1.43

Exhibit 5-3

The basis for this segregation of all the categories of costs previously discussed is described and explained in the following paragraphs:

Office Salaries. As was previously noted, some of the office salaries were allocated to the production departments on the basis of the number of employees in the three areas. These numbers could vary with production. Nevertheless, all office salaries were considered to be fixed costs since a sustained increase or decrease in overall volume of activity of 25 to 30 percent would not require any increase or decrease in office staff.

Office Expenses. Office expenses that varied with the number of production employees, for example, stationery used for payroll and personnel records, were considered to be variable costs. Those that were affected more by other factors than by production, for example, stationery used for production records, purchasing, and blueprint supplies, were considered to be fixed costs. Most of the office expenses were classified as fixed costs.

Foremen and Set-up Men. The salaries of all three production foremen were considered to be fixed costs. Since the work volume of the set-up men varied directly with production volume, this cost was classified as variable.

Maintenance Salaries. The portion of maintenance costs devoted to keeping the building in good repair was considered to be fixed. Maintenance of dies and equipment was considered to be a variable cost since it varied directly with production volume; the more hours the machines and dies were used the greater the wear and tear.

Depreciation. Depreciation costs were classified as fixed.

Supplies. The cost of indirect supplies was categorized as variable because usage was governed by volume of production.

Electricity. Analysis of electricity costs showed that one-third of the electric bill, on the average, represented demand charges. These charges were fairly consistent from month to month regardless of the volume of production. They were therefore classified as fixed. The remainder of the cost of electricity was considered to be variable.

Occupancy. Occupancy costs were classified as fixed since they did not vary with volume of production.

Fringe Benefits. Fringe benefits on direct labor were considered to be variable. Fringe benefits relating to indirect labor were split between fixed and variable in the same manner as the labor on which these costs were incurred.

PRODUCT COST

Once these analyses were completed it was a simple matter to calculate product manufacturing costs. The method used by the metal stamping company for developing this cost in the punch press department is illustrated in Exhibit 5-4.

Material cost was determined in the conventional manner through analysis of material requirements per one thousand parts. Direct labor, in the example shown, was costed at one-half the hourly rate of $2.70; since this particular operation required only half the operator's attention, he could tend another machine simultaneously.

Variable overhead is shown in Exhibit 5-4 as $.54. This is based on the hourly variable rate of $1.07 for punch presses multiplied by .5 hours per 1,000 pieces. The same principle applies to fixed overhead, i.e., .5 hours multiplied by the fixed overhead cost per hour of $2.46.

PRODUCT COST
PUNCHED PRESS DEPARTMENT

	Cost Per 1000
Material	$ .29
Direct labor (one operator for two presses)	1.35
Variable overhead (2000 pieces per machine hour)	.54
	$2.18
Fixed overhead (2000 pieces per machine hour)	1.23
Total Manufacturing Cost	$3.41

Exhibit 5-4

Separation of fixed and variable costs has many uses beyond product costing. It is necessary, for example, in the calculation of the breakeven point—and the small company's need to know its breakeven point is even greater than its larger competitor's. The same basic figures used in the breakeven analysis can be used to determine profitability at various volume levels.

BREAKEVEN ANALYSIS

Breakeven point analysis, this time for a company other than our previous example of the metal stamping company, is illustrated in Exhibit 5-5.

Note in Column 1 that the $59,000 profit represents a return of 14.8 percent on total sales. Column 2, which is the breakeven level, shows neither profit nor loss because the variable costs at this level of sales plus the total fixed costs exactly equal the sales income.

Column 3 analyzes the excess over breakeven. The "excess" sales are $129,670 while the variable costs are $70,670, leaving marginal income of $59,000. Inasmuch as the fixed costs of $123,000 have already been absorbed in the breakeven sales shown in Column 2, there are no fixed costs left. The entire $59,000 therefore becomes profit.

Since the profit of $59,000 applies to the sales above breakeven, the return on sales may be viewed not as 14.8 percent of $400,000 but as 45.5 percent of the sales above breakeven. Similarly, failure to attain breakeven sales may be viewed as resulting in a loss of 45.5 cents for each dollar by which sales fall short of the breakeven point.

BREAKEVEN ANALYSIS

		Dollars	Percent
Sales		$400,000	100.0%
Variable costs			
Material	$79,000		
Direct labor	85,000		
Variable overhead	54,000	218,000	54.5%
Marginal income		$182,000	45.5%
Fixed costs			
Fixed overhead		123,000	
Pre-tax profit		$ 59,000	
Breakeven point: $\dfrac{\$123,000}{45.5\%} =$		$270,330	

RECAP OF ABOVE

	From Above	Breakeven Level	Excess Over Breakeven
	(1)	(2)	(3)
Sales	$400,000	$270,330	$129,670
Variable costs (54.5% of sales)	218,000	147,330	70,670
Marginal income	$182,000	$123,000	$ 59,000
Fixed cost	123,000	123,000	—
Pre-tax profit	$ 59,000	—	$ 59,000
Return on Sales	14.8%	—	45.5%

Exhibit 5-5

MARGINAL CONTRIBUTION

Separation of fixed and variable costs is also useful in calculating the marginal contribution of individual products. The marginal contribution concept is useful in comparing the relative profitability of various products in the line because it evaluates products not on the basis of their full cost but rather on the basis of how much each product contributes to the liquidation of the fixed costs that exist regardless of the type of product being made.

This computation is made by calculating the profit after deducting variable costs from sales but before considering fixed or committed costs. The percentage of profit before fixed cost (usually referred to as marginal income) becomes an index of relative profitability. One type of such a calculation is demonstrated in Exhibit 5-6.

Product B has the higher selling price of the two products in Exhibit 5-6. Many salesmen might thereby infer that it would be more advantageous to "push" the higher-priced item. However, when the profitability of both products is evaluated in terms of the percentage of the sales dollar left to cover fixed costs, it becomes obvious that, sales dollar for sales dollar, Product A is the more profitable of the two.

MARGINAL CONTRIBUTION ANALYSIS

	Product A	Product B
Selling price	$30.00	$35.00
Variable Costs		
Material	$ 7.10	$ 9.70
Direct labor	1.94	2.42
Manufacturing overhead	3.86	4.83
Sales commissions	1.50	1.75
Total Variable Cost	$14.40	$18.70
% Variable Cost to Selling Price	48%	53%
% of Selling Price Left for Fixed Costs and Profit	52%	47%

Exhibit 5-6

Such an evaluation of relative profitability might also indicate to management that the design of the product or the method of manufacture should be changed in order to reduce the variable costs and thus leave a greater portion of the sales dollar available for fixed costs and profits.

Marginal contribution analysis can be useful in deciding whether to abandon or retain a product. This application is illustrated by the case of a plastics-product manufacturer that made combs and plastic ornaments. Evaluations of the financial results of the two products consistently showed the combs to be profitable and the ornaments unprofitable. The general manager's inclination, naturally enough, was to drop the unprofitable ornaments and concentrate on combs. However, he agreed to hold his decision in abeyance pending an impartial study.

This study produced quite different conclusions. In all the previous analyses the method of arriving at financial results had been to split selling, advertising, and the general and administrative costs between the two products on the basis of sales. This seemed a logical way to determine whether each product was standing on its own.

This approach, however, ignored one fact of life—that certain costs of being in business were unavoidable and could not be changed materially. The salesmen who sold the combs were the same salesmen who took orders for the ornaments. Elimination of the ornaments from the line would not materially reduce selling costs; they would remain about the same in the aggregate whether plastic ornaments were sold or not. The same held for advertising and for the general and administrative expenses.

The conclusion reached as a result of the marginal contribution study was that the ornaments, although showing a reported loss, were actually recovering some of the selling, advertising, and general administrative costs that would otherwise have to be borne completely by the combs. The tentative decision to get out of the plastic ornament business was therefore abandoned.

Although the marginal contribution approach has much value in product profitability analysis, a word of caution is in order. Indiscriminate use of this technique in pricing can be disastrous.

MARGINAL PRICING

A company manufacturing a brand name product that is fully priced is reasonably safe in introducing a private brand on a marginal contribution basis. The margin of safety lies in the fact that regular brand sales can be counted on to recover fixed costs fully, which makes even a relatively small contribution toward fixed costs by the private brand "plus" business.

Many companies, however, do not have the alternatives of brand name and private brand selling. In such cases selling at reduced prices carries the risk that too great a portion of the sales will be priced at a reduction with little or no fully priced sales to absorb the fixed costs.

If natural control such as that which can be exercised between regular brand and private brand products is lacking, all sales made at less than full cost must be closely monitored. One way to do this is to code all incoming orders taken on a reduced price basis so that sales analyses will continuously show the proportion of marginally priced business. When the percentage reaches a predetermined level, appropriate steps can be taken quickly.

CONCLUSION

Because of the tendency of management personnel in smaller companies to wear more than one hat, many decisions necessarily must be based on rule-of-thumb guides rather than on factually documented analyses. Such guides, used by individuals who have good business sense, have proved their worth time and again.

These overall guides save a company many dollars of clerical expense. There are times, however, when such guides should be subjected to scrutiny.

One such guide is the method used for costing products—a point of weakness in many small companies. Introduction of departmental machine-hour rates, coupled with a breakdown of fixed and variable costs, provides tools that are useful not only for measuring the profit potential of individual products but also for determination of breakeven points, profit/volume relationships, and marginal contribution.

The highly competitive business climate, in which small business finds its lot more and more difficult, makes the availability and use of such tools mandatory.

> Because of the tendency of management personnel in smaller companies to wear more than one hat, many decisions necessarily must be based on simpler guidelines than on the factually documented analyses. Such guides, used by individuals who have good business sense, have proved their worth time and again.

6

Balancing and Sequencing
a Cost Mix of Direct Labor
and Machine-Hour Rates

> A business whose unit of activity measurement is not the same throughout
> all its operations must be able to develop costing rates that provide the same
> answer as if there were complete consistency

This company is similar to Fabricators, Ltd., discussed in the previous chapter. It is similar in that extensive record keeping and sophisticated cost systems could not be justified. Because this company, Printing & Binding Co., Inc., has some differences in need, the approach must be different. For one thing, Fabricators did a relatively standard type of metal stamping and forming in which future orders could be anticipated and built to stock. Another difference is that in the preceding case, each of the three production departments was an entity unto itself—products that were made, were made entirely in one of the three production departments. In this case, all jobs are processed in most of the departments—moving from one to the other. There is also another difference in that the application of overhead in some of the production centers must be based on direct labor hours while in others it must be based on press or machine hours.

There are those who would argue that a direct labor base could be used on machines—that it isn't necessary to use machine hours simply because a rate is being developed for a machine. This is true in many cases. However, there are some machine operations in which the crew size can vary depending on the job, which is the case in Printing & Binding Co. For that reason, machine hours must be used as the basis for applying overhead.

The schedules that have been developed in providing this company with costing rates are as follows:

Schedule

A	Activity Base—Direct Labor and Machine Hours
B	Indirect Labor Requirements
C	Non-Labor Overhead Requirements
D	Allocation of Indirect Labor and Non-Labor Overhead
E	Determination of Hourly Costing Rates
F	Product Cost Estimate
G	Budget Formula for Overhead
H	Breakeven Analysis

The steps behind the preparation of these schedules are described below:

SCHEDULE A: ACTIVITY BASE—DIRECT LABOR AND MACHINE HOURS

The purpose of this schedule is to set forth the level of activity at which the business is expected to operate in the coming year, taking into account the important consideration that this will also be the level at which the fixed costs of business must be absorbed and still yield an acceptable return on investment.

A number of financial executives who were interviewed as to their practices in establishing the level of activity were found to favor forecasts of what was anticipated in the coming year. Others based the level on what they referred to as normal, or the expectation based on past history.

Schedule A

Printing & Binding Co., Inc.

Activity Base—Direct Labor and Machine Hours

	Shifts	Direct Labor Dollars	Direct Labor Hours
COMPOSITION			
3 Linotype Operators	1	$ 22,000	5,832
CUTTING AND FOLDING			
6 Operators	1	43,200	11,664

SEWING AND BINDING

5 Sewing Machine Operators	1	33,000	
3 Binders	1	21,600	
Total Sewing and Binding		54,600	15,550

PRINTING Machine

Letter Press Hours

6 Pressmen	2	54,000	
4 Helpers	2	30,000	
Total Letter Press		84,000	15,555

Offset Press

4 Pressmen	2	44,000	
4 Helpers	2	34,000	
Total Offset Press		78,000	7,776
Total		$281,800	

These approaches, in the author's opinion, are only partly correct—the important consideration that is frequently overlooked is the economics of the business. Economic considerations normally dictate that labor-paced operations would be carried on a single shift basis with some second shift work during peak periods. The printing presses, on the other hand, because of the capital investment, must be operated on a two-shift basis. If the company were to find it feasible to purchase automated composing equipment, it is likely that the economics would dictate a two-shift operation to justify the investment. In many companies, three-shift operations are mandatory. Plastics molding equipment and steel mills are an example of this.

Schedule A lists the production departments, the types of direct labor jobs within these departments, the number of shifts, the direct labor dollars and the direct labor hours for labor-paced operations and machine or press hours for the press operations.

SCHEDULE B: INDIRECT LABOR REQUIREMENTS

In this schedule, the labor segment of overhead is broken down by individual jobs as well as dollars. The breakdown by jobs is an important adjunct to the study of rates because it provides visibility to a fairly large portion of overhead.

The indirect labor of $106,000 plus payroll fringes of $27,600 in Schedule C account for about two-thirds of the total labor-related overhead cost of $212,400. In addition to the visibility aspect, it will be found in many cases that availability of the breakdown will facilitate a better allocation of costs.

Schedule B

Printing & Binding Co., Inc.

Personnel Requirements—Indirect Labor

Plant Operations

1	Factory Superintendent	$20,500	
1	Steno-clerk	8,500	
2	General Maintenance	16,000	$ 45,000

Accounting

1	Accountant	$14,000	
2	Cost Clerks	12,000	26,000

Production Control

1	Production Scheduler/Estimator	$15,000	
3	Expediters	20,000	35,000
			$106,000

SCHEDULE C: NON-LABOR OVERHEAD REQUIREMENTS

This schedule, like the preceding one, covers overhead expenses required for the level of activity shown in Schedule A. Identification of the individual items of overhead facilitates a more accurate allocation to production centers.

Schedule C

Printing & Binding Co., Inc.

Non-Labor Overhead Requirements

Payroll Fringes	$ 27,600
Ink	13,000
Freight	500
Rollers	4,300
Replacement Repair Parts	3,600
Oil Wipers	1,600

Electricity	5,600
Chemicals	3,000
Depreciation—Equipment	25,000
Depreciation—Building	12,000
Real Estate Taxes	8,200
Property Taxes	2,000
	$106,400

SCHEDULE D: ALLOCATION OF INDIRECT LABOR AND NON-LABOR OVERHEAD

This schedule serves as a "spread sheet" for allocation of all overhead costs to the production centers. The following bases of allocation were used:

Direct Labor: The bulk of the indirect labor was allocated to production departments on the basis of the direct labor in these departments. While some of the costs, such as production scheduling and expediting, would be more closely related to the number of operations that must be scheduled and expedited throughout the plant, it was found that there was a close correlation with direct labor hours. In the interest of simplicity, direct labor was used.

Floor Space: Those costs whose incidence is governed by the square footage of space occupied were allocated to the production centers on that basis. These included General Maintenance (building), building depreciation, real estate taxes and property taxes.

Direct and Indirect Labor: Payroll fringes, since they apply to both direct and indirect labor, were allocated to production centers on the basis of both the direct and indirect costs of the various production departments.

Number of Impressions: Such costs as ink, freight, rollers, oil and wipers were considered to be related exclusively to the printing press operations. The usage on letterpress work versus offset was broken down on the basis of the estimated number of impressions.

Estimated Usage: Replacement parts, electricity and chemicals were distributed on this basis. Since usage of replacement parts and chemicals was recorded on requisitions as these items were issued out of stock, a study of this history was used as a basis for assignment of this cost. Electricity usage was estimated by the amount required to run the equipment multiplied by estimated number of hours of running time.

Equipment Cost: The depreciation of the equipment was distributed to the various centers on the basis of the cost of the equipment.

Schedule D

Printing & Binding Co., Inc.

Allocation of Indirect Labor and Non-Labor Overhead to Cost Centers

Overhead Expense	Basis of Allocation	Amount	Composition	Cutting and Folding	Sewing and Binding	Printing Letter Press	Printing Offset Press
Indirect Labor							
Factory Manager	Direct Labor	$ 25,000)					
Cost Accountant	Direct Labor	12,000)					
Cost Clerks	Direct Labor	21,000)	7,440	13,950	17,670	27,900	26,040
Production Scheduling	Direct Labor	15,000)					
Expediting	Direct Labor	20,000)					
General Maintenance	Floor Space	13,000	3,120	2,340	1,950	2,600	2,990
		$106,000	10,560	16,290	19,620	30,500	29,030
Non-Labor Overhead							
Payroll Fringes	Direct and Indirect Labor	27,600	2,208	4,140	5,244	8,280	7,728
Ink	No. of Impressions	13,000				7,800	5,200
Freight	No. of Impressions	500				300	200
Rollers	No. of Impressions	4,300				2,580	1,720
Replacement Repair Parts	Estimated Usage	3,600	200	500	300	1,000	1,600
Oil, Wipers	No. of Impressions	1,600				960	640
Electricity	Estimated Usage	5,600	300	800	800	1,700	2,000
Chemicals	Estimated Usage	3,000				1,700	1,300
Depreciation—Equipment	Equipment Cost	25,000	2,600	4,200	4,100	6,900	7,200
Depreciation—Building	Floor Space	12,000)					
Real Estate Taxes	Floor Space	8,200)	5,328	3,996	3,330	4,440	5,106
Property Taxes	Floor Space	2,000)					
		$106,400	10,636	13,636	13,774	35,660	32,694
Total Overhead		$212,400	21,196	29,926	33,394	66,160	61,724

122

SCHEDULE E: DETERMINATION OF HOURLY COSTING RATES

(See page 124.)
The schedule develops the hourly costing rates in two steps:

1. The direct labor hours and press hours listed in Schedule A are adjusted downward to reflect the level of utilization. The factors used are 80% for labor hours and 70% for press hours.
2. These hours, after adjustment, are divided into the overhead costs for the respective cost centers to arrive at the hourly charging rate.

The utilization factors in (1) above, provide for the unavoidable types of delays that are a normal cost of doing business, such as downtime for equipment repair. In the case of press utilization, the 70% factor for presses does not include "make ready" (set-up) because such time is charged as part of the cost of the job.

SCHEDULE F: PRODUCT COST ESTIMATE

(See page 125.)
This is the product cost estimate format used to develop the cost of the job being quoted to the customer. The actual material costs and actual labor costs incurred are charged against each job. Upon completion of the job and shipment of the order, the relief out of inventory is made in two steps:

1. The product cost estimate or standard is recorded as cost of sales as well as the amount relieved out of inventory.
2. The difference between the standard and actual costs that were accumulated in the job are charged to cost of sales and indentified as variances.

The product cost estimate serves not only as a basis of determining what the selling price should be, but also as the standard for measuring deviations. These deviations provide a useful overview for management.

Schedule E

Printing & Binding Co., Inc.

Determination of Hourly Costing Rates

	Amount	Composition	Cutting and Folding	Sewing and Binding	Printing Letter Press	Printing Offset Press
Activity Base: (Per Exhibit A)						
Direct Labor Hours Available		5,832	11,664	15,550	--	--
Press Hours Available		--	--	--	15,555	7,776
Adjusted Activity Base						
Direct Labor Hours at 80% Utilization		4,666	9,331	12,442	--	--
Press Hours at 70% Utilization					10,886	5,443
Total Overhead Per Exhibit D	$212,400	21,196	29,926	33,394	66,160	61,724
Total Direct Labor Per Exhibit A	281,800	22,000	43,200	54,600	84,000	78,000
Total	$494,200	43,196	73,126	87,994	150,160	139,724
Hourly Costing Rates						
Overhead Cost Per Hour		$ 4.54	$ 3.20	$ 2.68	$ 6.08	$11.34
Direct Labor Cost Per Hour		4.71	4.63	4.39	7.72	14.33
Total Hourly Cost		$ 9.25	$ 7.83	$ 7.07	$13.80	$25.67

124

Schedule F

Printing & Binding Co., Inc.

Product Cost Estimate

		Cost Per M	
Materials:			
Paper—36 x 48 sheets		$166.05	
10% Spoilage		16.61	
Bindery Materials		108.75	
Total Material Cost			$291.41
Labor and Overhead:			
Cutting and Folding 14.0 Hours @ $7.83		109.62	
Sewing and Binding			
Gather	1.7 Hours		
Sew	4.9		
Trim	1.0		
Case-in	5.4		
	13.0 Hours @ $7.07	91.91	
Offset Press	27.0 Hours @ $25.67	693.09	
Total Labor and Overhead Cost			$894.62
Total Job Cost			$1,186.03
Markup—35% on Cost (26% on Selling Price)			415.11
Selling Price			$1,601.14

SCHEDULE G: BUDGET FORMULA FOR OVERHEAD

This budget formula for individual overhead costs is relatively simple to calculate since it utilizes the information already developed for determination of the charging rates. The categorization of fixed and variable costs is based on a management overview as to anticipated cost behavior.

All of the indirect labor except expeditors has been considered to be fixed, because it was deemed unlikely in the normal range of business activity that there would be any change in the amount of indirect labor cost. Since expediters were to some extent influenced by changes in activity, one of these was considered to be fixed and the other two, one of whom was employed part time, were considered as variable.

Schedule G

Printing & Binding Co., Inc.

Budget Formula for Overhead

	Annual Cost			Base for Variable Cost	Rate of Variable Cost to Base*
	Total	Fixed	Variable		
Indirect Labor					
1 Factory Superintendent	$ 20,500	$ 20,500	——		
1 Steno-Clerk	8,500	8,500	——		
2 General Maintenance	16,000	16,000	——		
	$ 45,000	$ 45,000	——		
Accounting					
1 Accountant	$ 14,000	$ 14,000	——		
2 Cost Clerks	12,000	12,000	——		
	$ 26,000	$ 26,000	——		
Production Control					
1 Scheduler/Estimator	$ 15,000	$ 15,000	——		
3 Expediters	20,000	7,200	$12,800	$281,800 (1)	4.54%
	$ 35,000	$ 22,200	$12,800		
Total Indirect Labor	$106,000	$ 93,200	$12,800		
Non-Labor Overhead					
Payroll Fringes	$ 27,600	$ 6,800	$20,800	$281,800 (1)	7.38%
Ink	13,000	——	13,000	23,331 (2)	$.56/MHR
Freight	500	——	500	281,800 (1)	$.17%
Rollers	4,300	——	4,300	23,331 (2)	$.18/MHR
Replacement Repair Parts	3,600	——	3,600	23,331 (2)	$.15/MHR
Oil, Wipers	1,600	——	1,600	23,331 (2)	$.07/MHR
Electricity	5,600	1,900	3,700	281,800 (2)	1.31%
Chemicals	3,000	——	3,000	23,331 (2)	$.13/MHR
Depreciation—Equipment	25,000	25,000	——		
Depreciation—Building	12,000	12,000	——		
Real Estate Taxes	8,200	8,200	——		
Personal Property Taxes	2,000	2,000	——		
	$106,400	$ 55,900	$50,500		
Total Overhead	$212,400	$149,100	$63,300		

(1) Total Plant Direct Labor

(2) Letterpress and Offset Press Machine Hours

*Note: This company has chosen to use unadjusted figures as the base for calculating the budget formula. The unutilized labor and machine hour costs are charged to a special variance account.

Payroll fringes were allocated between fixed and variable costs on the basis of direct and indirect labor. The direct labor fringes were considered to be entirely variable.

The demand portion of electricity was categorized as fixed and the balance variable.

Depreciation and taxes were classified as fixed while the various supply type items were considered variable.

Availability of this budget formula, expressed for variable costs as a rate per unit of applicable activity base and for fixed costs as so much per time period, provides a convenient basis for budgeting and forward planning.

SCHEDULE H: BREAKEVEN ANALYSIS

This breakeven analysis has been prepared on the assumption that the mix of business would be approximately the same as it had been during the last six months of the preceding year—that period reflecting certain equipment changes that were to be utilized henceforth.

Schedule H

Printing & Binding Co., Inc.

Breakeven Analysis

	Projected Volume		Percent	Breakeven Volume	Volume Above Breakeven
Sales		$1,200,000	100.00%	666,560	533,440
Variable Costs					
Material	$290,000				
Direct Labor	281,800				
Variable Overhead	63,300				
Sales Commissions	115,000	750,100	62.51%	416,660	333,440
* Contribution to Profit		449,900	37.49%	249,900	200,000
Fixed Costs					
Manufacturing Fixed Cost	149,100				
General & Administrative	100,800	249,900		249,900	—
Pre-Tax Profit		200,000		-0-	200,000

Breakeven volume equals $\dfrac{249,900}{37.49\%}$ equals $666,560

* Also referred to as Marginal Income and P/V Ratio

127

SUMMARY

The ever-increasing pressure on management to attain satisfactory profits, in light of increasing costs and vigorous competition, places a heavy responsibility on the company executives. The awareness of this responsibility has frequently lead to use of complex and costly techniques. The mathematical procedures for developing costing rates for product costing all follow principles that are basically similar. But in their application, these techniques must be tailored to the specific company's economics and its needs. Too many companies attempt to make the need fit the mathematics rather than make the mathematics become the vehicle for fulfilling the need.

> The product cost estimate for a customized product serves not only as a basis of determining what the selling price should be, but also as the standard for measuring deviations in cost. These deviations provide a useful overview for management.

7

Sophisticated Machine-Hour Rates
for a Highly Automated Operation

When an operation is highly automated, as in this company, a more sophisticated approach to machine-hour costing is mandatory

In American manufacturing the value of fixed investment per production worker is rising steadily. Whether you call this trend automation or merely a continuation of the mechanization that began with the Industrial Revolution, it is a fact of business life, with many implications for management planning and control.

Introduction of more and more costly equipment has substantially increased such overhead costs as depreciation and maintenance. As a result the proper assignment of overhead in product costing—never an easy task—has become both more difficult and more important than ever before.

Automation of manufacturing processes is not always followed by corresponding improvements in costing practices. All too many highly mechanized companies still cling to the traditional practice of using direct labor as the basis for applying overhead to the product. It is much more logical to use machine hours as a base since the overhead costs associated with the equipment are usually more closely related to the hours of running time than to the amount of direct labor required to operate the machine. Direct labor costs also should logically be applied to the product on the basis of machine hours.

To continue the use of direct labor as the base for applying overhead to the product can result in distorted product costs, particularly when the ratio of direct labor operators to machines varies from one product to another. Distorted product costs can produce serious errors in pricing.

Misapplication of overhead costs is not the only problem that automation creates in pricing, however. As mechanization increases, direct labor costs usually shrink in

129

relation to material and overhead costs. Since the end purpose of capital invested in a business is to obtain an adequate return on such investment, it follows not only that any procedures used to arrive at product costs should allow for differences in the investments associated with the various products but also that the application of a markup on each product should reflect a return on the investment employed to produce that product. Thus, pricing policies should recognize and provide for an adequate return on two major types of investment—inventories and fixed assets.

This chapter offers partial solutions to both the costing and pricing problems raised by automation. It describes a method for developing machine-hour rates for overhead costing, and it proposes a concept of pricing for return on investment.

MACHINE-HOUR RATES

A multiplicity of machine-hour rates must be developed to reflect differences in various types of automated equipment. In this case, unfortunately, the difficulty of accurately allocating large service department costs to small machine centers creates risk of distortions; a small percentage error in apportioning costs to a machine with a small machine-hour base can have a substantial effect on the rate.

To minimize such distortions, a two-step apportionment of costs is desirable. The first step is to apportion "basic" or general overhead to broad machine groupings. Then each type of equipment within the larger group should be charged with its share of such specifically assignable costs as depreciation, maintenance, and occupancy—all of which are measurable by machine types with a reasonable degree of precision. These specifically measurable costs are converted to a "differential" machine-hour rate that measures the cost difference from one class of equipment to another within the broad groups.

COMPUTING MACHINE-HOUR RATES

Exhibits 7-1 through 7-5 demonstrate the steps required for computation of the machine-hour rates. The function of each of these exhibits may be summarized as follows:

Exhibit 7-1 shows how the available machine hours are calculated and adjusted by a utilization factor to arrive at the total machine-hour base for the major machine groupings as well as for the individual types of machines within the groups.

Exhibit 7-2 summarizes the overhead costs that must be allocated to the machine groups and to the types of equipment within the groups.

In Exhibit 7-3 the total overhead summarized in Exhibit 7-2 is split between basic overhead and differential overhead. The computation of basic overhead rates by major groups is calculated in this schedule.

In Exhibit 7-4 the differential overhead calculated in Exhibit 7-3 is assigned to types of equipment to arrive at the differential rates.

In Exhibit 7-5 the basic and differential rates are consolidated into a single rate for each type of equipment. The labor cost per machine hour is determined, and the combined overhead and direct labor rate is adjusted for machine efficiency.

MACHINE-HOUR BASE

Exhibit 7-1 lists the production equipment for which machine-hour rates must be developed. Compression molding and injection molding are considered as separate major groups because of basic differences in the molding processes and types of equipment used. The compression molding group is then broken down by the types of equipment making up this major group. Within the injection molding group, the eight- and twelve-ounce machines are combined because the products of these machines are very similar—and frequently interchangeable.

The automatic and semi-automatic groups have been combined under the heading of Assembly because of similarity in costs and interchangeability of certain of the

CALCULATION OF MACHINE HOURS

Equipment	Machines Available For Prod.	Number of Shifts	Machine Hours Available Per Day	% Utiliza- tion of Equip.	Machine Hours Per Day Available for Production	Machine Hours Per Month (21 Days)
Compression Molding						
Rotaries	16	3	384	75%	288	6,048
Stokes	9	3	216	81	176	3,696
Transfer Press	8	3	192	63	121	2,541
Strauss	10	3	240	75	180	3,780
Total	43	3	1,032	74%	765	16,065
Injection Molding						
4 ounce	6	3	144	80%	115	2,415
8 & 12 Ounce	3	3	72	70	50	1,050
96 Ounce	1	3	24	60	14	294
Total	10	3	240	74%	179	3,759
Assembly						
Automatic Stakers	9	2	144	70%	168	3,528
Semi-Automatic & Hand Stakers	4	2	64			
Semi-Automatic & Hand Stakers	4	1	32			
Closure Liners	6	1	48	75%	36	756
Total	23	—	288	71%	204	4,284
Metal Fabrication						
Z & H — 9 ton Presses	18	1	144			
V & O — #0, #1, 25-ton, & 50-ton	8	1	64			
Minster — 22-ton	5	1	40			
Benchmaster — 4-ton & B&J	3	1	24	28%	81	1,701
Brandeis — 30-ton	1	1	8			
Henry & Wright — 60-ton	1	1	8			
Pin Machines	9	2	144	90%	124	2,604
Total	45	—	432	47%	205	4,305
Wheelabrator	1	1	10		9	189

Exhibit 7-1

products. Except for the pin machines, the equipment listed under Metal Fabrication has been grouped into a single center in this example.

Within each of the foregoing groups, the number of machines of each type is extended by the number of shifts to determine the available machine hours per day. Available machine hours are then adjusted to allow for normal downtime of equipment for interruptions such as those occasioned by repairs, adjustments, and changeovers. The daily running hours are then multiplied by 21 days to arrive at the number of hours in the average month.

ASSIGNMENT OF OVERHEAD

The average monthly overhead of $73,188 is listed by item of expense. Exhibit 7-2 allocates each of these expense items to the major equipment groupings on seven bases. Direct charges, which account for 43 percent of the overhead dollars, are represented by specific charges to a machine group. For example, indirect labor in the production department is a direct charge because such labor is native to the department and does not require allocation from a general pool. Maintenance is another such example. Here, historical records of maintenance costs have been used as a basis. Since manufacturing gas is used in only one center, it is specific to that center.

Floor space is used as the basis for allocating occupancy (rent-equivalent costs). Fringe benefits are distributed on the basis of the amount of direct and indirect labor payroll. Such costs as service department labor, small tools, and electricity are allocated on the basis of machine hours.

All the items listed in Exhibit 7-2 are categorized for convenience in identifying those that are fixed and those that are variable. Salaried labor, which includes supervision and clerical labor, would be considered as fixed while hourly paid labor would be treated as variable. Non-labor expenses are grouped as either fixed or variable. Availability of this type of breakdown provides management with analytical tools needed for determining breakeven points and the relative profitability of products in the line and for marginal contribution analyses.

CALCULATING THE BASIC RATE

The last line on Exhibit 7-2 becomes the first line on Exhibit 7-3. From this is subtracted $31,388 in differential overhead made up of items such as maintenance, manufacturing gas, and depreciation, which are specifically identifiable by individual type of equipment. Subtracting the breakdown of the $31,388 by major machine groupings from the breakdown of the total overhead of $73,188 results in a breakdown of the basic overhead. Dividing this by the machine hours of the major machine groups gives the basic overhead cost per machine hour for all types of equipment within the group.

Using injection molding for illustrative purposes, the total monthly overhead determined for this group in Exhibit 7-2 is $11,420. Subtracting from this the differential overhead in the amount of $5,604 leaves $5,816. This is the basic overhead

BREAKDOWN OF OVERHEAD BY MAJOR COST CENTERS

INDIRECT LABOR-PRODUCTION DEPTS.	Total Plant	Compr. Molding	Inject. Molding	Staking	Lining	Metal Fabr.	Allocation Code
Salaried	$ 1,757	$ 502	$ 431	$ 660	$ 164	$ —	
Hourly	3,992	274	136	2,552	638	392	
Total Indirect Labor	$ 5,749	$ 776	$ 567	$ 3,212	$ 802	$ 392	1
INDIRECT LABOR -SERVICE DEPTS.							
Salaried	$10,006						
Hourly	5,042						
Total	$15,048						
Less Transfers Out	1,114						
Net Charge	$13,934	$ 7,942	$ 1,811	$ 1,672	$ 418	$ 2,091	4
PROCESS ENGINEERING							
Salaried	$ 4,679						
Less Transfers Out	2,067						
Net Charge	$ 2,612	$ 1,489	$ 340	$ 313	$ 78	$ 392	4
MANUFACTURING EXPENSES							
VARIABLE							
Maintenance	$ 8,620	$ 1,795	$ 1,500	$ 1,900	$ 125	$ 3,300	1
Small Tools	200	114	26	24	6	30	4
Manufacturing Gas	1,000	1,000					1
Supplies	1,400	350	364	350	42	294	1
Total Variable Mfg. Expense	$11,220	$ 3,259	$ 1,890	$ 2,274	$ 173	$ 3,624	
FIXED							
Telephone & Telegraph	$ 550	$ 314	$ 71	$ 66	$ 16	$ 83	4
Miscellaneous	200	114	26	24	6	30	4
Power	2,000	1,140	260	240	60	300	4
Travel	550	314	71	66	16	83	4
Postage & Stationery	600	342	78	72	18	90	4
Water	125	63	62				7
Employee Insurance	700	231	105	252	42	70	3
Depreciation	7,200	2,808	1,512	1,584	216	1,080	1
Employee Service	85	28	13	31	5	8	3
Periodicals & Membership	15	9	2	2		2	4
Raw Material Losses	650	215	58	240	59	78	5
Mold Maintenance	4,818	4,818					1
Overhead Transfer	2,000		1,800	200			1
Professional Services	25	14	3	3	1	4	4
Occupancy	4,600	2,116	644	782	414	644	2
Discount Earned	(825)	(273)	(74)	(305)	(74)	(99)	5
New Equipment Design	1,260	403	164	478	76	139	6
Division Assessments	3,045	1,736	396	365	91	457	4
Warehousing Cost	3,150	1,040	283	1,165	284	378	5
Total Fixed Cost	$30,748	$15,432	$ 5,474	$ 5,265	$1,230	$ 3,347	
LABOR FRINGE BENEFITS							
Variable	$ 6,930	$ 2,287	$ 1,039	$ 2,495	$ 416	$ 693	3
Fixed	1,995	658	299	718	120	200	3
Total Labor Fringe Benefits	$ 8,925	$ 2,945	$ 1,338	$ 3,213	$ 536	$ 893	
Total Overhead	$73,188	$31,843	$11,420	$15,949	$3,237	$10,739	

BREAKDOWN OF ALLOCATION BY CODE

Code	AMOUNT	% of TOTAL
1 — Direct Charges	$30,787	43%
2 — Floor Space	4,600	6
3 — Direct & Indirect Payroll	9,710	13
4 — Machine Hours	23,731	32
5 — Material Consumed	2,975	4
6 — Adjusted Gross Sales	1,260	2
7 — Other	125	100%
	$73,188	

Exhibit 7-2

BREAKDOWN OF BASIC AND DIFFERENTIAL OVERHEAD BY MAJOR COST CENTERS

	Total Plant	Compression Molding	Injection Molding	Staking	Lining	Metal Fabr.
Total Monthly Overhead	$73,188	$31,843	$11,420	$15,949	$3,237	$10,739
Less Differential Overhead						
Maintenance	$ 8,620	$ 1,795	$ 1,365	$ 2,000	$ 160	$ 3,300
Manufacturing Gas	1,000	1,000	– –	– –	– –	– –
Depreciation	7,200	2,808	1,512	1,584	216	1,080
Mold Maintenance	4,818	4,818	– –	– –	– –	– –
Overhead Transfer	2,000	– –	1,800	200	– –	– –
Occupancy	4,600	2,116	644	782	414	644
Warehousing Cost	3,150	1,040	283	1,165	284	378
Total Differential Overhead	$31,388	$13,577	$ 5,604	$ 5,731	$1,074	$ 5,402
Total Basic Overhead	$41,800	$18,266	$ 5,816	$10,218	$2,163	$ 5,337
Total Machine Hours	28,413	16,065	3,759	3,528	756	4,305
Basic Machine Hour Rate		$ 1.14	$ 1.55	$ 2.90	$ 2.86 .	$ 1.24

Exhibit 7-3

for all the classes of equipment in injection molding. Dividing this figure by the total injection molding machine hours of 3,759 results in a basic rate of $1.55 for all types of equipment within this major grouping.

DETERMINING THE DIFFERENTIAL RATE

Following through with the illustration of the injection molding group, the $5,604 shown in the total differential cost column, which was determined to be the differential overhead, is assigned in Exhibit 7-4 to the various types of equipment within the major machine group.

The total of the differential overhead cost for each type of equipment is then divided by the machine hours of that type of equipment to arrive at a differential machine-hour rate.

COMBINING THE RATES

Exhibit 7-5 is the consolidation schedule, which brings the basic and differential rates together. For injection molding the basic rate is $1.55 per machine hour, while the differential rate is $1.05 per machine hour for the four-ounce equipment, $1.85 for the eight- and twelve-ounce, and $3.86 for ninety-six-ounce equipment.

To the overhead cost must be added the hourly cost of direct labor, which for the four-ounce machine is $.45 per machine hour, for the eight- and twelve-ounce, $2.21, and for the ninety-six-ounce, $2.30. Ordinarily the total overhead and direct labor per machine hour would be adjusted for machine efficiency to equate for productivity. In

BREAKDOWN OF DIFFERENTIAL OVERHEAD BY COST CENTERS

	Mainten-ance	Mfg. Gas	Depre-ciation	Mold Maint.	O. H. Transfer	Occu-pancy	Whse. Cost	Supplies	Power	Total Differen-tial Cost	Total Machine Hours	Differen-tial Machine Hour Rate
Total Plant	$8,620	$1,000	$7,200	$4,818	$2,000	$4,600	$3,150	$20	$50	$31,458*	28,502	
Total Compression Molding	1,795	1,000	2,808	4,818		2,116	1,040	20	50	13,647*	16,524	.84
Rotaries	700	1,000	2,364	3,151		727	676			7,618	6,048	1.26
Stokes	130		344	368		296	42			1,180	3,696	.32
Transfer Press	433		392	726		741	187			2,479	2,541	.98
Strauss	482		633	573		317	135			2,140	3,780	.57
Wheelabrator	50		75			35		20	50	230	189	1.22
Total Injection Molding	1,365		1,512		1,800	644	283			5,604	3,759	1.49
4 Ounce	550		529		1,080	277	92			2,528	2,415	1.05
8 & 12 Ounce	550		519		540	251	81			1,941	1,050	1.85
96 Ounce	265		464		180	116	110			1,135	294	3.86
Total Staking	2,000		1,584		200	782	1,165			5,731	3,528	1.62
Total Lining	160		216			414	284			1,074	756	1.42
Total Metal Fabrication	3,300		1,080			644	378			5,402	4,305	1.25

*Includes $20 for supplies and $50 for power to cover wheelabrator machine rate.

Exhibit 7-4

CALCULATION OF MACHINE RATES

	OVERHEAD						
	Basic Machine Hour Rate	Differential Machine Hour Rate	Total Machine Hour Rate	Labor Cost Per Machine Hour	Combined Machine Rate	Machine Efficiency	Adjusted Machine Rate
Compression Molding							
Rotaries	$1.14	$1.26	$2.40	$ .36	$2.76	95%	$2.90
Stokes	1.14	.32	1.46	.19	1.65	95	1.73
Transfer Press #1	1.14	.98	2.12	.54	2.66	95	2.80
Transfer Press #2	1.14	.98	2.12	1.40	3.52	90	3.91
Strauss	1.14	.57	1.71	.25	1.96	95	2.06
Wheelabrator	—	1.22	1.22	1.77	2.99	95	3.15
Injection Molding							
4 Ounce	1.55	1.05	2.60	.45	3.05	Allowance for machine
8 & 12 Ounce	1.55	1.85	3.40	2.21	5.61	efficiency included with
96 Ounce	1.55	3.86	5.41	2.30	7.71	% utilization of equip-ment. See Exhibit 1.
Staking							
Automatic	2.90	1.62	4.52	1.40	5.92	90	6.58
Semi-Automatic	2.90	1.62	4.52	2.10	6.62	90	7.36
Hand Staking	2.90	1.62	4.52	2.10	6.62	90	7.36
Lining	2.86	1.42	4.28	1.85	6.13	90	6.81
Metal Fabrication							
Pins	1.24	1.25	2.49	.26	2.75	85	3.24
Automatic	1.24	1.25	2.49	.39	2.88	85	3.39
Non-Automatic Metal	1.24	1.25	2.49	1.81	4.30	80	5.38

Exhibit 7-5

the case of the injection molding equipment, this allowance was included in the utilization allowance because the equipment had been newly installed and no definitive historical information was available to make a separate determination for machine downtime as opposed to machine productivity while running.

RETURN-ON-INVESTMENT PRICING

Many small fabricating companies have for years determined the selling prices of their products by doubling prime cost (material plus direct labor). As fabricating equipment has become more and more sophisticated in the last ten to fifteen years, direct labor has become the smallest of the three elements of cost, while overhead, on the other hand, has become substantially larger—often the largest of the three elements.

Since automated equipment and the associated support facilities represent a fairly large investment in capital assets, it seems logical that selling prices would be more appropriately based on a proper return on investment—inventory as well as fixed assets. Although fixed assets and inventory are not the only items making up total investment, they are very substantial in most automated factories. In addition to representing the predominant segment of invested capital, these two asset groups can be fairly well pinpointed to the product line for which the investment was incurred and are generally controllable by the factory manager since he is responsible for effective utilization of his facilities and proper turnover of inventory.

If it is agreed that fixed assets and inventory should be the basis for measuring return on investment, the problem then is to arrive at a vehicle for equating markup with return on inventory and with return on fixed assets.

CALCULATING THE DESIRED MARKUP

In the interest of simplicity, let us assume that a 20 percent return on inventory and fixed assets results in an adequate return on total assets. Exhibit 7-6 shows how the two markup factors would then be calculated.

If management's goal is an annual return of 20 percent on total inventory and fixed asset investment, then the amount to be recovered for the material content in inventory is $100,000, while the amount to be recovered for the labor and overhead content is $75,000. The amount to be recovered on fixed assets is $125,000.

The logical vehicle for recovering the first item of $100,000 is the material content of the product being sold. Let us assume for purposes of illustration that the amount of material consumed during the year (a turnover of four times per year) is two million. Dividing the desired return of $100,000 by two million results in a markup factor of 5 percent.

Labor plus overhead is the logical vehicle for recovering the investment on the balance of the inventory as well as the investment in fixed assets. The desired return to be recovered on a labor and overhead basis then is $200,000 ($75,000 on labor and overhead content in inventory and $125,000 on fixed assets). Assuming that labor and

CALCULATION OF MARKUP			
	Amount of Investment	% Return	Amount of Return
MATERIAL-RELATED INVESTMENT			
Inventory (material content)	$ 500,000	20	$100,000
INVESTMENT RELATED TO CONVERSION			
Inventory (labor and overhead content)	$ 375,000	20	$ 75,000
Fixed Assets	625,000	20	125,000
	$1,000,000	20	$200,000
TOTAL INVESTMENT	$1,500,000	20	$300,000

Exhibit 7-6

overhead content of products made in a normal year totals one million dollars, the markup would be 20 percent ($200,000 divided by $1,000,000).

Thus in costing up the product for sale, the cost and markup to arrive at selling price would be determined as shown in Exhibit 7-7. A pricing formula of the type illustrated is, at best, only a guide. Obviously no mathematical formula can be applied universally; it must be tempered by good business judgment. However, such a formula can be very helpful in maximizing profits through a more logical application of the factors that affect prices.

CALCULATION OF SELLING PRICE	
	Cost/M
Material (53 pounds @ $.10)	$5.30
Direct labor and overhead (.50 hours at $5.30/machine hour)	2.65
Total manufacturing cost	$7.95
Markup on material—5%	.27
Markup on labor and overhead —20%	.53
Selling price	$8.75
Note: In the interest of simplicity, only manufacturing costs are considered.	

Exhibit 7-7

Some basic principles of pricing products for maximum profits were summarized by Bertrand J. Belda, a partner in the firm of Ernst & Ernst, Cleveland, Ohio, in the following words:[1]

---

[1] *Illinois Certified Public Accountant,* vol. XXI, no. 2.

"Pricing products for maximum profits must take into account three fundamental factors: careful market analysis, sound costs, and markup techniques that are based upon carefully planned business objectives.

"The market analysis should include a penetrating study of product and territorial potentials, competitive conditions, and customer needs and desires. Costs for pricing purposes should be based upon current and future price levels and should be determined in a manner that will separate direct variable elements from fixed charges. Finally, profit markups should be calculated in a fashion that will recognize the significance of the varying investment factors involved in the production and sale of different products."

In an operation with a high capital investment, a return-on-investment approach to pricing is mandatory.

8

Linking Production Efficiency and Costing Rates to Machine Hours

> It will do little good for a company to automate its operations and then to cost and control its operations on a "horse and buggy" concept.

A high-speed automatic factory not under good control can turn out products at excess cost at tremendous rates of speed. On the other hand, automation provides a means for simplifying costing and cost controls.

Illustrative of a machine-paced operation is the company used in this case study. It is small enough to make allocation of die costs and heat treating difficult and yet it is sufficiently large to demonstrate how costs can be more closely controlled on a machine-hour basis than they would be if direct labor were used.

As a background for a better understanding of this case, a brief description of the manufacturing operation will be given; the problem of equitable distribution of die costs and heat treating will be discussed; the method of developing the hourly machine charging rates for labor and overhead will be explained; and finally, the subject of cost control will be covered. Drawn wire is the product.

WHAT IS WIRE DRAWING?

Wire drawing is a method of reducing ductile metals from a larger to a smaller diameter. This is accomplished by pulling the wire through a series of reducing dies. These are carboloy or diamond dies which contain a carbide compound or diamond stone with a contoured hole through the center. The die is housed in a circular steel disc about the size and appearance of the wheel on a child's roller skate. Dies are placed in the wire drawing machines in progressively smaller sizes so that the wire can be threaded and pulled through at the optimum speed required.

Each time the wire passes through a die, its diameter becomes smaller and smaller until the desired size is obtained. Wire may be hot-drawn or cold-drawn. When hot-drawn, it passes through a furnace before passing through the die. If cold-drawn, the wire will go through a series of dies without the prerequisite of heating. However, after a certain degree of reduction has been attained, heat treating is necessary before further reduction takes place, in order to bring about an equi-axed grain structure and to restore ductility. Each time the wire passes through a successive die, the tensile and yield strength increases while elongation decreases.

Proper temper is imparted by scheduling heat treatment at strategic points so that the reduction that follows will be of sufficient degree to bring about the desired hardness or temper. These vary with the products for which the wire is to be used. Such products are quite numerous. A few are:

Fences	Resistor wire in toasters
Springs	Filaments in light bulbs
Cables	Base pins in radio tubes
Nails	Electrical conductive wire
Wire for screens and weaving	Sponge wire for cleaning

COSTING PROBLEMS IN WIRE DRAWING; MACHINE-HOUR BASIS

Costing of the drawing of wire presents somewhat unique problems. The reason is that standards cannot readily be set on all the operations, particularly when a large variety of wire is drawn in relatively small lots. For one thing, heat treating (annealing) necessarily does not lend itself to time study. The amount of heat treating cost to be applied to each type of wire cannot be determined through the customary multiplication of production by the standard allowance. Die costs, likewise, present problems in allocation because the use of a die of a particular size is not confined to a specific size or type of wire. The allocation of die costs to types of wire is further complicated because of the tendency of different materials to have different rates of wear on the dies. Another peculiarity is that, in wire drawing, no material is added after the initial drawing.

A further characteristic is that, contrary to the frequent practice of using direct labor as a base for applying overhead, wire drawing utilizes machine hours as a base. Briefly, the number of machine hours is multiplied by the machine-hour rate which includes not only overhead but direct labor as well. However, this basis is not used blindly but with discretion and, as will be shown later, a separate machine-hour rate is set for differing types of equipment. This follows the circumstance that the operator of a wire drawing machine acts more as a machine attendant than an operator. His work consists of loading the machine, threading the wire through dies, and removing the finished spool. If a break occurs, he must rethread the wire. The time expended by an operator is such that he can easily attend two machines of a type in general use. The operator's effort does not vary with the pounds (or meters) of wire drawn but rather with the number of times he must load, unload, and rethread breaks in the wire.

In short, it is the number of hours that the wire drawing machine operates that varies in direct proportion to the amount of wire drawn. Direct labor is more in the nature of a fixed cost. Machine maintenance, die costs, depreciation, and the other items of overhead are, therefore, apportioned more equitably on a machine-hour base than on a direct labor base.

HEAT TREATING COSTS

Two costs accompanying wire drawing, and mentioned above, merit initial attention. For one, heat treating cost is difficult to assign to specific sizes of wire because of the fact that a good deal of the annealing is done in a pot furnace, i.e., various sizes, some on spools, some in unspooled coils, are heaped into the annealing pot which is sometimes half full and sometimes one-quarter or three-quarters full. Some wire is strand annealed, i.e., passed through furnace tubes in individual strands.

Although standards can be set on strand annealing, the pot annealing operation defies all attempts at time study and scientific allocation. For this reason, pot annealing costs are best treated as general overhead in the wire drawing operation and are allocated to the machines on the basis of machine hours.

The resulting costs will not be widely at variance with fact, because there is good correlation between the cost of heat treating and the number of machine hours of drawing time. The greater the degree of reduction, the greater the number of machine hours required to make the reduction. This also means that more frequent heat treating is needed, because ductility must be restored more frequently, for the harder the wire, the smaller the degree of reduction which can be made in each pass. More machine hours and more frequent heat treating will be required to draw hard wire to a given diameter, than softer wire.

It is recognized that the machine-hour basis of allocating heat treating costs as part of overhead results in a small amount of distortion in the cost of some types of wire which are sold as "soft," because this means that there is a heat treat operation without any further drawing or else there is a heat treat with only a small amount of subsequent drawing. However, to attempt to account for the cost of heat treating on each type of wire drawn would mean a prohibitive amount of clerical expense. Selling prices do not distinguish hard or soft.

DIE COSTS

We come now to die costs. The allocation of die costs to types of wire drawn presents a problem in a plant where numerous metals are used and where there is frequent interchange of types of wire on the various machines. Carboloy dies are generally used in drawing wire down to .020", while diamond dies are used for diameters under .020". As soon as a diamond die gets "out of round," it is ground down and used again for the next larger diameter. The procedure is repeated until the die is finally so large it can no longer be used.

Die wear will be affected by the temper and type of wire as well as by the type of lubricant used. Generally, hard wires will wear dies faster. However, certain soft materials will wear them out as fast as the hard materials. Also, some types of wire like aluminum, nickel, chromium, and titanium have oxides present which cause rapid wear. Using the correct lubricant for each type of wire will aid in reducing die wear. However, it is not practical to empty out the lubricant and refill with the right kind when the type of wire is changed frequently. For this reason, some all-purpose lubricant is ordinarily used.

In a large wire drawing operation where the volume of each type of wire drawn is large enough to warrant the use of specific machines for wires having similar properties, it would be possible to determine die costs by types of wire drawn, with a high degree of accuracy. However, in a small operation there is no choice but to allocate die costs on the basis of the number of machine hours required to draw each type of wire and then to apply correction factors based on an engineering estimate.

TWO PRODUCTS—AND THE DEVELOPMENT OF RATES

It might be well at this point to describe briefly the steps in drawing wire for two particular uses and to comment on the costing of the wire so drawn. Wire to be used for base pins in radio tubes and for sponge wire used in kitchen cleaning pads has been selected for this purpose.

The wire used for these two products is a special alloy consisting of nickel, chrome and iron. For purposes of this illustration, it will be assumed that the wire is purchased at a diameter of .150" and cold drawn down to .051", at which dimension it is ready to be cut into proper lengths for use as finished base pins. The cold drawing is done in two steps, down to .100" on the bull block and down to .051" on the 6-7 Pass Vaughn, with heat treating following each drawing.

The same alloy is then used for drawing sponge wire. This is accomplished by drawing .051" wire down to .020" on the 6-7 Pass Vaughn and then putting the .020" wire through a fine wire drawing unit called the CF-1. This machine draws the wire down to .0055", at which point the wire is ready for sale.

Overhead is assigned to the various machines on the most appropriate basis to determine sound machine-hour rates for each type. Maintenance records indicate the amount of maintenance required for each machine. Depreciation is likewise known for each kind of machine. All rent-equivalent or occupancy expenses, such as heat, light, building depreciation, taxes, and building maintenance, are allocated on the basis of floor space occupied. The expense of carboloy dies is allocated to the equipment used for drawing down to .020", while the cost of diamond dies plus the cost of die maintenance is charged to the remaining drawing machines on the basis of machine hours. Indirect labor is charged to each machine on the basis of percentages estimated by the departmental supervisors, in cases where a machine-hour allocation would not be equitable.

After all overhead is distributed to machines, the monthly machine hours at which it is anticipated that each machine will be operated are divided into the monthly overhead to obtain the overhead rate per machine hour. The resulting figures are:

Bull Block	$2.50	per	machine	hour
6-7 Pass Vaughn	4.50	"	"	"
12 Pass Vaughn	5.15	"	"	"
CF-1	3.50	"	"	"

Direct labor is determined for each machine on an hourly basis and then added to the hourly overhead rate to obtain a combined rate.

Calculations for direct labor are illustrated by the following example:

MACHINE LABOR RATES

	Hrly. D.L. Cost Per Shift	No. Mach.	Hrly. D.L. Cost Per Machine	Allow- ances	D.L. Cost Per Mach. Hour
Bull Block	$1.32	1	$1.32	10%	$1.47
6-7 Pass Vaughn	1.37	1	1.37	10%	1.52
12 Pass Vaughn	1.37	3	.46	10%	.51
CF-1	1.37	3	.46	10%	.51

The overhead rate is then added and also the rates for heat treating. In the interest of simplicity, strand annealing, like pot annealing, is assumed to be in the nature of a general overhead item. The total direct labor in both these operations is added to arrive at a total and then divided by the total machine hours for all wire drawing machines. Using the overhead and direct labor rates cited above and assuming $0.35 for heat treating, the combined machine rates became as follows:

MACHINE LABOR AND OVERHEAD RATES

	Labor	Overhead	Heat Treat.	Total
Bull Block	$1.47	$2.50	$.35	$4.32
6-7 Pass Vaughn	1.52	4.50	.35	6.37
12 Pass Vaughn	.51	5.15	.35	6.01
CF-1	.51	3.50	.35	4.36

WIRE DRAWING STANDARDS

We have now developed the means through which labor and overhead costs (including heat-treating) are applied, i.e., as a rate per hour, depending on the type of machine used. Thus, if we know the machine types and times involved in particular kinds of wire, we are in a position to set product standards for labor and overhead from the machine rates. If we again take base pins for radio tubes and sponge wire as examples, we find the following pounds per hour (very fine wire is measured in meters) convertible into hours per cwt.

MACHINE PRODUCTION RATES

	Wire Drawn From	to	Lbs. Per Hour	Conversion to Hrs. Per Cwt.
Base pins for radio tubes				
Bull Block	.150″	.100″	400	.25
6-7 Pass Vaughn	.100″	.051″	200	.50
Additional drawing to get sponge wire				
6-7 Pass Vaughn	.051″	.020″	.50	2.00
CF-1	.020″	.0055″	.20	5.00

Thus it takes only combined use of machine cost rates and the production rates appearing in the last column of the two tables above to give labor and overhead product standards costs, as follows:

LABOR AND OVERHEAD STANDARD DRAWING COSTS

	Size From	to	Hours Per Cwt.	Machine Rate	Cost Per Cwt.	Cumulative Cost Per Cwt.
Base pins for radio tubes						
Bull Block	.150″	.100″	.25	$4.32	$ 1.08	$ 1.08
6-7 Pass Vaughn	.100″	.051″	.50	6.37	3.19	4.27
Addition drawing to get sponge wire						
6-7 Pass Vaughn	.051″	.020″	2.00	6.37	12.74	17.01
CF-1	.020″	.0055″	5.00	4.36	21.80	38.81

From the final column of this table it will be seen that the labor and overhead standard cost of wire drawn down to base pin thickness will be $4.27 per 100 lbs. and that the two additional drawings needed for sponge wire bring the labor and overhead standard cost for that product to $38.81 per 100 lbs.

To these standards we need to add the cost of material. Since no material is added in the process of wire drawing, material costing is fairly easy, inasmuch as material in one pound of .150″ wire is exactly the same as in .020″, the only varying factor being the amount of shrinkage caused through snarling, breakage, and poor drawing because of worn dies or improper annealing.

DAILY PRODUCTION REPORT FOR CONTROL

Because the presence of the operator of each group of machines is required, regardless of whether all or only one machine of his group is in operation, direct labor is a fixed cost in wire drawing operations. Therefore, the problem of controlling direct labor variances is similar to the problem of keeping the fixed overhead costs under control. The principal accounting means for this control is a production report issued daily, weekly, and monthly. This is illustrated in Exhibit 8-1 and compares actual with

Daily Production Report

Machine	Material	Size From	to	Production	Hrs.	Actual Prod. Hr.	Std. Prod. Hr.
Bull Block	A Nickel	.125″	.100″	10,300 lbs.	26.5	388 lbs.	370 lbs.
" "	A Nickel	.250″	.194″	13,900 "	35.0	397 "	385 "
6-7 Pass Vaughn	S Nickel	.100″	.040″	1,500 lbs.	13.0	114 lbs.	115 lbs.
" " "	#4 Alloy	.100″	.051″	2,700 "	14.0	193 "	200 "
" " "	* #4 Alloy	.030″	.020″	2,000 "	21.5	93 "	102 "

* Non-standard Draw.

Exhibit 8-1

standard production hours. The information is also accumulated from month to month, so that the report can be compiled on a quarterly, semi-annual, or even annual basis, if need be. The comparison of the actual production per hour with the standard production per hour furnishes the wire department foreman with a quick analysis of each day's operation.

THE PROBLEM OF THE NON-STANDARD DRAW

Our concern with the control problem may be illustrated by the following typical example. Let us assume that the foreman's schedule requires that he draw 2,000 lbs. of .051″ wire down to .020″. Since the time standard for this operation is two hours per hundred pounds, the foreman's total allowance would be 40 hours. Let us assume that because of pressure to get out production, 0.30″ wire (intended for another purpose) is drawn down to .020″. Obviously, it takes fewer machine hours to draw wire down from .030″ than from .051″. The budget will, therefore, show a favorable variance, even though this non-standard operation is costlier. It is costlier because it requires almost the same set-up time and the same amount of effort in loading and unloading, whether the draw is .051″ to .020″ or .030″ to .020″.

The problem resolves itself into two parts. The first is an analysis of each day's production, in such fashion as to highlight any nonstandard draws. The daily production report does this. Second, in the event that a nonstandard draw is made, the budget allowance should be based only on the degree of reduction which actually takes place. This presents a difficulty, because standards are not set on reductions which are uneconomical.

The last line in Exhibit 8-1 displays such a nonstandard draw. The problem as to how the variance can be measured when .030″ wire rather than .051″ is drawn down to .020″, resolves itself into a problem of interpolation. (This is how the necessary standard figure of 102 pounds per hour was provided for the applicable line on Exhibit 8-1.) Probably the graphic method is the simplest way to arrive at the answer. The 6-7 Pass Vaughn utilizes seven dies, each die bringing about a 15 to 20 percent reduction in the wire being drawn. Since the percentage reduction for each die in a given machine is the same, logarithmic graph paper should be used in preference to the conventional scale, because equal percentage changes will show as a straight line. (On the conventional graph scales, equal percentage changes would result in a curved line which would make interpolation less accurate.)

Exhibit 8-2 shows the cost of .051" wire plotted at $4.27 and .020" wire plotted at $17.01. By connecting these two points with a straight line and interpolating at .030" we arrive at a cost of $10.75 for .030" wire. Subtracting $10.75 from $17.01, we get $6.26 per 100 pounds as the allowable cost for drawing between .030" and .020". Since the rate for this machine is $6.37 per hour, we need only divide $6.26 by $6.37 to arrive at the allowable machine hours for drawing .030" wire down to .020". The result of the division is .98 machine hours per 100 pounds. The allowance for drawing 2,000 pounds, therefore, would be 19.6 hours.

The standard production per hour would be obtained by dividing 19.6 hours into 2,000 pounds, the production quantity involved, thus arriving at 102 pounds per hour as the allowance. This is the figure shown in the last column of the production report, asterisked to indicate a nonstandard draw. Highlighting nonstandard draws discloses uneconomical practices.

Interpolation for Cost of Drawing .030″ Wire to .020″

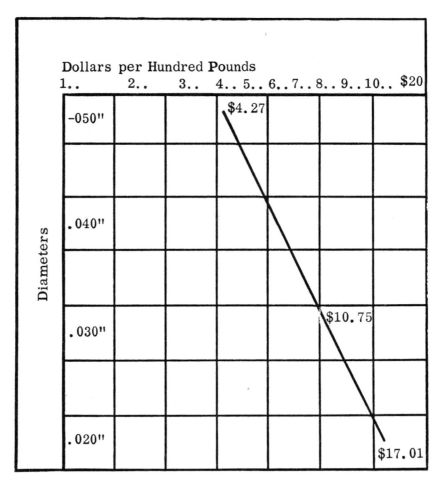

Exhibit 8-2

SUCCESSFUL COST CONTROL

Wire drawing is an operation in which good control can be exercised through use of a single index, i.e., comparison of actual production per hour with standard production per hour. The reason that this single index will work effectively is that material, labor and overhead are closely tied together. Material is put into process only once. Labor and overhead are applied in a single rate.

An inspection of the production report on a particular day in which shrinkage was high in drawing nickel from .125" to .100", for example, will show that the production per hour was less than the standard allowance per hour. It would follow that labor and overhead costs would also be in excess of standard. (Incidentally, if the .100" wire referred to above were taken out of stock at a later time to be drawn further, the material cost would then be the accumulated material, labor and overhead cost at the end of the .125" to .100" draw.)

It is true that exercise of control through comparison of actual production per unit of time with the standard allowance, is fundamental to cost control in industry as a whole. However, it is especially applicable to wire drawing because of the correlation among material, labor and overhead in the process. In the manufacture of products with many components, this correlation seldom exists to the same extent. One component might take a large amount of material, with very little labor, and might require a large automatic machine utilizing a great amount of overhead. Another component of the same product might require only a small amount of material with little overhead but a great deal of hand labor.

Thus, although wire drawing presents definite problems in the treatment of annealing and die cost, particularly in a low volume operation, good overall cost control is possible through use of the daily production report, which will reflect drawing efficiency broken down by type of material drawn, by type of machine used, and by range of reduction which took place. The test of good control is whether or not the inefficiency is localized so that further study can be made. The daily production report meets this test for the wire drawing process, and should have useful application in other processes.

CONCLUSIONS

As industry modernizes its manufacturing processes, improvements in cost controls frequently lag because of a tendency to cling to the traditional concept of recognizing direct labor as the logical activity base.

Cost control procedures in companies that have automated their processes should capitalize on these innovations. This requires:

1. Recognition that cost controls must be harnessed to machine hours, which, to a greater extent than direct labor, are highly sensitive to production activity and are therefore a better basis for controlling costs.

2. Machine-hour rates for costing the product must be determined for homogeneous groups of equipment, rather than utilizing a single all-inclusive rate.
3. The machine-hour rate should include direct labor as well as overhead.

> A high-speed automatic factory can turn out products at tremendous rates of speed. Without good cost control, the same high-speed automatic factory will turn out unprofitable products at the same rate of speed.

9

A Case Study in Costing
a New Product Successfully

Product cost—material, direct labor and overhead—account for 65% to 80% of sales in many manufacturing companies.

The preceding chapters on costing rates for various types of operations are condensed into a case study. This study embodies not only the conversion costs—direct labor and overhead—but also includes material requirements, allowances for losses in production, and die and mold maintenance and amortization. The manufacturing process and the problems encountered in manufacturing will be covered to demonstrate the reasons for making these allowances in product cost buildup. The operating levels and utilization of equipment will also be discussed from the viewpoint of setting selling prices for this highly competitive newly acquired product.

THE PROBLEMS OF ACQUISITION

The acquisition of a new product line is not an everyday occurrence. However, when it does occur every department in the organization is affected by new and unpredictable problems.

The engineering staff will work feverishly for many weeks checking the drawings and tools of the newcomer; the maintenance group will evaluate the condition and maintenance requirements of the newly acquired equipment; industrial engineers will review the methods, while the purchasing and material control groups evaluate the condition and quantity of raw material and finished stock on hand.

The controller, in his role as financial coordinator and guardian of the assets, must evaluate the financial implications resulting from these investigations. He must establish procedures for costing the new product to assure that inventory valuations will be correct. He must also establish acceptable cost-selling-price relationships which will provide reliable bases for pricing new products or variations of existing products which will subsequently be introduced into the line.

Although the controller's role is many faceted, this chapter will concern itself only with the costing and the establishment of cost-selling-price relationships, for a product peculiar to the electronics industry. Since the heart of an electronic system is the electron tube, let us assume that the socket into which such tubes are plugged was selected as the candidate for acquisition. The company which has been acquired is a small producer whose costing procedures are informal because of the tendancy of the owner and his partner to substitute personal opinion and judgment for accounting techniques—a practice which is inconsistent with the principle of professional management.

THE NEW PRODUCT

The sockets fall into two broad categories: the molded line and the laminated line. The molded type is the more rugged of the two and is the more widely used. The laminated socket is used for some commercial applications such as radio and television set manufacture where failure would not be critical. Although the procedures which will be explained apply to the sockets specifically, numerous other products also make up the line. Examples of these are the plastic bases used at the base of the electron tube, terminal boards such as those used for printed circuits, and terminal strips. To provide a better understanding of the costing problems, it might be well to give a brief description of the method of manufacturing both the molded and laminated sockets, and later, to show the differences in method of costing.

MANUFACTURE OF THE MOLDED SOCKET

The molded body (insulator) used in molded sockets is made by placing plastic powder in the cavities of a mold. (There may be anywhere from one to 30 cavities, depending on volume.) The two halves of the mold come together, applying heat and pressure to the powder for a period of from a minute to a minute and a half. Upon completion of this molding cycle, as it is known, the socket bodies are ejected. The next step in the process is to insert contacts into the openings in the molded body and to crimp a metal saddle around the body. The saddle has two holes through which the socket is riveted to the chassis of the equipment.

MANUFACTURING PROBLEMS—ALLOWANCES IN COSTS

The principal problems of manufacture arising in the molding process are: (1) wearing of the mold which results in heavy flash (flash is the thin skin of plastic which covers the openings and overlaps the edges)—this causes difficulty in assembly because it requires more than average pressure to push the contacts through the flash covering the contact passageway; (2) porosity—this is caused by an insufficient amount of powder in the cavity or insufficient heat; (3) blistering—caused by too much heat;

(4) excessive or insufficient shrinkage of the molded parts because of too rapid or too slow cooling of the mold, and (5) flash burns—wherein a piece of flash will burn the molded body causing a pit.

In the automatic assembly process, the most frequent source of trouble is insecure or missing contacts. To allow for the difficulties explained above, a two percent allowance for spoilage is made in costing up the molded part and one percent in costing up the assembly.

MANUFACTURE OF THE LAMINATED SOCKET

Where the molded socket uses a molded body to hold the contacts, the laminated socket uses two plates punched out of bakelite. The bakelite is purchased in sheets four feet square. These sheets are first heated (to eliminate fracture marks and rough edges when sheared) and then sheared into strips of proper width for punching out the plates. Each socket has a top and a bottom plate which when secured together hold the contacts in place. No metal saddle is used as in the case of the molded sockets because two holes are provided in the plates for riveting the socket in place. This is one of the cost-saving features of the laminated socket. In the costing of the molded body, such factors as cycle time, number of cavities, and weight of powder are the principal considerations. In costing the laminated socket plates, only the weight of material and press speed are required.

LAMINATED SOCKETS—ALLOWANCES IN COSTS

In making laminated plates the greatest loss is in: (1) the trimming operation which just precedes shearing; (2) blanking scrap such as rounded areas and holes, and (3) spoilage due to end-pieces which are not of sufficient size to punch out a full plate. Since all of the above losses are not the result of improper fabrication, the allowance is made only in the amount of material provided. The allowance, therefore, does not include the labor and overhead of the punching operation.

More spoilage is encountered in assembling the laminated socket than the molded type. The laminated product uses an L-shaped contact, the short part of the "L" being held between the plates, and the long end extending through the lower plate for contact. An incorrect angle in the bend can cause jams in the machine, thus preventing subsequent contacts from feeding. As a rule, salvage operations are performed on such sockets. Frequently, the addition of one contact and a hand eyeletting operation will complete the socket. In our illustration of how a laminated socket is costed, a two percent allowance will be made to allow for spoilage in assembly.

FACTORS AFFECTING THE COSTING PROGRAM

Upon addition of a new product, programs may be instituted to achieve automation. Dies may be equipped with automatic controls which stop the press electronically as soon as the material jams, or when the material runs out. Thus, one operator could service five or six presses with ease, where previously each machine required a full-time operator. This mechanism, which is used in connection with metal punching dies, is permanently attached to the die and moved with it. The cost would be carried in the die and mold account and amortization taken over the life of the die. In the case of presses used for punching laminated parts, a program to build automatic feeds which would heat the bakelite and feed the strips automatically might be pursued by management in order to fully exploit cost savings potentials.

The engineering department may find it desirable to redesign parts and to alter the manufacturing procedure. Thus, because of the cumulative effect of the various changes, existing cost figures, to the extent that they are available, may be obsoleted almost immediately upon acquisition. The accounting department must therefore restudy the entire costing structure with a view toward arriving at manufacturing costs so a current cost-selling price comparison can be made.

The first step would be the development of up-to-date press rates and the screening out of the unusual maintenance and rearrangement costs. Although the ideal program would be to develop a flexible budget in connection with the development of press rates, expediency might dictate analysis of all expenses at one level of operation and setting temporary press rates on that basis until a more complete job can be done at a later date, when more experience would be available.

COSTING THE MOLDED SOCKET

The molded part of the socket is costed first with allowances being made for spoilage. The cost of the molded part is then taken as material in costing up the assembly operations. Let us assume the following figures in costing a 7-contact molded socket (all costs are on a per 1000 basis):

Material required	5.5#
Material cost	$.22 per pound
Curing cycle	90 seconds
Number of cavities	30

COST OF MOLDED BODY

	Cost Per 1000
Material	
5.5# powder @ $.22	$1.21
Labor & Overhead	
Cycle time of 90 sec. = 40 cycles/hr.	
40 cycles x 30 cavities =	
1200 socket bodies per hour	
1200 socket bodies @ press rate of $2.40/hr	2.00
Other	
Mold Amortization	.26
Mold Maintenance	.04
2% allowance for spoilage	.07
Total cost per 1000 socket bodies	$3.58

COSTING THE ASSEMBLY OPERATION

Let us assume the following statistics in connection with the assembly cost: production rate of 2000 per hour with press rate including labor at $6 per hour. The cost of the molded body @ $3.58 per 1000 is taken from above and considered as part of the material cost on the socket assembly sheet.

COST OF THE ASSEMBLED SOCKET

	Cost Per 1000
Material	
1 Molded body	$ 3.58
1 Saddle	1.50
7 Contacts	7.00
	$ 12.08
Labor & Overhead	
2000 assembled per hour @ $6.00/hr	3.00
Other	
1% allowance for spoilage	.15
Total cost per 1000 completed sockets	$15.23

COSTING THE LAMINATED SOCKET

Material weight is determined by multiplying the width by pitch (length) by thickness by density. The cost of shearing is shown on a flat charge basis regardless of the width of the strip sheared. The reason for this is the fact that the bulk of the shear hand's time is spent loading the oven, unloading, trimming the sheets, and getting more material from the local storage area. Overhead is not applied on the shearing labor because it is included in the press rate.

COST OF TOP PLATE

	Cost Per 1000
Material	
1/32XP Bakelite 1.50# @ $.90 lb.	$1.35
Labor & Overhead	
Labor cost of shearing	.05
Production—8000/hr. @ press rate of $3.20	.40
Other	
Die Amortization	.02
Die Maintenance	.05
Total cost per 1000 top plates	$1.87

COST OF BOTTOM PLATE

	Cost Per 1000
Material	
3/64 XP Bakelite 2.25# @ $.70	$1.58
Labor & Overhead	
Labor cost of shearing	.05
Production—8000/hr. @ press rate of $3.20	.40
Other	
Die Amortization	.02
Die Maintenance	.07
Total cost per 1000 bottom plates	$2.12

Although the top and bottom plates are the same size, the bottom plate weighs more because it is thicker. Punching costs are the same because the punching speed which has been assumed in the above example is the same for both. Die maintenance for the bottom plate is greater because the bottom plate has more holes and is thicker than the top plate.

COSTING THE ASSEMBLY OPERATION

As in the case of the molded sockets, it was found that the same form could be followed in costing up the assembly operations for the laminated socket. Here again, as in the case of the molded body, the total cost of the top and bottom plates was picked up as material in the assembly operation.

COST OF THE ASSEMBLED SOCKET

	Cost Per 1000
Material	
1 Top Plate	$ 1.87
1 Bottom Plate	2.12
7 Contacts	7.00
2 Eyelets	.70
	$11.69
Labor & Overhead	
3000 assembled per hour @ $6.00/hr.	2.00
Other	
2% allowance for spoilage	.27
Total cost per 1000 completed sockets	$13.96

THE PROBLEM OF COMPETITIVE PRICING

The development of a formula for pricing the new product, particularly when competitive pressures are intense, is one of the most difficult problems.

As supply approaches demand, prices are forced downward; purchasers become more exacting in their requirements and suppliers find that returns from customers are on the increase.

Costs of inspection and process controls become increasingly great. Customers begin to demand that the supplier, rather than they, maintain inventories for release on short notice. Thus, as prices are squeezed downward, costs are forced upward.

The need for changes in costing and pricing practices cannot be predicted in advance so that revisions can be scheduled in an orderly fashion. On the contrary, as in changes in the business cycle, one suddenly becomes aware of new forces which have come into play almost imperceptibly.

The Sales Department will get the first inkling as to these changes through greater difficulty in making sales at existing prices. Increased returns from customers will serve as another clue. While these indicators or barometers are recognizable in varying degrees, the transition is gradual. No one can say, as of a certain week or month, that new basic forces have become predominant. Too often profit erosion is well advanced before management has realized the full magnitude of the problem it now has on its hands.

PHILOSOPHY OF PRICING

The philosophy of pricing in our competitive economy was best expressed by the elder Henry Ford:

> ... Our policy is to reduce the price, extend the operations, and improve the article. You will notice that the reduction of price comes first. We have never considered any costs as fixed. Therefore we first reduce the price to the point where we believe more sales will result. Then we go ahead and try to make the prices. We do not bother about the costs. The new price forces the costs down. The more usual way is to take the costs and then determine the price, and although that method may be scientific in the narrow sense, it is not scientific in the broad sense, because what earthly use is it to know the cost if it tells you that you cannot manufacture at a price at which the article can be sold? But more to the point is the fact that, although one may calculate what a cost is, and of course all of our costs are carefully calculated, no one knows what a cost ought to be. One of the ways of discovering ... is to name a price so low as to force everybody in the place to the highest point of efficiency. The low price makes everybody dig for profits. We make more discoveries concerning manufacturing and selling under this forced method than by any method of leisurely investigation.

Apropos of this philosophy, it is important that pricing be based on optimum levels of manufacturing activity and efficient operations.

OPTIMUM UTILIZATION OF
EQUIPMENT—ECONOMICS OF MANUFACTURE

Optimum level or normal capacity for the majority of companies is based on a five-day week. Utilization of equipment within that period, however, is governed by the economics of manufacture. Annealing furnaces and large molding presses, for example, would be scheduled on a 24-hour basis because it is cheaper to keep production going 'round the clock than it would be to wait several hours for the equipment to come up to temperature.

Expensive fabricating equipment would likewise be operated 'round the clock to minimize depreciation charges. A simple bench assembly operation (except for bottleneck operations) would ordinarily be limited to a single shift. But development of an expensive automatic machine to replace hand assembly might require a two- or three-shift operation (depending on the capacity of the machine) in order to obtain an adequate return on investment. Each type of operation has its own peculiar economics which can be determined without too much difficulty. Taking these economic factors into consideration will yield overhead absorption rates based on an optimum sales level.

LEVELLED PRODUCTION A PREREQUISITE TO
OPTIMUM OPERATING EFFICIENCIES

The accumulation of inventories during the low period of the seasonal cycle as a means of levelling out the peaks and valleys of production is a necessary prerequisite to attainment of optimum operating efficiencies. Levelled production is especially important in companies producing a large variety of parts that require tooling. Metal stamping and molding are good examples. Scheduling the part for production means that availability of tools must first be checked. If tools are available, then availability of the proper machine must be checked. If a multipurpose tool is being used for stamping one of a family group of parts, or if the tool requires modification of repair, a suspense file must be carried until the tool becomes available.

This seems simple enough under normal conditions when there is not too much pressure for production. But let's take the situation of a company which perhaps because of limited working capital, loose production control methods, or unbalanced inventories, has large fluctuations in activity because production is geared directly to incoming orders. During the slow period, when demand is low, production runs are relatively short. Frequent changeovers from type to type result in a large amount of downtime and, consequently, higher costs of production. When volume increases at the high point of the seasonal cycle, six and seven day work-weeks become the order of the day. However, changeovers and downtime remain high because more and more types are required. Because inventories become unbalanced, production must be interrupted frequently to run all the types required.

Production control and planning functions become bogged down with the problem of re-scheduling accumulated orders because of complaints from customers and urgent requests from the sales department to expedite new orders. Because of the terrific pressure, quality suffers, returns from customers increase, and what should be a season of high profits becomes a period of confusion with the resulting lower profits and probable losses of future business.

LEVELLED PRODUCTION MEANS MORE PRODUCTIVE LABOR

Fluctuations in production mean fluctuations in employment, and the resulting labor inefficiency. People whose employment is contingent upon seasonal demand are not likely to develop either the skill or the interest needed to do more than a passing job. The secure, happy employee who can depend upon year-round employment is much more likely to think beyond starting and stopping the machine to which he is assigned. He will become curious as to why certain defects occur; he will begin to wonder how he can prevent them from recurring; and as time goes on, he will get the "feel" or his machine in much the same way one gets to know one's automobile. In short, instinctive know-how will take the place of mechanical boredom.

THE MARKUP FACTOR IN PRICING

No discussion of costing and pricing would be complete without a review of the nature of markup. The markup factor is not a standard figure, as it is frequently assumed to be, applicable to all the companies of a particular type of manufacture. Since markup is the difference between manufacturing cost and selling price, markup merely measures this difference.

A company which bases its customer quotations on optimum standards, the method recommended, would use a higher markup than a company using historical costs. The following illustrates this point:

PRODUCT A

	Historical Costs	Optimum Standards
Material	$23	$20
Direct Labor	10	8
Variable Burden	20	18
Fixed Burden	10	7
Total Cost	$63	$53
Markup	6	16
Selling Price	$69	$69

Markup may even vary within a line of products. These differences in pricing procedure and inconsistencies in markup practices point up the importance of developing standards based on optimum levels and optimum efficiencies.

Standards developed in this manner will tend to be more consistent than historical or adjusted historical costs because of the tendency to "freeze" inefficiencies into the latter.

With pricing accomplished on the basis of optimum standards, the next step would be to break down the entire line of products into family groups. Thus, when the markup for a family group has been established, any new additions to the family would be priced using the markup for the group as a guide.

Exhibit 9-1 shows the costs of seven battery sockets of a "family." Four types have been in the line for some time, but three types, 43-2424, 43-2425, and 45-2507, are variations of the existing types for which selling prices must be established.

All costs are based on optimum volume and optimum efficiencies, therefore they represent costs which are competitive. To arrive at selling prices for the three new types, the percentage of cost to selling price was first calculated for the existing types. This percentage showed that the high volume sellers which were in great demand had a 79% and 80% ratio of cost to selling price while the lower volume 4-contact socket, which required a large investment in equipment and inventories per unit, had a 76% ratio.

This indicated that the market would allow only 79% to 80% of the selling price to cover manufacturing costs when the item was in general demand and sold in large volume. However, in the case of the 4-contact socket, which is not manufactured in large volume runs, as are the other types, the price recognizes that the higher investment per unit must be repaid through a higher selling price, as evidenced by the fact that costs consume only 76% of the sales dollar in the two 4-contact sockets compared with 79% and 80% for the 2-contact sockets.

In determining the selling prices for the three new types, an evaluation would first be made of investment requirements and potential volume of these types.

In the case of 43-2424 and 43-2425 it was felt that the 76% ratio which applies to the 44-2467 and 44-2447 should apply to these; the potential volume and investment requirements being about the same. The 76% was then divided into the cost of $18.15 to arrive at a selling price of $24.00 per thousand. For the 45-2507 the anticipated industry volume was somewhat lower than any of the other sockets because the number of applications for this socket were fewer. Volume would be lower and investment would therefore be higher per unit than for any of the others. While a 72% or 73% ratio would have been desirable, this would have resulted in a selling price which would have exceeded the selling price of a 2-contact plus a 3-contact socket. Therefore, a 74% ratio was chosen.

CONCLUSIONS

The costing and pricing of various products in a line is not a simple arithmetical task which can be delegated on a routine clerical basis.

To obtain historical actual costs with inefficiencies "frozen in" can be misleading to management and can lead to erroneous conclusions, particularly in the setting of competitive selling prices. Product costs must be logically developed from component to finished assembly on the premise that the manufacturing operation is completely competitive and that the customer cannot be expected to pay for inefficiencies.

Battery Sockets
Comparison of Cost with Selling Price
Per 1000

Material	2 Contacts		3 Contacts		4 Contacts		5 Contacts
Top Plate	42-2511	42-2440	43-2424	43-2425	44-2467	44-2447	45-2507
12-2524 1/32 XP	3.60						
12-2466 1/16 XP		3.74					
12-2448 1/16 XP			5.62				
12-2460 1/32 XP				5.62			
12-2440 1/32 XP					7.50		
12-2423 1/32 XP						7.50	
12-2412 1/32 XP							9.37
Bottom Plate							
13-2524 1/16 XP	4.00						
13-2466 3/64 XP		4.24					
13-2448 3/64 XP			6.37				
13-2460 3/64 XP				6.37			
13-2440 3/64 XP					8.50		
13-2423 3/64 XP						8.50	
13-2412 3/64 XP							10.62
Contacts							
10-431	2.00	2.00					
10-562			3.00				
10-567				3.00			
10-632					4.00	4.00	
10-636							5.00
Eyelets							
46	.60	.60	.60	.60			
48					.70	.70	.70
Total component cost	$10.20	$10.58	$15.59	$15.59	$20.70	$20.70	$25.69
Assembly labor and overhead	2.00	2.00	2.20	2.20	2.40	2.40	2.40
Spoilage allowance	.24	.25	.36	.36	.46	.46	.56
Total cost	$12.44	$12.83	$18.15	$18.15	$23.56	$23.56	$28.65
Selling price	15.75	16.00	24.00 *	24.00 *	31.00	31.00	38.75 *
% cost to selling price	79%	80%	76% *	76% *	76%	76%	74% *

* New types
NOTE: Selling prices rounded off to nearest $0.25

Exhibit 9-1

Setting prices requires a knowledge as to the type of customer for whom the product is intended. When the product is sold to another manufacturer, who in turn uses it in his manufacturing process, specification requirements are usually more rigid than they are for the replacement market. In spite of more rigid requirements, selling prices are generally lower because of larger sized orders and bulk packaging. Thus, the same basic product will be sold at one price to the manufacturer and at another to the replacement market even though the cost of manufacture may be exactly the same for both.

Another factor which must be taken into account is market willingness or unwillingness to pay a particular price. The existence of an alternate type of material or component made by a completely different process may create a buyer's market. In such a case, a management decision will be required to determine what the selling price should be. And after establishment of a price, tighter competition may force additional reductions.

Investment requirements in the launching of a new product type may justify a higher selling price than the normal cost/selling price relationship. Again, management judgment, rather than formula, enters the picture to appraise such factors as:

1. elasticity or inelasticity of demand
2. how high a selling price will yield a fair return on investment without "holding an umbrella" over potential competitors
3. available substitute products
4. potential size of the market

To assure success in obtaining business which is uniformly profitable, factors such as these must be carefully evaluated, particularly in the newer industries where stability has not been attained. The management which comes closest to anticipating the customer's willingness to pay a specific price will have a distinct advantage over its competitors—an advantage tantamount to monopoly.

> When a new company is acquired, costing procedures and pricing policies are frequently found to be informal—a real challenge to the new management.

SECTION III

Inventory Accountability and Valuation

10

Product Costing in Motion–
Inventory Accountability
and Valuation

Many companies using manual procedures to account for inventories must take shortcuts. These shortcuts frequently result in year-end surprises when the physical inventory is compared with the general ledger balance.

An important reason for good product costing is to assure sound inventory valuation. When inventories are not correctly valued, serious discrepancies can occur which affect the reliability of reported profits. It is surprising how many writers and speakers overlook proper inventory accountability and valuation as an important ingredient to reliable financial reporting.

Perhaps there is a lack of awareness of the hundreds of manufacturing companies which, at year-end, find that an eleven-months' profit has seriously deteriorated because of a large discrepancy between "physical" and "book."

"$5 million inventory shortage
at ABC Corporation; several
lawsuits in the offing."

Only the inventory shortages that result in lawsuits make the headlines. These represent only the tip of the iceberg. The average executive is not aware of the many occurrences because there is no tabulation available. In fact, the embarrassment to the financial executive tends toward suppressing rather than publicizing the occurrence. Most times the shortages are not real losses—the discrepancy being the result of a poor cost system that under-relieves inventories during the year, requiring adjustment at year-end.

This raises several questions:

1. Why is correct inventory valuation so important?
2. How do the discrepancies occur?
3. What is the solution?

This chapter will be devoted to answering these questions.

WHY IS PROPER INVENTORY VALUATION SO IMPORTANT?

Good inventory accountability is necessary to assure correct reporting of profits during the interim periods as well as at year-end.

a) There is nothing more disconcerting to the general manager responsible for the profit goals of his operation than to go along for eleven months of the year under the illusion that he is meeting his business plan—only to find in the twelfth month that a large inventory difference between physical and book wipes out a large part of the profit. Often when this happens, a promising career can be demolished overnight. This can happen not only to the financial executive, but to the general manager of the operation as well.

Often, a defensive stance is taken, wherein it is argued that the discrepancy between physical and book is only one half of one percent of throughput (flow of production). The implied question is, "How much more accuracy can you expect with the massive movement of material and parts that takes place in the course of a year?"

While it seems logical to equate the magnitude of the discrepancy with the volume of throughput, the more frequently used measure in the real world of business is the impact on profits. The difference is demonstrated in the two illustrations below:

	Company A	Company B
Annual throughput (Factory Cost of Production)	$20,000,000	$20,000,000
Inventory discrepancy	200,000	200,000
Percent to throughput	1%	1%
Pretax profit	2,000,000	400,000
Percent discrepancy to profit	10%	50%

Obviously, a greater unfavorable reaction can be expected from Company B's management and stockholders than from Company A's even though the amount of inventory discrepancy and throughput are exactly the same.

b) Another reason for the need for proper inventory accountability is the requirement for quarterly submissions to the Securities Exchange Commission. A company whose inventory is overstated on its books may show overstated profits in the first three quarters and a relatively poor performance for the fourth quarter. This does not represent acceptable reporting.

c) Stock analysts who make recommendations to their clients on the basis of reported earnings can be greatly misled by incorrect profits resulting from overstated earnings. This can work to the detriment of a company seeking to raise capital.

HOW DOES IT HAPPEN?

There are a number of ways in which inventory discrepancies occur. The case studies which follow are illustrative of the more typical occurrences.

Company A

This company had one inventory pool in the books. There was no breakdown among raw material, work-in-process and finished goods.

Input into inventory was based on the actual cost of material purchased and the actual direct labor as recorded on the payroll. Overhead was applied on the basis of a predetermined overhead rate on direct labor.

Output. Relief to inventory was determined on the basis of "standard" costs that were applied to shipments. These were developed to approximate actual costs. As the rate of cost escalation accelerated during the year, the standards used for costing sales fell far short of actual costs. As a result, the book inventory was substantially higher than the value of the physical inventory, resulting in a substantial reduction in profits that were reported in the earlier months.

Company B

This company did not have a formal standards program.

Input. In an attempt to approximate a standard cost system, actual labor costs were factored by estimated efficiency factors. Material input was based on standard prices.

Output. To arrive at the cost of sales, an historically experienced percentage was applied to each month's sales. As in the case of Company A, the basis of output was not consistent with input. The percentage applied to sales was 51%. The actual cost of sales turned out to be 57%. Because of this under-relief of 6% there was an inventory discrepancy of approximately a million dollars.

In both Company A and B, the requirement was to establish standards that would be used for both input and output.

Company C

Company C did have a formalized standard cost system. The same standards used for costing individual operations added up to the total standard product costs used for arriving at cost of sales. However, because losses in production were not fully accounted for, this company found at year end that it had an inventory shortage between physical and book amounting to $465,000.

Reporting production losses through direct paper work is easier said than done. Frequently, such losses occur because material thickness and widths (particularly in metal stamping) exceed the specifications called for. Since the end product in this company costs approximately $.15 per unit, this is certainly not enough to warrant an expensive monitoring procedure to assure that all losses are correctly and fully accounted for. The solution is to report the good finished components and subassemblies only when accepted into stock, thus excluding spoilage. This approach which is applicable to many companies will be discussed in a later section.

Company D

Because of a defect in a newly launched product, customers were authorized to return the product for replacement of the defective part. As the returns began accumulating, paperwork fell behind. The controller therefore resorted to a physical inventory each month as a means of accounting for the backlog of returned products. This resulted in an overstatement of inventory since most of the items were still the property of the customers.

Company E

A certain amount of rework is characteristic of many products. In doing rework, it is important to carefully monitor the production count to assure that double-counting is avoided—once when the original work is done and again when the defect is corrected.

Company E made a product that was subject to about 10% rework. Its controls to assure accurate counting were somewhat weak. As a result, double-counting caused an inventory buildup on the books that was unknown until the book and physical inventories were compared at year-end.

The experiences of Companies A, B, C, D, and E are illustrative of what can occur in causing a large inventory discrepancy. The number and variety of such possible occurrences are almost limitless. Positive steps that give consideration to the variations in cost flow must be taken to minimize the potential causes of discrepancies.

VARIATIONS IN COST FLOW

The nature of the inventory accounting procedures is dependent on the type of cost flow. Cost flow, in turn, should be based on the actual production flow of the product being manufactured.

A custom product is an entity unto itself—production flow being patterned around making specific products for specific customers. The flow of material, labor and overhead is directed toward satisfying the requirements for making that specific product. When completed, it is shipped to the customer out of work-in-process rather than out of a finished goods warehouse. In a number of instances companies make custom products from standard components that are interchangeable. Thus, the production flow for the components can be quite similar to the flow in making standard products for stock while the assembly of the finished unit can be quite similar to that of custom products.

A standard product is usually built to stock and sold out of finished goods. The production flow can be pictured as a steady stream of material, labor and overhead flowing into work-in-process through the various operations. From work-in-process, the flow is through the finished goods inventory from which shipments are made.

Job Costing

The job costing system utilizes two basic inventory accounts:

1. raw material
2. work-in-process (jobs in process)

While purchases are normally directed into the raw material inventory account and then issued to jobs as needed, this is not always the case; material purchased specifically for a job can bypass the raw material inventory account. Direct labor is charged directly against the job on which the work is performed.

Inventory accountability under job costing is relatively simple; as each job is completed, all accumulated costs that were charged to that job are cleared out of inventory, leaving no unaccounted-for residual quantities. If relief is made at the standard cost of the finished job (or estimated cost), the resulting residual quantity represents a variance. This would be cleared out of work-in-process as a separate step. (See Exhibit 10-1.)

There are disadvantages to the job costing method, however, because such a system requires substantially more work than a process cost system. As an example, a company with annual sales of less than $10,000,000 could have as many as 500 jobs in process. There is also a tendancy in job shops to "borrow" from one job to meet priority requirements of another. When such borrowing is done without paperwork documentation, the accuracy of the inventory value carried on the books becomes questionable. While process costing is simpler and therefore less costly, it cannot be substituted for job costing when customized production is required.

The type of product or service dictates the type of cost system required. When the product or service is unique and its specific cost must be known, then the job cost system is mandatory. In a process type business in which standardized products are built to stock, rather than to order, a standard cost process flow type of system is more suitable.

Standard Costing in a Process Flow

In a process (repetitive) type business, three basic inventory accounts are required:

1. raw material
2. work-in-process
3. finished goods

Many companies that have greatly improved the credibility of their financial statements through better inventory accountability are still vulnerable to year-end discrepancies because of incipient problems that are not reflected in the paperwork that documents the various transactions affecting the inventory. Examples are over-reporting of production, excessive use of material that is unreported, and rejects that are not completely accounted for.

As will be illustrated later, the work-in-process account should be broken down further to identify those items that are being stored in a controlled stockroom and those that make up the floor work-in-process. Accounting systems rarely recognize this breakdown in work-in-process, and thereby miss an opportunity for better accountability of inventory.

Most of the foregoing problems that result in under-relief of inventory in a process flow system occur in work-in-process. Efforts to correct the reporting

TWO BASIC COST FLOWS

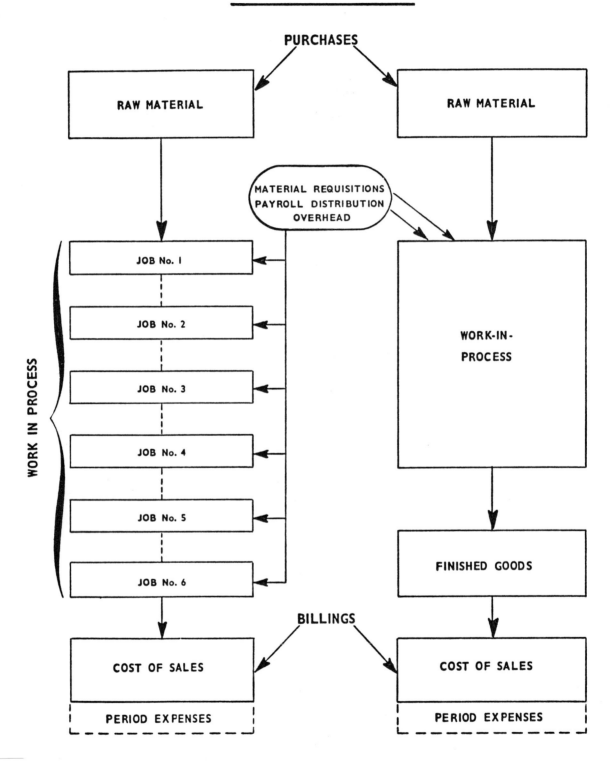

Exhibit 10-1

frequently become highly frustrating exercises because the cost of the cure often far exceeds the benefits. This is particularly true when low unit values are involved. What, then is the solution?

WHAT IS THE SOLUTION?

True accountability of inventory requires two steps:

- accountability for the physical units
- assigning dollar values to the physical units accounted for

The accounting department rarely has the tools necessary for good physical accountability. This capability is possessed by the production and inventory control group whose major responsibility is to:

- issue requisitions for purchase of material
- issue shop orders for production of components and subassemblies as well as the finished product
- maintain perpetual records of items in inventory.

With the introduction of the computer in maintaining perpetual records of all stockroom inventories and, in many cases, status reports of floor inventories, it behooves the accountant to make better use of the same paperwork that is used for moving material in and out of the various stores accounts.

The big hangup of many accounting departments lies in the work-in-process inventory. The accountant looks upon this as a single pool of costs. The production and inventory control group, on the other hand, identifies work-in-process in at least two segments—finished parts in work-in-process stores and floor work-in-process. Exhibit 10-2 illustrates a work-in-process inventory that contains three stockrooms:

- components
- subassemblies
- unpacked goods (finished goods that have not yet been packed)

The components and subassembly stockrooms are enclosed areas while the unpacked goods are in an open area located at the end of the production line. Although the latter area is not enclosed, it is closely controlled as are the other two.

Receipts into all three areas are based on counts of items that have been inspected and accepted by the inspector. The smaller items are weighed and scale counted through use of conversion factors. The larger items are accounted for individually.

The tickets representing receipts into stock and issues out of stock are sequentially numbered. Each day's receipts and issues are batched and forwarded to the data processing department for processing. the preprinted numbers are listed sequentially for both the receipts and issues to determine if any tickets are missing. In the event that there is a gap, the issuer of the ticket is asked for an accounting. It is usually found that missing numbers are tickets that were voided and thrown out. Insistence of

PRODUCTION FLOW

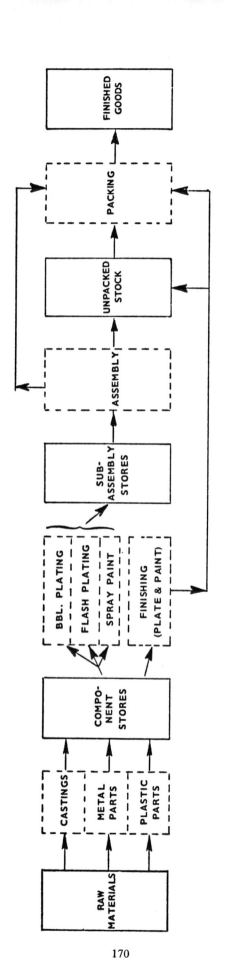

SOLID LINES — CONTROLLED STORES

DOTTED LINES — FLOOR WORK-IN-PROCESS (FLOAT)

Exhibit 10-2

170

full accountability serves as a disciplinary reminder to all new personnel that every transaction must be documented.

The quantities received into each of the controlled areas as well as the quantities issued out of these areas are used as the basis for adjusting the "on hand" figures on the perpetual inventory status report for each stockroom (same procedure followed for raw material and finished goods). The same paperwork used for adjusting the perpetual inventories should be the basis for input into inventory on the books. Before discussing accountability for the floor work-in-process, let us cover cycle counting–the assurance that physical inventories are correct.

Importance of Cycle Counts

No perpetual inventory can be run ad infinitum without regular verification. The preferred method is to use cycle counting–so named because of the systematic selection of items to be counted. The selection illustrated here established priorities according to the following four categories:

– A items

– B items

– C items

– D items

The 18,250 different items making up these four categories in one company break down as follows:

	Number of Items	% of Total Items	% of Total Value
A items	1,350	7.4%	48%
B items	2,300	12.6	26
C items	3,200	17.5	16
D items	11,400	62.5	10
	18,250	100.0%	100%

The frequency cycle for taking cycle counts is based on the following table:

A items	Every 2 months
B items	Every 3 months
C items	Every 6 months
D items	Every 12 months

Since the A and B items account for 74% of the total inventory value and require counting only 20% of the total number of items, cycle counts for these two categories are scheduled more frequently. The D items, which represent over 60% of the total number of items and only 10% of the total value, can safely be scheduled for counting once a year. Over and above verification through cycle counting, there is an automatic verification of each item in which an issue reduces the balance unrealistically—to a negative value, for example. In such instances, it may be found out that an erroneous identification of an item number resulted in the incorrect reduction of one item and overstatement of another. For this reason, when negative values are found, they should not automatically be restored to "zero" or to some other value. The impact of restoring negative values to "zero" unilaterally is to write up the inventory—an action that should be avoided unless the offsetting error is also corrected.

Accounting for Floor Work-in-Process

Once the stockroom work-in-process inventories are accounted for, only the floor inventories remain to be discussed. These are the raw materials that have not yet been processed but are lying around the work places awaiting processing. Floor work-in-process will also include items that have been partially processed as well as those awaiting acceptance into stockrooms.

If the floor work-in-process is in the nature of "pipeline stock," it is possible that it can be properly accounted for by carrying a fixed dollar value on the books. If there are "expansion points" at which fluctuations in amount of floor inventories occur, it may be necessary to take physical inventories at such points and to adjust the fixed value carried on the books.

Some production and inventory control departments account for floor work-in-process through shop orders which utilize "travelers" or shop orders to identify the production at each point of the process as well as the number of units that have been lost through defective workmanship or materials. Where such information exists, the balances on the travelers or shop orders can be costed to arrive at the value of the floor work-in-process.

Some accountants monitor floor inventories by attempting to account for movement from cost center to cost center. While this method seems to be theoretically proper, it can result in a fictitious buildup on the books with the resulting discrepancy at year end when the book value is compared with the physical value.

The weakness in this method is that production figures on an operation-by-operation basis, even if correct, would result in input into inventory of costs that would be too high because of losses in later operations. If such losses were removed from the inventory, the net result would be approximately correct. However, in the real world, reporting of production losses is one of the weak links in inventory accountability. It is a rare company that can boast of reliability in reporting of such losses—leaving as the most reliable alternative the acceptance into book inventory of only the costs of those items that are accepted in the various stores accounts.

The procedures for developing the cost data for use in the valuation of transactions will be discussed in another chapter.

Good inventory accountability requires two steps: first, recognizing good production only, based on parts and finished products accepted into controlled stores areas; and second, accounting for floor work-in-process as a separate operation.

11

Computerizing the Cost
System for Better
Inventory Control

This chapter © 1976 by Thomas S. Dudick.

> The proliferation of items carried in inventory by modern-day business makes accountability through manual procedures obsolete and inaccurate.

In recent years the explosive increase in demand for a proliferation of products and product types, coupled with the trend toward larger and larger manufacturing units, has resulted in a massive increase in the number of different items carried in inventory by many companies. This does not apply to finished goods and raw materials alone—it applies to the multiplicity of components, assemblies and subassemblies in various stages of completion as well. A fairly common mass-produced product can have as many as 20,000 items in inventory. An "order of magnitude" analysis by raw material, work-in-process and finished goods might typically show the following breakdown of the total of 20,000:

Raw Material	500
Work-in-process	14,500
Finished goods	5,000
	20,000

When manufacturing units were smaller and the items in inventory fewer in number, accountability for physical units and dollar value could be accomplished manually. But as the number of items expanded, companies found it more and more difficult to achieve proper accountability. Production and inventory control records were laboriously posted by hand. Accountants responsible for preparing financial statements found it exceedingly difficult to apply dollar values to movement of inventories through the production processes and through cost of sales. To develop such costs without a computer would require the manual treeing-up of costs from raw material through the various components and subassemblies to the cost of the finished product.

Such treeing-up on a manual basis would require a day to a day and a half, at a minimum, for each finished product. Even if this were a practical approach for 5,000 end products, it would be impossible—except at a highly prohibitive cost—to achieve proper inventory valuation. The reason is that even if the costs for the 20,000 items were available, the tracking of physical movement through the process for the various operations would be very burdensome. Many production and inventory control departments that have not yet instituted a computerized approach find it impossible to follow production through work-in-process except in overall terms. Since this function, which has the responsibility for filling customer orders, must take arbitrary approaches for physical accountability, it is difficult to imagine how the accounting function can find a more sophisticated valuation method.

With the advent of the modern computer, the process of physical accountability and valuation of the physical quantities can be achieved in a fraction of the time that manual approaches would require. Once the computerization has been accomplished, the accounting values placed on inventory can be directly related to and documented by the physical units making up the production and inventory control records.

OVERVIEW OF COMPUTERIZATION

The Engineering Bill of Material is the "blueprint" of how the product is made. It provides a list of the various material items, processes, and processing times at the different stages of production. Just as a bill of material is important to the physical production process in the manufacture of a product, so is the computerized bill of material the central point in a computerized inventory control system. Exhibit 11-1 diagrammatically illustrates the relationship of the input and output documents to the computerized bill of material (referred to in this company as the indented bill of material). On the input side, it shows the various types of transaction documents that are run against the bill of material information to produce such output documents as product costs, transaction costing, cost of sales and variance analyses. Also as an important part of the computerized procedures are the ongoing and year end maintenance programs, the edit lists to assure accurate input of information, and the "where-used" information.

This chapter will detail the content of the indented bill of material, where the information comes from, and how the product cost is developed. It will also illustrate transaction lists and describe the procedure for summarizing these and developing the closing journal entries.

INDENTED BILL OF MATERIAL

The end product used to illustrate the indented bill of material is a piece of

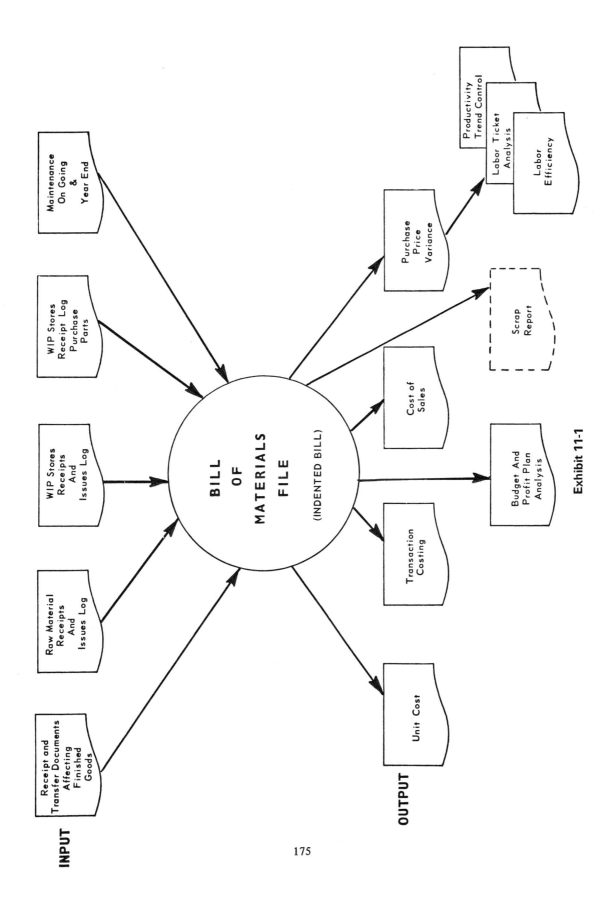

INPUT

Maintenance On Going & Year End

WIP Stores Receipt Log Purchase Parts

WIP Stores Receipts And Issues Log

Raw Material Receipts And Issues Log

Receipt and Transfer Documents Affecting Finished Goods

BILL OF MATERIALS FILE (INDENTED BILL)

OUTPUT

Productivity Trend Control

Labor Ticket Analysis

Labor Efficiency

Purchase Price Variance

Scrap Report

Cost of Sales

Budget And Profit Plan Analysis

Transaction Costing

Unit Cost

Exhibit 11-1

175

machined brass rod about two inches long and .280 inches in diameter. This has affixed at one end a plastic disc. The operations include the mixing of the plastic ingredients, forming the plastic disc, making the brass stem, and then combining the plastic disc and the stem through a molding operation. After some drilling and reaming operations, the item is packed and labeled.

This product, 01 02608 5036, was selected because of its simplicity. The treeing-up process for this product is illustrated in Exhibit 11-2. Note that only five levels are required to diagram the process; the more complex products would require numerous sheets of paper to illustrate the treeing-up process and would require as many as 14 levels of complex interrelationships of components and subassemblies.

Exhibit 11-3, Indented Bill of Material, illustrates how the treeing-up process is reflected in the computer. The columnar headings in this exhibit are explained on pages 178 and 179.

TREEING UP THE PROCESS

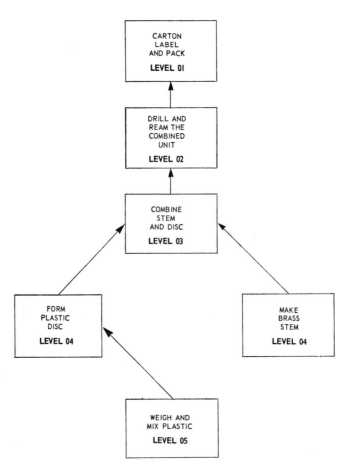

Exhibit 11-2

INDENTED BILL OF MATERIAL

FOR PRODUCT 01-02608-5036

PRODUCT ID	OPR NO.	BM LEVL	QUANTITY	START OPN.	COST CNTR.	STND HRS/M	LABOR RATE	VARBLE OVHEAD	FIXED OVHEAD	R/M CODE	R/M GROSS	R/M NET	SCRAP RECOVY	STANDARD R/M COST	U M
01-02608-5036	010	01	1.00000	010	1369	.02	2.497	1.749	3.407	018751				128.6900	2
01-02608-5036	010	01	1.00000	010						011856				8.0500	2
01-02608-5036	020	01	1.00000	020	1369	.05	2.497	1.749	3.407						
. 01-02608-0537	010	02	1.00000	010	0267	1.67	2.473	2.093	3.678						
. 01-02608-0537	020	02	1.00000	020	0267	1.18	2.473	2.093	3.678						
.. 01-02608-0005	010	03	1.00000	010	0568	.05	2.752	6.022	4.282						
.. 01-02608-0005	020	03	1.00000	020	0981	1.16	2.790	1.942	3.237						
... 01-02608-0008	010	04	1.00000	010	0447	.15	1.335	4.182	7.121	202800	37.800	17.000	313.75000	638.1700	2
... 01-02608-0008	020	04	1.00000	020	0450	.50	1.335	4.182	7.122						
... 01-02608-0008	030	04	1.00000	030	0761	.81	3.396	3.326	4.933						
... 01-02608-0008	050	04	1.00000	050	0568	.07	2.752	6.022	4.282						
.... 01-02608-0002	010	04	1.00000	010	1294	.08	2.773	2.978	4.413						
..... 97-00019-0000	010	05	.00990	010	1291	4.65	2.773	2.978	4.413	059562	350.75000	350.75000		250.0000	2
..... 97-00019-0000	010	05	.00990	010						055401	17.54000	17.54000		88.0000	2
..... 97-00019-0000	010	05	.00990	010						051202	3.86000	3.86000		530.0000	2
..... 97-00019-0000	010	05	.00990	010						058110	4.56000	4.56000		530.0000	2
..... 97-00019-0000	010	05	.00990	010						057326	7.02000	7.02000		34.5000	2
..... 97-00019-0000	010	05	.00990	010						054202	35.08000	35.08000		260.0000	2
..... 97-00019-0000	010	05	.00990	010						057320	87.69000	87.69000		114.2100	2
..... 97-00019-0000	010	05	.00990	010						055407	86.64000	86.64000		160.0000	2
..... 97-00019-0000	010	05	.00990	010						057315	3.51000	3.51000		225.0000	2
..... 97-00019-0000	010	05	.00990	010						059536	70.15000	70.15000		102.5000	2
..... 97-00019-0000	010	05	.00990	010						059537	224.48000	224.48000		60.0000	2
..... 97-00019-0000	010	05	.00990	010						051214	21.05000	21.05000		11.7500	2
..... 97-00019-0000	010	05	.00990	010						054213	87.67000	87.67000		72.5000	2

Exhibit 11-3

PRODUCT ID. As is typical in many companies reverting to the computer, difficulties arose in this company in trying to use existing product identification numbers. There was no consistency in the numbering procedures which had been developed over the years. In many instances a combination of numerals and alphabetical designations had been used. In some, additional digits were added for designation of special finishes or colors. To avoid the problems of attempting to use these, a new four-digit "machine code" was added to the regular number. Thus, the old number—familiar to the operating people— would always print out with the machine code used in the computer for identification purposes. In the indented bill of material, the existing number used in past years is illustrated by the first seven digits. The machine code follows as the next four digits.

OPR NO. To identify the product further, by stage of completion within each level, an operation number is introduced. Operation numbers are shown as 010, 020, 030, 040, 050, etc. 010 may identify a drilling operation in one cost center but in another the same number would mean a coating process. Generally, however, each number within a cost center would stand for the same operation on all products going through that center.

The "BM LEVL" corresponds with the level of manufacture illustrated in Exhibit 11-2. Note that the indentation of the Product ID is represented by dots preceding the number. The top level—the finished product—is not preceded by a dot. The next lower level is preceded by a single dot, the next level by two, etc.

"QUANTITY" specifies how many of the specific item are required per completed item at that level. This must be viewed in conjunction with the last column, "UM," which stands for Unit of Measure. In this instance, the code 2 under "UM" means per thousand. The quantity of 1.00000 therefore means that 1,000 components, for example, are required per 1,000 units that are completed at that level. When two units are required per finished unit, the quantity will be shown as 2.00000. In the case of raw materials shown as the 97 series of items at the bottom portion of the indented bill, the quantity is shown as .00990. This means that .00990 pounds of material are required per thousand units of product.

"START OPN." The operation number in this column identifies the point in the process at which processing starts on an incoming component. Note in Exhibit 11-3 that the first operation in cost center 1369 relates to raw material (packaging and labels). The first operation for these incoming materials is Operation 10, which consists of making up the carton and applying the label. The incoming component (from Level 2) is packaged in Operation 20. Thus the start operation for the latter is indicated as 020.

"COST CENTER" refers to the natural departmental area in which related manufacturing processes take place. The first two digits identify the overall department while the second two identify various work centers within the department. Availability of the four digits facilitates the application of machine-hour rates to smaller segments within the department. Although physical inventories are costed at the point at which the latest operation has been completed, the monthly transaction listings do not attempt to follow production from work center to work center within a department. They identify "issues to" and "transfers from" by the two-digit departmental designation.

"STND HRS/M" specifies the number of hours per thousand units that it should take to perform an operation. This figure represents labor hours when a hand operation is required. When a machine-paced operation is involved, these are machine hours. (Machine hours could be synonymous with labor hours when there is a full-time operator for each machine.)

"LABOR RATE" quantifies the labor cost per hour for performing the particular operation. This rate, multiplied by the hours, provides the standard direct labor cost.

"VARBLE OVHEAD" is the variable portion of indirect costs. It is based on a flexible budget which identifies separately those costs that are likely to fluctuate with changes in volume of production. Variable overhead would include such costs as supplies, material handling, and equipment servicing.

"FIXED OVHEAD" is also determined through the flexible budget. This category includes such costs as occupancy, supervision and depreciation. Segregation of the variable and the fixed overhead facilitates additional analysis beyond that provided in the routine cost system procedures.

"R/M CODE" identifies the material to which no labor has yet been applied. Included in this coding in the indented bill of materials illustrated by Exhibit 11-3 are the following:

- cartons and labels used at Level 1
- brass rod used for making the stem in Level 4
- ingredients required for making the plastic disc (Level 5)

"R/M GROSS" refers to the starting quantity of material for making the component or assembly. When material is unavoidably lost in the processing of a component, the finished weight shows under "R/M NET." An illustration of this is Operation 10 of Level 4. Here, the brass rod must be drilled out and threaded. The gross weight of the rod is shown as R/M Gross while the finished weight is indicated as R/M Net.

"SCRAP RECOVY" shows the standard cost per thousand pounds of metal recovered from the process.

"STANDARD R/M COST" shows the standard cost of the raw material used in the product.

The indented bill of material contains the "formula" for costing the product at the various stages of production. The document providing this basic data must be so organized that there will be a natural flow of information not only on existing products but also on new products and on basic changes that are made to present items. The source of this data will be discussed next.

SOURCE OF MANUFACTURING DATA

Basic manufacturing data eminates from two sources—the product development group in the engineering organization and the industrial engineering section.

Product Development

This function may not always be identified by the term product development—it may be part of engineering without bearing any special nomenclature. The function is to develop and maintain specifications on the various products made by the company. This covers the specifications of the material to be used, the quantity per unit, and in some instances the vendor source. In addition, the specifications for product performance are also part of the function of this group.

Industrial Engineering

Sometimes called Manufacturing Engineering, this group includes a function which specifies the equipment on which the product and its components will be made, the time requirements for processing and the labor category required to perform the work.

In organizing for computerization of the cost accounting system, this data must be assembled for all active products on a document that will act as a funnel to transmit the information. In some companies, the material is summarized on engineering Bills of Material while the processing data is shown on a Route sheet. In the example illustrated in this case study, both material and processing data are included in a single document called the Manufacturing Process Sheet. An example is shown in Exhibit 11-4. This exhibit lists the raw materials used in making up the batch of plastic required in a later operation to form a circular plastic disc. In addition to the raw materials, this process sheet also shows the time requirements for weighing out and mixing these ingredients. Since only one processing step is required, only one operation is indicated (Operation 010). This is performed in Cost Center 1291. The weighing out and mixing should take 4.65 hours per thousand pounds and the labor grade to be used is 8.

The Manufacturing Process Sheets must be developed in a manner that fits into the level-by-level progression of the manufacturing operation. This is demonstrated in Exhibit 11-5 for the product shown in Exhibit 11-3 (Indented Bill of Material).

The tie-in of the manufacturing process sheets to the treeing-up of the manufacturing process shown in Exhibit 11-5 is also illustrated with the indented bill of materials in Exhibit 11-6, entitled "Data Source for Indented Bill of Materials." Two manufacturing process sheets are used in this example: the weighing out of the plastic ingredients at Level 5 and the fabrication of the stem at Level 4.

Exhibit 11-6 identifies on both the indented bill of materials and the process sheets such items as the cost center, operation number, level of manufacture, standard hours per thousand, raw material code, and the weight of the brass used in making the stem.

Since the computerized bill of materials contains all the basic manufacturing information as well as the appropriate direct labor grade, overhead and material costs, it contains all the elements needed to develop the product cost.

MANUFACTURING PROCESS SHEET

SHEET 1 OF 2

ISSUE DATE	ISSUE NO	SUPERCEDED DATE	P.C.	BASIC	LINE NO	MACH CODE	REFERENCE	SHOP ORDER NO.
	4		97	00019	0000	0000		

DRAWING NO.

PART NAME: PLASTIC D785A

MATERIAL CODE	KIND	SIZE	DATE ISSUED
SHAPE	SPEC.	TEMPER	HARDNESS	QTY TO MAKE
UNIT	PER/M GROSS	PER/M NET		RAW MATERIAL REQ
ROUTING				REQUIRED COMPLETION DATE

MOLDING

LEVEL 05

OPER. NO.	OPERATION DESCRIPTION	EQUIPMENT	DEPT	SET-UP HRS	LAB GRD	PROD. HRS/M	LAB GRD	NO. MACH	NO. MEN	Cost Center
010	Weigh out and mix plastic ingredients (listed below)	Bench w/scale, Mixer Mold				4.65	8		3	1291

MATERIAL CODE	DESCRIPTION	POUNDS PER "M"
05-9562	Plastic #276	350.75
05-5401	Magnesium LT	17.54
05-1202	Z46	3.86
05-8110	LML	4.56
05-7326	Carbon 6	7.02
05-4202	Alumina 205	35.08
05-7320	Single Ply MM	87.69
05-5407	Black Oxide	86.64
05-7315	Acetone	3.51
05-9536	UPO Black #362	70.15
05-9537	M-34 Black	224.48
05-1214	Gr. Phosphate	21.05
05-4213	Hexo Cl	87.67

Total Pounds of Ingredients   1,000.00

PROCESS ENGINEER

STANDARD ENGINEER

Exhibit 11-4

181

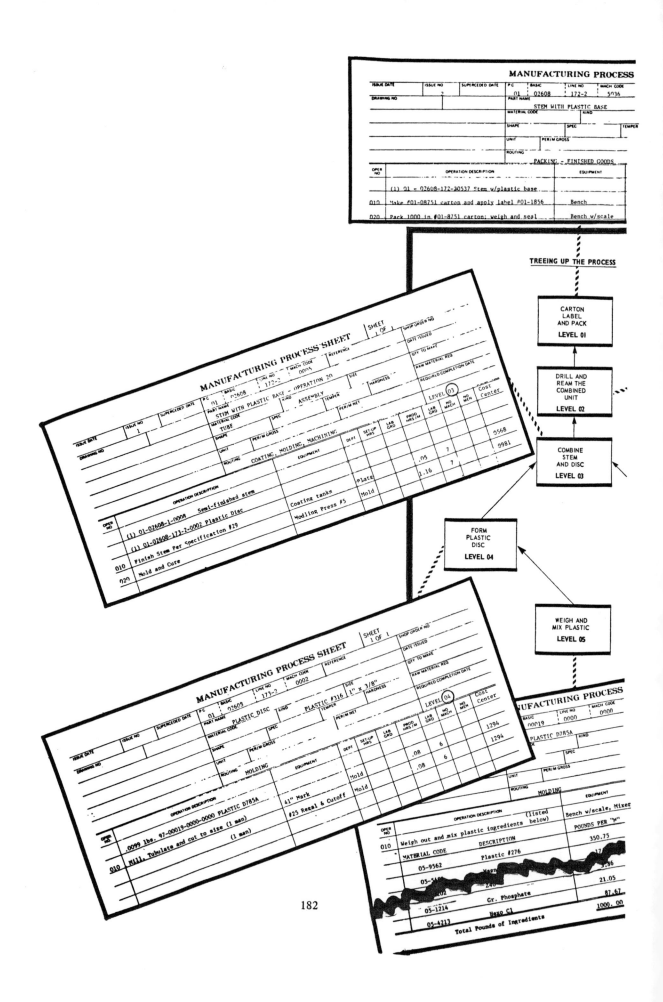

182

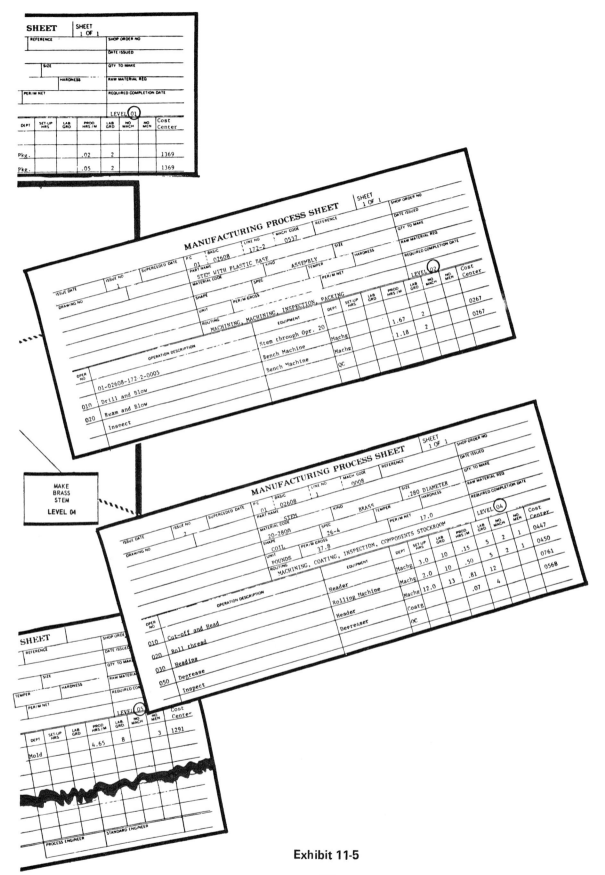

Exhibit 11-5

183

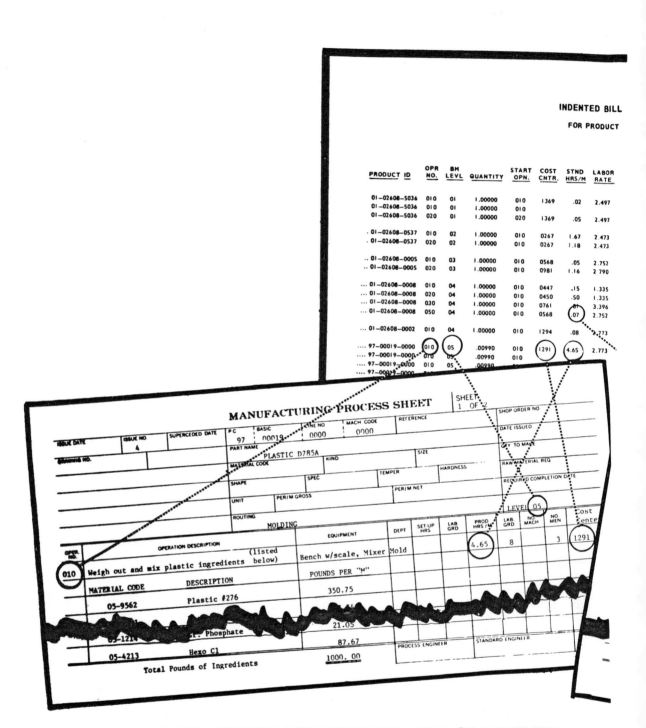

DATA SOURCE FOR INDENTED BILL OF MATERIAL

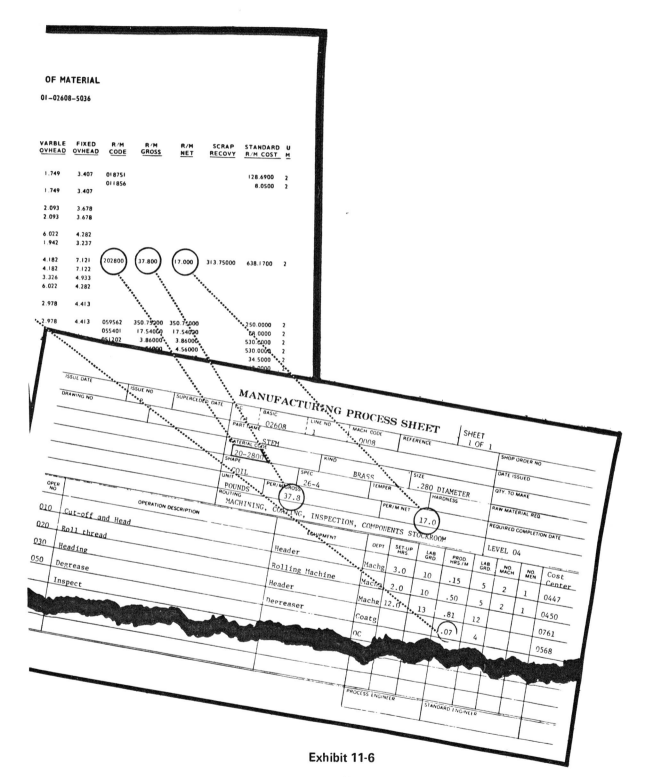

Exhibit 11-6

185

DEVELOPING THE PRODUCT COST

Exhibit 11-7 shows how the material elements are combined to arrive at the total cost of the brass used in making the stem. The starting size of brass rod needed to make a thousand stems weighs 37.8 pounds. In making the finished brass stem, it is necessary to hollow out the rod, to tap it and to thread the outside. The net weight of the finished stem is 17 pounds per thousand; 20.8 pounds, or 55% of the starting weight representing "necessary" scrap. The starting weight is costed by the standard cost of brass, which is $638.17 per thousand pounds of rod. The lost brass of 20.8 pounds is costed by the standard cost of scrap brass, which is $313.75 per thousand pounds. When the value of the scrap recovered is subtracted from the starting cost, the resulting cost of brass per thousand finished units is $17.60.

Exhibit 11-8 illustrates the procedure for arriving at the labor cost for product 01-02608-5036. The standard hours per thousand units are added up for all operations in all cost centers. These hours are multiplied by the labor grade applicable to the operations to arrive at a total labor cost by cost center. The addition of the total labor cost by cost center results in a total labor cost of $14.76 per thousand units of product. The variable and fixed overheads are applied on the basis of the same hours per thousand used to calculate the labor cost. The non-brass material for this product, amounting to $1.67, is the cost of cartons and labels used in the packaging operation in Level 1. The total standard product cost, then, is $73.05 per thousand units.

The figures contained in the product cost reports for the various levels are the same figures that are used for costing sales, issues and transfers.

Before discussing the transaction documents referred to above, it would be well to first review two more exhibits, 11-9 and 11-10. Exhibit 11-9 is illustrative of the "Where Used" file which identifies where the various components are used within the product line. Component #06100746, for example, is used in 749 different end products. In making a change in any of the elements of this component, it is obviously necessary to know which products will be affected by the change. The "Where Used" file serves this purpose.

Exhibit 11-10 illustrates an Edit Listing. This relates to the group of transactions identified as #9. The departments involved in the transfers are shown, as well as the quantities involved. The ticket numbers are listed sequentially so that missing numbers can be identified. The edit process for this month (August), would also "kick out" any transactions that were made to an incorrect department.

TRANSACTION LISTINGS

Transaction listings are the audit trails from which summaries and exception reports are derived. All material issued to the various production areas, all product movement between departments, transfers into and out of work-in-process stockrooms, and movements into and out of finished goods must be accounted for in terms of both physical units and dollar values on transaction runs. These provide the basis for maintaining inventory status reports as well as providing the documentation to support values carried on the accounting books.

Exhibit 11-11 illustrates the floor layout in which the various production departments and stockrooms are shown. These include:

Raw Material Stockroom
Primary work-in-process
    Automatic Machines
    General Machinery
    Plastics Molding
    Plating, Cleaning and Coating
Fabricated and Purchased Components Stockroom
Secondary work-in-process
    Hand Assembly (including packaging)
    Automatic Assembly (including packaging)
Finished Goods Stockroom

Raw materials issued out of the stockroom include brass rod to the automatic machines and plastic ingredients to the plastics molding department.

The fabricated brass stems and molded discs are moved to the Fabricated and Purchased Components Stockroom until scheduled for assembly. At that time, the two components are moved back into primary work-in-process for combining through a further molding and curing operation. At this point, they usually move into the secondary work-in-process area. Although this move bypasses the Fabricated and Purchased Components Stockroom, the paperwork reflects transfers into and out of the stockroom as if the product had moved through a storage area. In the secondary production area, the product will flow either to the Automatic Assembly or the Hand Assembly Department and will be packaged for shipment, after which it moves into the finished goods stockroom.

Some illustration of the transaction listings follow:

Raw Material Issues

Exhibit 11-12 shows a listing of raw material that was issued to production. The items have been listed in sequence by part number showing the unit of measure, quantity and standard unit cost at which they were carried in inventory. The column headed "Extended Cost" shows the total standard cost of the various materials issued. Note that item 96-5408 shows a negative quantity and therefore a negative cost—indicating either a return to stock or a correction of a previous issue. The page of the transaction listings used in this exhibit shows the total value of raw material issued in the period. This amount, $346,340.81, will be shown later in a journal entry relieving the raw material inventory account.

Fabricated Parts Transferred into the Stockroom

Most companies of this type utilize a work-in-process stockroom as a storage and staging area for the primary components and subassemblies. When the finished product

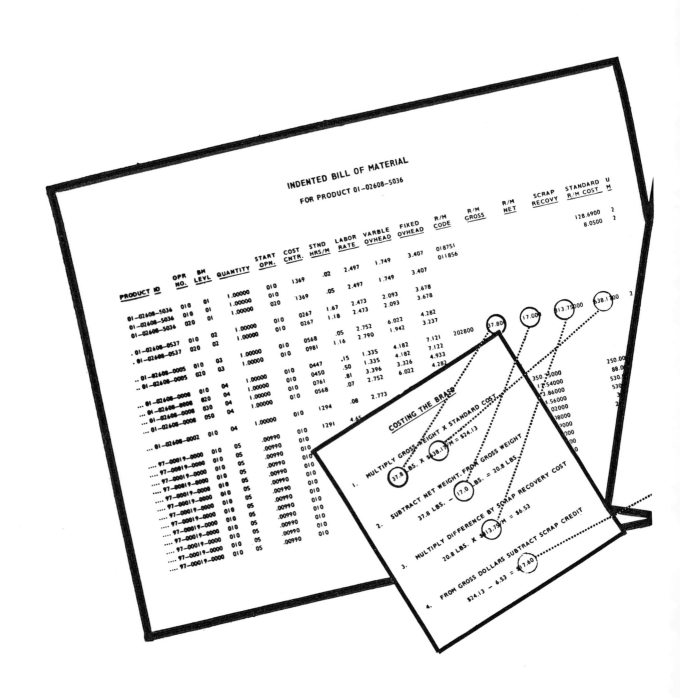

INDENTED BILL OF MATERIAL

FOR PRODUCT 01-02608-5036

COSTING THE BRASS

1. MULTIPLY GROSS WEIGHT X STANDARD COST
   37.8 LBS. X $638.17/M = $24.13

2. SUBTRACT NET WEIGHT FROM GROSS WEIGHT
   37.8 LBS. - 17.0 LBS. = 20.8 LBS.

3. MULTIPLY DIFFERENCE BY SCRAP RECOVERY COST
   20.8 LBS. X $313.73/M = $6.53

4. FROM GROSS DOLLARS SUBTRACT SCRAP CREDIT
   $24.13 - 6.53 = $17.60

PRODUCT COST REPORT

PRODUCT AND OPN	ID #	BRASS WEIGHT CRUDE WT	FINISH WT.	BRASS	SALVAGE	NON BRASS MATERIAL	LABOR	VARIABLE OVERHEAD	CUMULATIVE COST	FIXED OVERHEAD	TOTAL COST
01 0972 R											
010 R		27.80	17.00								
020 R		37.80	17.00	17.60	6.53	1.53	11.66	12.26			
030 R		42.80	18.70	17.60	6.53	1.53	18.74	18.24	43.05	19.59	62.64
S		.56	.27	20.34	7.56	2.22	24.00	24.31	56.11	30.11	86.22
W		.73	.66	.75	.10				72.32	39.92	112.24
040 R		42.80	18.70	.70	.03						
S		.98	.51	20.34	7.56	14.77	29.17	28.99			
W		.73	.66	1.06	.17				95.03	47.39	142.42
050 R		42.80	18.70	.70	.03						
S		.98	.51	40.34	7.56	14.77	34.12	33.17			
W		.73	.66	1.06	.17				104.16	54.75	158.91
060 R		42.80	18.70	.70	.03						
S		.98	.51	20.34	7.56	23.66	40.89	38.91			
W		.73	.66	1.06	.17				125.56	64.83	190.39
01 02608 172		5036		.70	.03						
010 R		37.80	17.00	17.60	6.53	1.67	14.63	14.76			
020 R		37.80	17.00	17.60	6.53	1.67	14.76	14.85	48.66	24.00	72.66
01 03621 181		5040							48.88	24.17	73.05
010 R		69.20	30.09	13.26	23.66	49.62	49.30				
S		.98	.51	1.06	.17				154.43	81.32	235.75
W		.73	.66	.70	.03						

LEGEND FOR PRODUCT ID: R = Rod.   S = Strip;   W = Wire.

DEVELOPING THE PRODUCT COST-MATERIAL

Exhibit 11-7

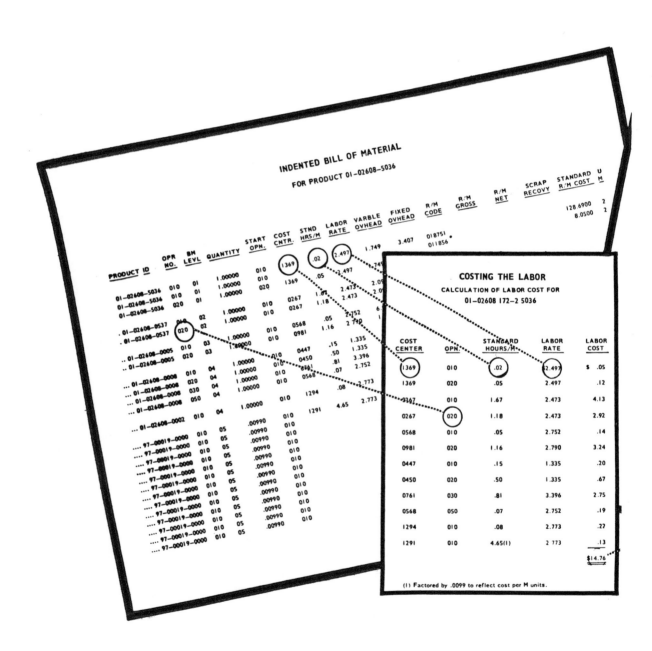

INDENTED BILL OF MATERIAL

FOR PRODUCT 01-02608-5036

PRODUCT ID	OPR NO.	BM LEVL	QUANTITY	START OPN.	COST CNTR.	STND HRS/M	LABOR RATE	VARBLE OVHEAD	FIXED OVHEAD	R/M CODE	R/M GROSS	R/M NET	SCRAP RECOVY	STANDARD R/M COST	U M
														128.6900	2
														8.0500	2
								1.749	3.407	018751					
				010	1369	.02	2.497	1.749		011856					
01-02608-5036	010	01	1.00000	010	1369	.05	2.497	2.09							
01-02608-5036	010	01	1.00000	020			2.473	2.0							
01-02608-5036	020	01	1.00000	010	0267	1.67	2.473	2.0							
		02	1.00000	010	0267	1.18	2.752								
. 01-02608-0537	010	02			0568	.05	2.740								
. 01-02608-0537	020	02		010	0981	1.16									
.. 01-02608-0005	010	03	1.00000	010	0447	.15	1.335								
.. 01-02608-0005	020	03	.00000	010	0450	.50	1.335								
			1.00000	010	0761	.81	3.396								
... 01-02608-0008	010	04	1.00000	010	0568	.07	2.752								
... 01-02608-0008	020	04	1.00000	010		.08	2.773								
... 01-02608-0008	030	04	1.00000	010	1294		2.773								
... 01-02608-0008	050	04	1.00000	010	1291	4.65	2.773								
... 01-02608-0002	010	04	.00990	010											
.... 97-00019-0000	010	05	.00990	010											
.... 97-00019-0000	010	05	.00990	010											
.... 97-00019-0000	010	05	.00990	010											
.... 97-00019-0000	010	05	.00990	010											
.... 97-00019-0000	010	05	.00990	010											
.... 97-00019-0000	010	05	.00990	010											
.... 97-00019-0000	010	05	.00990	010											
.... 97-00019-0000	010	05	.00990	010											
.... 97-00019-0000	010	05	.00990	010											
.... 97-00019-0000	010	05	.00990	010											
.... 97-00019-0000	010	05	.00990	010											

COSTING THE LABOR

CALCULATION OF LABOR COST FOR
01-02608 172-2 5036

COST CENTER	OPN.	STANDARD HOURS/M	LABOR RATE	LABOR COST
1369	010	.02	2.497	$ .05
1369	020	.05	2.497	.12
0267	010	1.67	2.473	4.13
0267	020	1.18	2.473	2.92
0568	010	.05	2.752	.14
0981	020	1.16	2.790	3.24
0447	010	.15	1.335	.20
0450	020	.50	1.335	.67
0761	030	.81	3.396	2.75
0568	050	.07	2.752	.19
1294	010	.08	2.773	.22
1291	010	4.65(1)	2.773	.13
				$14.76

(1) Factored by .0099 to reflect cost per M units.

PRODUCT COST REPORT

PRODUCT AND OPN	ID #	BRASS WEIGHT CRUDE WT.	FINISH WT.	BRASS	SALVAGE	NON BRASS MATERIAL	LABOR	VARIABLE OVERHEAD	CUMULATIVE COST	FIXED OVERHEAD	TOTAL COST
01 0972 R											
010 R		27.80	17.00								
020 R		37.80	17.00	17.60	6.53						
030 R		42.80		17.60	6.53	1.53	11.66				
S		.56	18.70	20.34	7.56	1.53	12.26	18.74	43.05		
W		.73	.27	.75	.10	2.22		18.24		19.59	62.64
040 R	42.80		.66	.70	.03		24.00	24.31	56.11	30.11	86.22
S		.98	18.70	20.34	7.56	14.77		24.31	72.32	39.92	112.24
W		.73	.51	1.06	.17		29.17	28.99			
050 R	42.80		.66	.70	.03	14.77			95.03	47.39	142.42
S		.98	18.70	40.34	7.56		34.12	33.17			
W		.73	.51	1.06	.17	14.77			104.16	54.75	158.91
060 R	42.80		.66	.70	.03	23.66	40.89	38.91	125.56		
S		.98	18.70	20.34	7.56					64.83	190.39
W		.73	.51	1.06	.17						
01 02608 172			.66	.70	.03						
010 R	5036	37.80	17.00	17.60	6.53	1.67	14.63		48.66	24.00	72.66
020 R		37.80	17.00	17.60	6.53	1.67	14.76	14.85	48.88	24.17	73.05
01 03621 181							(14.76)				
010 R	5040	69.20	26.95	30.09	13.26	23.xx	49.62	49.30	154.43	81.32	235.75
S		.98	.51	1.06	.17						
W		.73	.66	.70	.03						

LEGEND FOR PRODUCT ID: R = Rod; S = Strip; W = Wire

DEVELOPING THE PRODUCT COST-LABOR

Exhibit 11-8

"WHERE USED" FILE

COMPONENT #06100746 USED IN 749 END PRODUCTS

02026910209	02026910307	02026910308	02026910309	02052950002
02054310003	02054310004	02054310020	02054310198	02054310209
02054310298	02054320003	02054320004	02054330001	02054330002
02054330129	02054340001	02054340002	02054340197	02054350002
02054350003	02054350020	02054350021	02054350197	02054350209
02054350210	02054360002	02054360003	02054360197	02054360198
02054360200	02054360209	02054360210	02054370003	02054370020
02054380003	02054380020	02055720002	02055720003	02055720019
02055720020	02055720021	02055720209	02055720210	02055730002
02055730003	02055730019	02055730020	02055730021	02055730209
90057620099	90057620090	90057620092	90057620096	90057620197
99009900099	99009900100	99052880336	99052890126	99052932401
99053880097	99052453212	99052567820	99061880132	99073201063
99132647761	99133677642	99213674541	99224675132	99567362111

COMPONENT # 061001001 USED IN 3 END PRODUCTS

39031001001	39076160419	39078131335

Exhibit 11-9

is scheduled for production, the required primary components are issued to the secondary departments for further processing.

Exhibit 11-13 is illustrative of a typical transaction listing of components and subassemblies transferred to the work-in-process stockroom. Since no production operations are performed in the stockroom, the operation number used is 999. Note that the columnar format for identifying the costs follows the same breakdown used in the product cost breakdown. Note also that the costs transferred to the stockroom are totaled at the lower part of the listing as "TO." The "FROM" totals reflect the costs at which these items were relieved from primary floor work-in-process; these are exactly the same. This type of summarization is done for all transaction listings to assure consistency in valuation.

Cost of Sales

Exhibit 11-14 shows the listing of finished products taken out of the finished goods stockroom for shipment. Product 01 02608 5036 shows a sale of 2,255 units. The costs under the various categories reflect the extended standard cost of these 2,255 units. Brass, for example, was shown as $17.60 per thousand units in the Product Cost Report. Extending this amount by 2,255 gives $39.68, the amount indicated for the product under the Brass column.

192

EDIT LISTING

TR	Product ID	To	From	OP	Quantity	Ticket[1]	Mo
9	02 07752 0105	73	61	999	1,300	49638	8
9	03 05858 0005	73	61	999	29,000	49639	8
9	21 00423 5305	73	61	999	3,750	49640	8
9	02 07792 0131	73	61	999	4,500	49641	8
9	02 07907 0038	73	61	999	6,600	49642	8
9	02 00150 0715	73	61	999	4,750	49643	8
9	07 00135 0118	73	61	999	4,000	49644	8
9	02 07792 0131	73	61	999	2,400	49645	8
9	21 00416 6299	73	61	999	8,550	49646	8
9	21 50017 9900	73	61	999	180	49647	8
9	21 90001 9901	73	61	999	1,190	49648	8
9	02 07792 0105	73	61	999	1,600	49649	8
9	02 07907 0038	73	61	999	1,100	49650	8
9	21 00413 5299	73	61	999	7,200	49651	8
9	21 00418 0010	73	61	999	1,800	49652	8
9	21 00413 0021	73	61	999	42,500	49653	8
9	34 00316 5217	73	61	999	400	49654	8
9	02 07793 0036	73	61	999	1,300	49655	8
9	06 04374 0013	73	61	999	800	49656	8
9	06 04374 5101	73	61	999	1,000	49657	8
9	01 00015 0009	73	61	999	4,000	49658	8
9	21 00423 5309	73	61	999	9,600	49659	8
9	11 90014 9900	73	61	999	450	49660	8
9	01 00131 0013	73	61	999	8,000	49661	8
9	01 00151 0005	73	61	999	8,000	49662	8
9	21 00413 5090	73	61	999	138,000	49663	8
9	21 03575 5545	73	61	999	15,000	49664	8
9	21 03060 0004	73	61	999	10,000	49665	8
9	01 00131 0013	73	61	999	14,500	49666	8
9	21 00423 5309	73	61	999	3,700	49667	8
9	21 00055 5299	73	61	999	8,000	49668	8
9	21 00418 0010	73	61	999	3,560	49669	8
						*	
9	21 00419 0212	73	61	999	2,496	49671	8

[1] Missing numbers indicated with an asterisk.

Exhibit 11-10

The percentages across the bottom of this exhibit reflect the percentage breakdown of the various elements of cost for each of the product families sold. This facilitates analysis to determine the material, labor and overhead content of the various product groupings. Such a breakdown is frequently helpful in highlighting changes in mix.

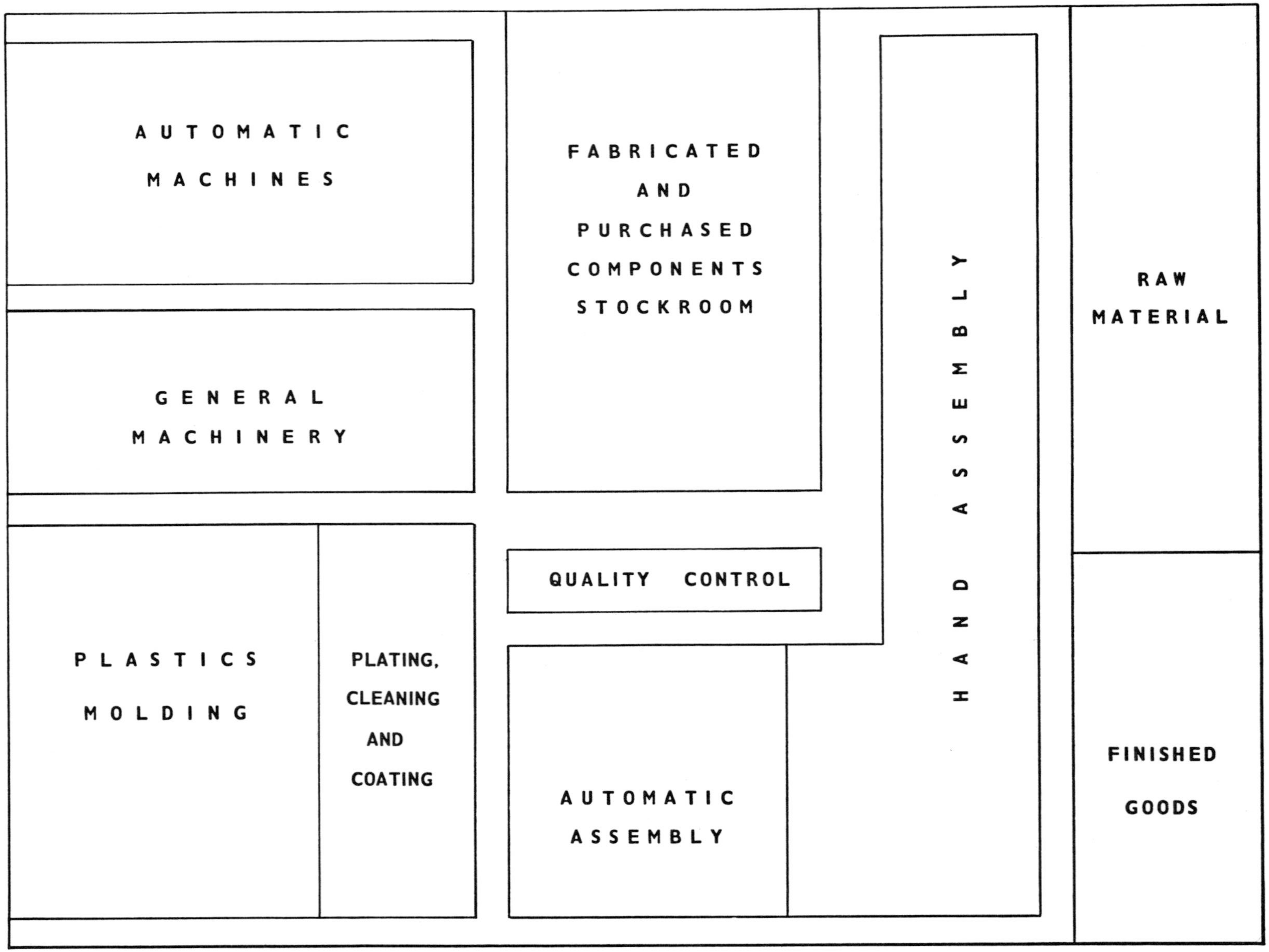

RAW MATERIAL

FINISHED GOODS

HAND ASSEMBLY

FABRICATED AND PURCHASED COMPONENTS STOCKROOM

QUALITY CONTROL

AUTOMATIC ASSEMBLY

AUTOMATIC MACHINES

GENERAL MACHINERY

PLATING, CLEANING AND COATING

PLASTICS MOLDING

Exhibit 11-11

RAW MATERIAL ISSUES

Chemicals	Description	U/M	Quantity	Unit Cost	Extended Cost
96-5408	POWDER = 6 H	2	30-	4750.0000	142.50-
			30-		142.50- *
96-5410	TETRAFLOUREOTHYLENE RESIN = 6	2	184	4750.0000	874.00
96-5410	TETRAFLOUREOTHYLENE RESIN = 6	2	138	4750.0000	655.50
96-5410	TETRAFLOUREOTHYLENE RESIN = 6	2	221	4750.0000	1,049.75
96-5410	TETRAFLOUREOTHYLENE RESIN = 6	2	140	4750.0000	665.00
			683		3,244.25 *
96-5411	NAPTHA	2	30	45.0700	1.35
96-5411	NAPTHA	2	60	45.0700	2.70
96-5411	NAPTHA	2	30	45.0700	1.35
			120		5.40 *
			2,062		3,313.98 **
					346,340.81 **

Exhibit 11-12

195

FABRICATED PARTS TRANSFERRED TO
FABRICATED AND PURCHASED PARTS STOCKROOM

Product ID		Opr No.	Quantity	Brass	Non-Brass Material	Labor	Variable Overhead	Cumulative Operating Cost	Fixed Overhead	Total Cost
31 05163	0009	999 R	360	3.16	4.54	34.96	43.52	86.18	70.52	156.70
33 00798 D15	0016	999	250		13.13	.00	.00	13.13	.00	13.13
39 01451 198	0019	999 R	1,900	2.36	.00	27.49	3.49	34.87	4.52	39.39
		W		1.53						
39 04414 6	0019	999 R	710	4.36	2.65	18.59	7.40	33.19	9.90	43.09
		S		.19						
39 09155 6	0048	999 R	830	1.75	8.78	51.24	12.54	74.37	21.36	95.73
		W		.06						
41 00931 5	0049	999	300		.17	1.84	1.62	3.63	2.74	6.37
51 01593 4	0029	999	1,000		25.55	9.68	11.15	46.38	13.38	59.76
53 07642 2	0019	999	1,000		2.61	.00	.00	2.61	.00	2.61
53 08385 A3	0109	999	41,620		19.98	155.02	129.55	304.55	223.07	527.62
67 03670 197	0079	999	10		5.85	.00	.00	5.85	.00	5.85
67 08600 16	0119	999	8		.15	.11	.06	.32	.12	.44
67 08600 22	0159	999	7		.24	.57	.63	1.44	1.00	2.44
67 08600 23	0169	999	7		.11	.67	.81	1.59	1.32	2.91
67 08600 45	0269	999	9		.57	.49	.68	1.74	.83	2.57
67 08601 12	0089	999	10		5.20	.00	.00	5.20	.00	5.20
"TO" DEPT. TOTALS		R	48,021	11.63	89.53	300.66	211.45	615.05	348.76	963.81
		S		.19						
		W		1.59						
"FROM" DEPT. TOTALS		R	48,021	11.63	89.53	300.66	211.45	615.05	348.76	963.81
		S		.19						
		W		1.59						

LEGEND: R = Rod; S = Strip; W = Wire

Exhibit 11-13

COST OF SALES

Product ID	Opr No.	Quantity	Brass	Non-Brass Material	Labor	Variable Overhead	Cumulative Operating Cost	Fixed Overhead	Total Cost
01 00131 AP1 0004	000 R	315,000	4,191.36	17.71	310.16	731.31	5,250.54	837.66	6,088
01 00131 A1782 0013	000 R	57,500	773.78	240.59	481.82	524.23	2,020.42	756.87	2,777
01 00131 17829 0017	000 R	243,800	3,167.79	899.12	2,187.49	2,315.74	8,570.14	3,324.75	11,894
01 00152 17829 0005	000 R	45,500	591.20	248.82	407.35	437.68	1,685.05	631.78	2,316
01 01651 UAH1 0086	000 R	277,500	3,605.67	15.45	287.09	676.08	4,584.29	760.57	5,344
01 02870 7913 5179	000 R	757	12.58	5.29	31.35	20.25	69.47	27.18	96
01 02608 1727 5036	000 R	2,255	39.68	3.77	33.28	33.49	110.22	54.50	164
01 03407 0178 5032	000 R	8,550	137.70	29.88	148.94	186.67	503.19	241.74	744
PRODUCT TOTALS	R	952,062	12,535.35	1,472.22	3,904.79	4,940.38	22,852.74	6,655.99	29,508
PERCENT OF TOTAL COST			42.49	4.99	13.23	16.75	77.46	22.54	100.00

LEGEND: R = Rod

Exhibit 11-14

197

The breakdown of variable and fixed costs is helpful in profit contribution analysis. The cost system provides for full costing of inventories and at the same time shows the fixed cost content of the various components and finished products, so that internal statements can be presented on a direct costing basis.

JOURNALIZING THE TRANSACTIONS FOR THE COST SYSTEM

There are eleven standard journal entries used in this company's cost system for purposes of closing the books. These can be broken down into eight categories.

- Purchase price variances on material
- Issues of raw material
- Costing production
- Issues out of WIP stores
- Completed production transferred to Finished Goods
- Determining the production variances
- Costing shipments
- Closing out the variance accounts

Purchase Price Variance. Most companies siphon off the purchase price variance at time of purchase of the material. The transaction run from which the amount of variance is determined is shown as Exhibit 11-15. The run lists the actual and standard costs of each item as well as the amount of variance. Unfavorable variances are indicated with a minus sign. The total variance shown in Exhibit 11-15 is $16,191.67. This amount identifies that portion of the variance that applies to materials booked into the raw material inventory account. Another segment of the listing, not shown here, indicates that $160.87 of variance applicable to purchased components was incurred on materials purchased into the Fabricated and Purchased Parts stockroom. The resulting journal entry to book the purchase of material into inventory at standard cost is:

Journal Entry #1

	Dr.	Cr.
Material Variance		16,191.67
Raw Material Inventory	16,352.54	
Fabricated and Purchased Stores (WIP)		160.87

The net effect of the above entry is to increase the inventory value by $16,352.54 because the purchase prices at actual cost fell short of standard cost by that amount.

The transaction listings of purchases should not be limited to the accounting application only. Since material represents an important element of cost, such information should be used for control purposes as well as accounting documentation. Illustrative of three uses to which the purchases listings can be put are the following:

- −Purchase Price Variance by Major Item
- −Purchased Parts Price History

PURCHASE PRICE VARIANCE BY ITEM

P.O. No.	Item Code	Quantity	U/M Code	U/M	Unit Cost	Actual Cost	Standard Cost	Variance
49999	03 3472	3346	2	LBS	702.700	2,754.43	2,351.23	403.20-
50344	20 2980	810	2	LBS	620.190	490.21	502.35	12.14
49760	21 3190	1851	2	LBS	625.000	1,110.97	1,156.88	45.91
50134	21 3476	4372	2	LBS	625.000	2,733.37	2,732.50	.87-
50333	21 3476	7378	2	LBS	625.000	4,428.28	4,611.25	182.97
50050	21 3650	344	2	LBS	724.490	206.47	249.22	42.75
50217	21 4450	555	2	LBS	580.000	306.75	321.90	15.15
49799	21 4450	1238	2	LBS	580.000	684.24	718.04	33.80
50591	22 0781	127	2	LBS	1,287.780	109.83	163.55	53.72
50218	22 1562	110	2	LBS	828.000	89.56	91.08	1.52
49215	22 1660	1000	2	LBS	828.000	814.20	828.00	13.80
49216	22 1660	6018	2	LBS	828.000	4,899.86	4,982.90	83.04
49216	22 1660	4383	2	LBS	828.000	3,130.34	3,629.12	498.78
49185	23 0245	6810	2	LBS	625.000	4,087.36	4,256.25	168.89
49186	23 0245	26689	2	LBS	625.000	16,152.18	16,680.63	528.45
49186	23 0245	17314	2	LBS	625.000	10,391.86	10,821.25	429.39
49186	23 0245	7859	2	LBS	625.000	4,716.97	4,911.88	194.91
49186	23 0245	20517	2	LBS	625.000	12,416.89	12,823.13	406.24
48958	23 0332	6614	2	LBS	630.000	4,002.79	4,166.82	164.03
48958	23 0332	3726	2	LBS	630.000	2,329.50	2,347.38	17.88
49398	23 0437	7152	2	LBS	585.000	3,988.67	4,183.92	195.25
48971	23 0437	13939	2	LBS	585.000	7,773.78	8,154.32	380.54
49996	23 0438	534	2	LBS	585.000	297.81	312.39	14.58
49670	23 0467	2522	2	LBS	585.000	1,454.44	1,475.37	20.93
50345	23 0531	5066	2	LBS	576.000	2,777.18	2,918.02	140.84
49659	23 0625	1010	2	LBS	549.000	524.90	554.49	29.59
50222	23 0625	1520	2	LBS	549.000	789.94	834.48	44.54
						232,934.06	249,125.73	16,191.67

Exhibit 11-15

Purchase Price Variance by Major Item. The accounting listing developed for accumulation of the total purchase price variance for the month is far too detailed for analytical purposes. Exhibit 11-16 illustrates a weekly report that selects only the major purchase price variances that should receive management attention. The guideline for selection in this company is a variance of 10% plus any items in which the variance is over $100 per item purchased. This approach has the advantage in that it monitors purchases more frequently and highlights the variances on an exception basis.

Purchased Parts Price History. Generally, the price information on purchases in many companies is maintained in the purchasing department files. To make any meaningful appraisal would require burdensome manual analysis which would be both time consuming and costly. Introduction of the computer provides an excellent opportunity to develop a price history by individual items over a period of time. Exhibit 11-17 illustrates an example of two items for which such an analysis is made. The items are Part No. 01-2868 and Part No. 43-9267. These part number purchases are listed sequentially by date of purchase. The unit cost of each purchase can be compared with prior purchases of the same part. The number of units is also shown—providing a means for roughly correlating unit cost differences with the quantities ordered.

No standard price is shown because the intent of this control is to monitor price trends. A material price history, properly used, can be helpful not only for reviewing price trends, but also for:

- revising material price standards
- providing current costs for price estimating
- highlighting frequently purchased high cost items for cost reduction considerations

As in any automated report, there must be an alertness to variations in practice. In listing the individual purchases and the quantities ordered, care must be exercised to assure that partial shipments are not confused with the total quantity ordered. A code such as a letter "p" could be used to identify incomplete orders.

Vendor Delivery Performance. Vendor performance is measured not only in terms of price; timely delivery is also an important consideration. Timeliness means delivery on schedule—not late and not too early. The objection to late delivery is obvious; to early delivery, not so obvious. It is to the advantage of the vendor to ship to the contumer as soon as possible—even if ahead of schedule. The vendor thus reduces the amount of capital tied up in inventory and improves his return on investment. While advantageous to the seller, this practice has the opposite effect on the buyer. If the buyer company receives the shipment ahead of schedule, its investment is needlessly increased and its return on investment reduced.

A report that can be used for monitoring vendor delivery performance is illustrated in Exhibit 11-18. The basis of the report is to compare the scheduled delivery date, contained in the purchase order data base, with the date of receipt of the

PURCHASE PRICE VARIANCE BY MAJOR ITEM

P.O. No.	Item Code	Quantity	U/M Code	U/M	Unit Cost	Actual Cost	Standard Cost	Variance
49999	03 3472	3346	2	LBS	702.700	2,754.43	2,351.23	403.20-
50333	21 3476	7378	2	LBS	625.000	4,428.28	4,611.25	182.97
50050	21 3650	344	2	LBS	724.490	206.47	249.22	42.75
50591	22 0781	127	2	LBS	1,287.780	109.83	163.55	53.72
49216	22 1660	4383	2	LBS	828.000	3,130.34	3,629.12	498.78
49185	23 0245	6810	2	LBS	625.000	4,087.36	4,256.25	168.89
49186	23 0245	26689	2	LBS	625.000	16,152.18	16,680.63	528.45
49186	23 0245	17314	2	LBS	625.000	10,391.86	10,821.25	429.39
49186	23 0245	7859	2	LBS	625.000	4,716.97	4,911.88	194.91
49186	23 0245	20517	2	LBS	625.000	12,416.89	12,823.13	406.24
48958	23 0332	6614	2	LBS	630.000	4,322.79	4,166.82	164.03
49398	23 0437	7152	2	LBS	585.000	3,988.67	4,183.92	195.25
48971	23 0437	13939	2	LBS	585.000	7,773.78	8,154.32	380.54
50345	23 0531	5066	2	LBS	576.000	2,777.18	2,918.02	140.84

Exhibit 11-16

PURCHASED PARTS PRICE HISTORY

Part No.	Vendor	Invoice No.	P.O. #	Invoice Date	Quantity	U/M	Total Actual Cost	Actual Unit Cost
01-2868	Ajax Supply Company	42367	02873	2/2	100	ea.	53.80	.538
01-2868	Ajax Supply Company	42367	05091	3/5	400	ea.	215.20	.538
01-2868	Ajax Supply Company	42646	03047	3/6	100	ea.	53.80	.538
01-2868	Ajax Supply Company	43359	06068	5/7	100	ea.	53.80	.538
01-2868	Ajax Supply Company	43363	06949	6/7	900	ea.	522.90	.581
01-2868	Ajax Supply Company	43424	06729	6/8	300	ea.	176.40	.588
01-2868	Ajax Supply Company	43426	07657	7/12	600	ea.	352.80	.588
01-2868	Ajax Supply Company	43468	07657	8/18	600	ea.	352.80	.588
01-2868	Ajax Supply Company	43686	07729	9/12	300	ea.	176.40	.588
01-2868	Ajax Supply Company	45898	07892	10/13	500	ea.	345.00	.690
01-2868	Ajax Supply Company	46667	07884	10/16	502	ea.	376.50	.750
01-2868	Ajax Supply Company	48882	08861	11/23	501	ea.	375.75	.750
01-2868	Ajax Supply Company	52601	08960	12/14	500	ea.	375.00	.750
					5403		3,430.15	.635
43-9267	Berkshire Products	41031	02802	1/30	25	ea.	408.17	16.327
43-9267	Berkshire Products	42308	02815	2/5	125	ea.	2,040.85	16.327
43-9267	Berkshire Products	42309	05020	2/18	25	ea.	408.17	16.327
43-9267	Berkshire Products	42656	03023	3/6	50	ea.	816.34	16.327
43-9267	Berkshire Products	42333	05621	4/2	75	ea.	1,224.51	16.327
43-9267	Berkshire Products	43852	06842	5/9	25	ea.	408.17	16.327
43-9267	Berkshire Products	43962	06731	6/17	25	ea.	416.50	16.660
43-9267	Berkshire Products	43975	07662	7/12	35	ea.	583.10	16.660
43-9267	Berkshire Products	44502	07894	8/14	85	ea.	1,416.10	16.660
43-9267	Berkshire Products	45652	07992	9/16	65	ea.	1,082.90	16.660
43-9267	Berkshire Products	46867	08012	10/18	15	ea.	249.90	16.660
43-9267	Berkshire Products	49001	08862	11/21	56	ea.	932.96	16.660
43-9267	Berkshire Products	51621	09002	12/16	57	ea.	949.62	16.660
					663		10,937.29	16.496

Exhibit 11-17

VENDOR DELIVERY PERFORMANCE

Week Ending _____/_____/_____

Vendor	Part No.	Purch. Order Number	Description	Qty.	U/M	Total Standard Cost	Scheduled Delivery Date	Received Date	Vendor Performance[1]
ABC Corp.	1440 202	C45100	Angle	1,440	In	504.00	5 17 75	5 23 75	6
ABC Corp.	1452 316	C45101	Channel	2,400	In	1,200.00	5 22 75	5 19 75	3-
ABC Corp.	1535 360	C45205	Flat	2,400	In	1,320.00	5 22 75	5 23 75	1
						3,034.00 *			
ABZ. Corp.	1440 220	C45100	Angle	1,440	In	576.00	5 15 75	5 22 75	7-
						576.00 *			
B.Z. Co.	1535 274	C45206	Flat	240	In	144.00	5 09 75	5 20 75	11
B.Z. Co.	1622 334	C46170	Bar Round	240	In	120.50	5 15 75	5 21 74	6
B.Z. Co.	1622 342	C46275	Bar Round	240	In	132.00	5 16 75	5 23 75	7
						3,996.50 **			

[1] Indicates the number of days ahead of or behind schedule.

Exhibit 11-18

material. The last column, headed "Vendor Performance," indicates the number of days that the delivery was made ahead of or behind the authorized delivery date. Such a report can be useful in determining which vendors come closest to approximating the authorized receipt date. Those who habitually make delivery several days ahead of time can be dealt with by:

1. refusing to accept the material
2. accepting the material but basing payment and discount (if applicable) on the authorized delivery date.

Like many control reports, this one can be prepared on an exception basis–listing only those items whose cost is above a prescribed amount.

Input into Production

Several of the journal entries relate to costs incurred in production. This includes not only costs transferred into work-in-process but also transfers out of work-in-process. Since in a standard cost system, actual costs and actual performance must be compared with standard, it is necessary to use a clearing account to measure the difference. This clearing account, in some companies, is called "Manufacturing Cost Control"; in others, including this one, the terminology "Variance" is used. In this case study, the variance account is broken down into three accounts:

• Material Variance
• Labor Variance
• Indirect Labor and Overhead Variance

The actual costs are generally charged to these accounts. The standard cost of the finished production is credited to the same accounts. The difference between the two, then, becomes the variance.

Raw Material Issues. Exhibit 11-12 lists the raw material issues for the period. It shows a total of $346,340.81 issued to production. The Journal entry to show the charge into production and relief of inventory is:

Journal Entry #2

	Dr.	Cr.
Material Variance	346,340.81	
Raw Material Inventory		346,340.81

Fabricated Parts Transferred into Stock. The following schedule summarizes the transaction run to show by department the standard cost of primary components and subassemblies transferred to WIP stock. The summary shows a category referred to as "uncosted." This means that some items that have been produced did not have costs in the computer file, and it was necessary to cost them separately. Steps being taken to link the order entry system into the scheduling procedure will eliminate this problem when implementation is completed.

From	Brass	Non-Brass	Direct Labor	Variable Overhead	Fixed Overhead	Total
01	$ 13.41	89.53	300.66	211.45	348.76	963.81
02	1.50	38.12	4.08	3.20	4.75	51.65
03	2,085.47	81.80	302.92	678.81	1,029.06	4,178.08
04	4,098.41	11,926.58	2,080.78	2,055.62	2,889.39	23,050.78
05	229,804.96	16,932.22	39,916.46	69,870.01	93,891.07	450,414.72
06	2,913.91	591.33	1,796.39	2,041.96	2,879.65	10,223.24
07	1,408.39	63.53	388.42	433.52	654.23	2,948.09
08	15,413.32	2,473.79	10,881.12	14,917.32	22,872.35	66,557.90
09	541.54	1,204.47	3,340.78	3,096.48	4,880.48	13,063.75
10	97.36	246.72	26.32	28.35	39.43	438.18
11	1,390.27	1,611.96	539.96	628.49	950.28	5,120.96
12	–	36.72	–	–	–	36.72
Total Costed	257,768.54	35,296.77	59,577.89	93,965.23	130,439.45	577,047.88
Uncosted items	6,666.95	2,003.78	1,495.59	2,368.74	3,444.58	15,979.64
	$ 264,435.49	37,300.55	61,073.48	96,333.97	133,884.03	593,027.52
	(264,435.49)	264,435.49	–	(96,333.97)	96,333.97	–
		301,736.04	61,073.48		230,218.00	593,027.52

The first two columns, which add up to $301,736.04, represent the standard material cost of production. Direct labor represents $61,073.48 while variable plus fixed overhead amounted to $230,218.00. These three figures are the credits to the respective variance accounts while the total of the three becomes a charge to the fabricated and purchased parts inventory account. This is summarized in the journal entry which follows.

Journal Entry # 3

	Dr.	Cr.
Fabricated and Purchased Parts Inventory	593,027.52	
Material Variance		91,736.04
Labor Variance		61,073.48
Indirect Labor and Overhead Variance		230,218.00

To record production of fabricated parts transferred into fabricated and purchased parts stores.

Transfers from Finished Goods to WIP Stockroom. Primary components are sometimes sold as replacement parts. They are also sold to companies that purchase the components and make their own assemblies. Such sales are usually made out of finished goods because the cost of sales entry automatically relieves the finished goods inventory. At times, there are returns to work-in-process stock when there are too many of the items in the finished goods storeroom. There are also occasions when the parts in finished inventory must be further modified prior to sale. In such instances they are returned to production through the work-in-process stockroom The summary transaction shown here represents the current month's transfers. The journal entry is also shown.

	Brass	Non-Brass	Direct Labor	Variable Overhead	Fixed Overhead	Total
Total Costed	$47.72	537.22	217.03	188.69	273.50	1,264.16
Uncosted items	31.60	471.41	69.30	47.90	72.19	692.40
	$79.32	1,008.63	286.33	236.59	345.69	1,956.56

Journal Entry # 4

	Dr.	Cr.
Fabricated and Purchased Parts Inventory	1,956.56	
Finished Goods Inventory		1,956.56
To record transfers from finished goods to fabricated and purchased parts stores.		

Transfers from WIP Stockroom. The transaction run summary shown below summarizes by department the primary components, purchased parts and subassemblies issued to the production floor. Some of the components and purchased parts have been transferred to the primary production area such as Department 01—Automatic Machinery, and 04—General Machinery. Department 05 is the Plating, Coating and Cleaning department. Many of the primary components in the stockroom are sent to this department prior to transfer to the secondary departments for assembly.

To	Brass	Non-Brass	Direct Labor	Variable Overhead	Fixed Overhead	Total
01	$ 48,524.50	21,270.43	18,750.18	23,636.47	32,404.98	144,586.56
02	14,120.43	5,520.33	9,464.68	13,374.62	20,628.73	63,108.79
04	2,454.31	15,257.61	1,861.74	2,285.78	3,029.04	24,888.48
05	152,774.51	6,920.74	14,377.23	24,868.29	34,414.69	233,355.46
06	5,803.94	15,186.86	1,737.66	2,538.59	3,463.66	28,730.71
07	25,787.14	495.34	9,930.40	21,765.50	28,195.78	86,174.16
08	189.76	565.40	41.22	50.95	70.46	917.79
11	1,769.73	373.78	1,077.12	1,791.47	1,738.56	6,750.66
12	14,507.04	59,294.59	5,319.20	7,813.14	10,714.46	97,648.43
13	.34	–	.07	.11	.17	.69
Total Costed	265,931.70	124,885.08	62,559.50	98,124.92	134,660.53	686,161.73
Uncosted items	4,389.27	1,867.91	1,208.45	1,969.62	2,788.12	12,223.37
	$270,320.97	126,752.99	63,767.95	100,094.54	137,448.65	698,385.10

Journal Entry # 5

	Dr.	Cr.
Work-in-Process Floor Inventory	698,385.10	
Fabricated and Purchased Parts Inventory		698,385.10
To record issues of fabricated and purchased parts to production floor.		

Customer Returns

Customer returns for which credits have been issued are covered by Journal Entry #6. Because there were no credits issued in the current period, this journal entry is not applicable.

Components in Finished Goods Stock Returned to Production

These transactions are similar to those covered by Journal Entry #4 except that the items are being returned directly to production for immediate processing.

To	Brass	Non-Brass	Direct Labor	Variable Overhead	Fixed Overhead	Total
01	$ 347.41	119.19	243.64	277.24	413.38	1,400.86
02	16.48	96.01	17.43	15.64	25.46	171.02
04	13.08	1.58	28.39	29.87	46.15	119.07
06	–	61.99	.50	.35	.68	63.52
07	37.87	.12	1.57	3.41	5.69	48.66
08	.05	.21	.50	.37	.57	1.70
11	315.01	850.44	213.87	215.11	333.43	1,927.86
12	1,637.18	1,887.21	1,504.84	1,419.30	2,173.41	8,621.94
32	21.28	77.66	21.30	20.58	31.88	172.70
41	1.42	1.92	2.27	2.20	3.26	11.07
42	.58	.49	.51	.66	.81	3.05
43	1.12	1.06	.62	.60	.93	4.33
47	269.84	63.51	172.31	186.96	289.44	982.06
Total Costed	2,661.32	3,161.39	2,207.75	2,172.29	3,325.09	13,527.84
Uncosted items	547.84	85.95	40.25	47.92	19.42	741.38
	$3,209.16	3,247.34	2,248.00	2,220.21	3,344.51	14,269.22

Journal Entry # 7

	Dr.	Cr.
Work-in Process Floor Inventory	14,269.22	
Finished Goods Inventory		14,269.22
To record items in finished goods transferred to the production floor.		

Completed Production Transferred to Finished Goods

The transaction summary below shows the costs of finished products that have been transferred to finished goods inventory. The applicable journal entry is also shown.

	Brass	Non-Brass	Direct Labor	Variable Overhead	Fixed Overhead	Total
Total Costed	$214,710.48	123,008.74	108,217.04	121,741.51	181,154.82	748,832.59
Uncosted items	7,264.81	5,825.78	5,386.64	5,965.95	8,725.37	33,168.55
	$221,975.29	128,834.52	113,603.68	127,707.46	189,880.19	782,001.14

Journal Entry # 8

	Dr.	Cr.
Finished Goods Inventory	782,001.4	
Work-in-Process Floor Inventory		782,001.14
To record production transferred to finished goods.		

Floor Work-in-Process

Some cost systems calculate their standard cost of inventory input on an operation-by-operation basis. As production is reported at each operation, the number of units completed at that operation is extended by standard cost.

Other cost systems calculate input when the last operation is completed in each department. The product is then moved to the next department.

The problem with recognizing input into floor work-in-process is that the components and assemblies recognized as good production at an earlier stage might later be scrapped. While the textbook would say that such spoilage should be recorded and then relieved from inventory, the real world is quite different from the book.

Unless dealing with a large and expensive unit, companies generally do not closely enforce discipline for reporting of rejects, because of the expense that could be involved. An automated machine that spews out parts by the hundred or even thousand per hour, will lose hundreds of components in the course of a shift. These drop down under the machines and cannot be readily recovered and counted. In operations in which parts can be recycled, such as plastics molding or die casting, rejects can be counted as production and then thrown back in for remelting. In many such instances, production can be doubled up. Monitoring to avoid double counting can be expensive.

What then is the solution? Very simply, the solution is not to recognize input into production until the component or subassembly is accepted into the work-in-process or finished goods stockrooms. This leaves only the floor work-in-process to be accounted for. This becomes a two-step process: first, net out the production that was transferred into finished goods with the issues of components and subassemblies that were transferred out of the stockrooms to the production floor; second, account for the "pipeline" inventory on the floor through either a constant floor inventory, a shop-order type accountability if practical, or if all else fails, a physical inventory of major items on the floor.

The transactions summarized below relate to the first of the above.

	Brass	Non-Brass	Direct Labor	Variable Overhead	Fixed Overhead	Total
Finished Goods Produced:	$221,975.29	128,834.52	113,603.68	127,707.46	189,880.19	782,001.14
From Finished Goods to Production Floor:	3,209.16	3,247.34	2,248.00	2,220.21	3,343.51	14,268.22
From Fabricated Stores to Production Floor:	270,320.97	126,752.99	63,767.95	100,094.54	137,448.65	698,385.10
	(51,554.84)	(1,165.81)	47,587.73	25,392.71	49,088.03	69,347.82

Journal Entry #9

	Dr.	Cr.
Work-in-Process Floor Inventory	69,347.82	
Material Usage Variance (Brass & Non-Brass)	52,720.65	
Labor Variance		47,587.73
Indirect Labor and Overhead Variance		74,480.74
To record standard cost of production.		

The company used as the subject for this case study establishes the "pipe-line" value of its floor inventory by establishing a constant value and adjusting this each month by the results of physical counts taken at key points where buildups can occur.

Shipments During the Month

The cost of sales transaction format was shown in an earlier section of this chapter. Like all transactions, the cost breakdown indicates all the elements of cost shown on the Product Cost Sheet. The journal entry is:

Journal Entry #10

Cost of sales	753,596.69	
Finished Goods Inventory		753,596.69
To record shipments made during month.		

Variance Analysis

An earlier section referred to the use of a clearing account for charging actual costs and crediting the standard costs charged into inventory. The net of the three clearing accounts (Material Variance, Labor Variance, and Indirect Labor and Overhead Variance) is the amount of variance. At the end of the period, these three variance accounts must be closed out to cost of sales. This is done in Journal Entry #11.

Journal Entry # 11

Cost of Sales	62,364.67	
Indirect Labor and Overhead	40,740.02	
Material Variance		81,133.75
Labor Variance		21,970.94
To close out variance accounts		

All eleven journal entries are summarized in Exhibit 11-19. Exhibit 11-20 breaks these entries down into "T" accounts. This provides a summary of each of the accounts showing the effect on the various journal entries.

From the foregoing journal entries and "T" accounts, the standard cost of sales and total variances provide the basis for preparation of the abbreviated income statement shown below:

SALES	$1,260,350
STANDARD COST OF SALES	753,597
STANDARD GROSS PROFIT	506,753
VARIANCES	62,365
ACTUAL GROSS PROFIT	$ 444,388

The breakdown of total variances can be categorized further to show the total material, direct labor, and total indirect labor/overhead. This categorization corresponds with the breakdown of the three variance accounts used for clearing actual costs against standard.

MATERIAL		
PURCHASE PRICE	$(16,192)	
MATERIAL USAGE	97,326	81,134
DIRECT LABOR		
RATE	6,534	
EFFICIENCY	15,437	21,971
OVERHEAD		
SPENDING	12,887	
VOLUME	(53,627)	(40,740)
		$ 62,365

JOURNAL ENTRIES

(1)

	Debit	Credit
Material Variance	16,352.54	
Raw Material Inventory		16,191.67
Fabricated and Purchased Stores (WIP)		160.87
To record purchase price variance		

(2)

	Debit	Credit
Material Variance	346,340.81	
Raw Material Inventory		346,340.81
To record issues of raw material to production floor.		

(3)

	Debit	Credit
Fabricated and Purchased Parts Inventory	593,027.52	
Material Variance	301,736.04	
Labor Variance	61,073.48	
Indirect Labor and Overhead Variance	230,218.00	
To record production of fabricated parts transferred into fabricated and purchased parts stores.		

(4)

	Debit	Credit
Fabricated and Purchased Parts Inventory	1,956.56	
Finished Goods Inventory		1,956.56
To record transfers of items in finished goods to fabricated and purchased parts stores.		

(5)

	Debit	Credit
Work-in-Process Floor Inventory	698,385.10	
Fabricated and Purchased Parts Inventory		698,385.10
To record issues of fabricated and purchased parts to production floor.		

(6)

No entry this month.

(7)

	Debit	Credit
Work-in-Process Floor Inventory	14,269.22	
Finished Goods Inventory		14,269.22
To record items in finished goods transferred to the production floor.		

(8)

	Debit	Credit
Finished Goods Inventory	782,001.14	
Work-in-Process Floor Inventory		782,001.14
To record production transferred to finished goods.		

(9)

	Debit	Credit
Work-in-Process Floor Inventory	69,347.82	
Material Usage Variance	52,720.65	
Labor Variance		47,587.73
Indirect Labor and Overhead Variance		74,480.74
To record standard cost of production.		

(10)

	Debit	Credit
Cost of Sales	753,596.69	
Finished Goods Inventory		753,596.69
To record shipments during month.		

(11)

	Debit	Credit
Cost of Sales	62,364.67	
Indirect Labor and Overhead Variance	40,740.02	
Material Variance		81,133.75
Labor Variance		21,970.94
To close out variance accounts		

Exhibit 11-19

"T" ACCOUNT SUMMARY

Raw Material Inventory

Debit		Credit	
(1)	16,352.54	(2)	346,340.81

Fabricated and Purchased Parts Inventory

Debit		Credit	
(3)	593,027.52	(1)	160.87
(4)	1,956.50	(5)	698,385.10

Work-in-Process Floor Inventory

Debit		Credit	
(5)	698,385.10	(8)	782,001.14
(7)	14,269.22		
(9)	69,347.82		

Finished Goods Inventory

Debit		Credit	
(8)	782,001.14	(4)	1,956.56
		(7)	14,269.22
		(10)	753,596.69

Material Variance

Debit		Credit	
(2)	346,340.81	(1)	16,191.67
(9)	52,720.65	(3)	301,736.04
		(11)	81,133.75

Labor Variance

Debit		Credit	
Actual Labor	130,632.15	(3)	61,073.48
		(9)	47,587.73
		(11)	21,970.94

Indirect Labor and Overhead Variance

Debit		Credit	
Actual Overhead	263,958.72	(3)	230,218.00
(11)	40,740.02	(9)	74,480.74

Cost of Sales

Debit		Credit	
(10)	753,596.69		
(11)	62,364.67		

Exhibit 11-20

The further breakdown of variances would identify them by areas of responsibility. Purchase price variances, for example, would be the responsibility of the purchasing department. The transaction listings would identify the price variances by type of material on which the variance was incurred—giving some indication of purchasing effectiveness based on the predetermined standard price. It is possible that because of short lead times given to the buyer he may not have been able to negotiate out of strength. The purchase price variances, in such instances, should be identified as to the specific reason for their occurrence and given visibility. This would provide information as to the additional cost of orders taken with short lead times.

Material usage, that is, quantity actually used versus quantity that should have been used, can also be identified by type of material. However, it would be more important to identify the responsible foreman so that he would be prompted to take corrective action.

MATERIAL RELATED VARIANCES

Responsibility of:

Purchasing Department	PURCHASE PRICE VARIANCE	
	BRASS	$(16,598)
	OTHER METALS	632
	PLASTICS	(342)
	PACKING MATERIAL	116
		$(16,192)
Departments Using Material	MATERIAL USAGE	
	BRASS	$ 73,499
	PLASTICS	22,168
	PACKING MATERIAL	1,659
		$97,326

Once the labor rate variances have been isolated (just as the purchase price deviation was), then the labor efficiency variances can be identified by responsible department heads.

DIRECT LABOR EFFICIENCY RELATED VARIANCES

Responsibility of:

Department Foremen	AUTOMATIC SECTION	$ 5,162
	GENERAL MACHINERY	(872)
	PLATING AND COATING	1,242
	HAND ASSEMBLY	6,842
	AUTOMATIC ASSEMBLY	3,063
		$15,437

Once the overhead volume variance has been determined and the cause localized—was it lack of sales or inability to get out the product, for example—the overhead spending variance can be identified by responsibility. Some of these can be directly identified by specific departments. Others are most appropriately identified on an overall basis. Electricity, for example, can not be measured by department because of the impracticality of metering each department and measuring usage of such services as high and low pressure air. In this instance the chief electrician would monitor the invoices coming in from the utility company and make recommendations for reducing usage. He might, for example, recommend that certain high users of electricity be scheduled at such times when the peak load allowances are not exceeded and thus avoid the extra demand charges. Although this company monitors maintenance department costs on an overall basis, future plans are to monitor the costs of jobs so that each department will be measured by a maintenance budget which will be compared with the actual charges incurred.

<u>OVERHEAD SPENDING RELATED VARIANCES</u>

Department		
Foremen	AUTOMATIC SECTION	
	INDIRECT LABOR	$ 1,842
	FRINGE BENEFITS	98
	O/T PREMIUM	165
	SUPPLIES	50
	SMALL TOOLS	86
		$ 2,241
	GENERAL MACHINERY	
	INDIRECT LABOR	$ 672
	FRINGE BENEFITS	121
	O/T PREMIUM	(22)
	SUPPLIES	65
	SMALL TOOLS	41
		$ 877
	PLATING AND COATING	
	INDIRECT LABOR	$ (25)
	FRINGE BENEFITS	(5)
	O/T PREMIUM	–
	SUPPLIES	155
	SMALL TOOLS	5
		$ 130
	HAND ASSEMBLY	
	INDIRECT LABOR	$ 3,065
	FRINGE BENEFITS	260
	O/T PREMIUM	128
	SUPPLIES	87
	SMALL TOOLS	62
		$ 3,602

AUTOMATIC ASSEMBLY

INDIRECT LABOR	$	214
FRINGE BENEFITS		35
O/T PREMIUM		10
SUPPLIES		12
SMALL TOOLS		22
	$	293

OVERALL PLANT

Chief Electrician	ELECTRICITY	795
Plant Manager	REAL ESTATE TAXES	360
Plant Engineer	MAINTENANCE DEPARTMENT	4,414
Personnel Manager	DUES AND SUBSCRIPTIONS	175
TOTAL OVERHEAD SPENDING VARIANCES		$12,887

While the overall variances are determined directly through the transaction summaries that are the basis for the journal entries, the more detailed variances by responsibility must be determined through separate supplementary subsystems that are not discussed in this chapter.

The cost of achieving a computerized system is not small. A company that is interested in computerizing its cost system should computerize its production and inventory control system as well. The reverse is also true. Cost accounting and inventory control are inextricably tied together. The physical units reported in the transaction listings and providing the basis for inventory status reports (perpetuals) should be the same units that are valued by the cost department in arriving at general ledger inventory balances.

As competitive pressures intensify more and more, inventory management will become even more important to the economic survival of many companies. The steps for computerizing, outlined in this chapter, provide a framework which should support management's needs for effective inventory management for some time to come.

> Computerized procedures, if not properly designed, can spew out reports as if they were the end product of the business.

SECTION IV

How to Develop Realistic Measurements of Performance

12

Direct Costing–Handle
with Care

Contrary to common belief, direct costing was in use prior to 1906 although
it was not referred to by this name. This predates absorption costing which
was the outgrowth of mass production.

Although direct costing is new to the modern large company,
variations of the direct costing concept have been used by a number of small
companies for some time. Many small fabricators have for years set selling prices by
adding a markup factor to prime cost.

Direct costing provides statements that are easier to understand because of the
exclusion of volume variances. Even though the modern manager is a professional, his
knowledge and understanding of the flow of costs in an absorption accounting system
is limited. The closer correlation of profits with sales–a characteristic of direct
costing–provides the manager with a more understandable financial picture than
absorption accounting which tends to correlate profits with volume of production.

Direct costing also demonstrates quite forcefully the impact of period cost on
profits, providing a financial statement which spells out the profit-volume relationship.
Although the author is a strong advocate of direct costing for internal reporting and
analysis, he feels the need for urging caution in the use of this system. This chapter will
develop the reasons.

INTEREST IN DIRECT COSTING

The impetus given to direct costing stems from the ever-increasing mechanization
of American industry. With automation on the increase, overhead becomes an even
larger element of cost. Since a substantial portion of this element is largely non-variable

in nature, seasonal variations in production and sales tend to cause a distortion in profit which is difficult to justify when preparing income statements for management. When production volume is on a steep incline, fixed costs tend to build up in the inventory, thus reducing the amount of the current period's costs until such time as the inventory is sold. During this period of heavy production, profits may be high even though sales are low. During the reverse cycle, the opposite will usually be true.

Under direct costing, inventories would be valued at direct or variable costs while fixed costs would be charged directly to expense in the current period. The basic difference in the income statement format between the absorption principle (in which fixed costs are included in inventory) and direct costing (which includes only direct or variable costs) is illustrated in the simplified examples shown below:

INCOME STATEMENT
Absorption Costing Format

Net Sales	$100,000
Less Cost of Sales	80,000
Gross Profit	$ 20,000
*Administration	4,000
*Selling	6,000
Total Administrative & Selling	$ 10,000
Pre-tax Profit	10,000

*Normally considered period cost even in an absorption accounting system.

INCOME STATEMENT
Direct Costing Format

Net Sales		$100,000	100%
Less Variable Costs			
Material	$18,000		
Direct Labor	21,000		
Variable Overhead	21,000	60,000	60
Balance Left for Fixed Cost		40,000	40%
Fixed Costs			
Manufacturing Overhead	$20,000		
Administration	4,000		
Selling	6,000	30,000	
Pre-tax Profit		$ 10,000	

THE DIRECT COSTING FORMAT BECOMES
A BREAKEVEN ANALYSIS

Because separation of fixed and variable costs is a natural byproduct of the direct costing format, calculation of the breakeven point based on each accounting period's mix of sales becomes fairly simple. Using the above example, the variable or direct costs amount to 60% of the month's sales—leaving 40% of the sales dollar to cover fixed costs and profits. Dividing the fixed costs of $30,000 by 40%, the breakeven sales would be $75,000.

Calculation of the profit at various levels between the breakeven point and $100,000 can be accomplished quite simply:

Breakeven sales	Additional sales above breakeven	Total sales	40% profit on the addit'l sales
$75,000	—	$ 75,000	—
75,000	5,000	80,000	2,000
75,000	10,000	85,000	4,000
75,000	15,000	90,000	6,000
75,000	20,000	95,000	8,000
75,000	25,000	100,000	10,000

The above calculations assume that a range of activity from $75,000 to $100,000 can be considered a normal range and that the fixed costs would remain relatively stable within this range.

Calculation of losses *below* breakeven would be calculated in the same manner:

Breakeven sales	Sales fell short of breakeven by:	Total sales	40% loss on sales deficiency
$75,000	5,000	$70,000	2,000
75,000	10,000	65,000	4,000
75,000	15,000	60,000	6,000

While the mathematics will usually fall into a clear pattern as illustrated above, it is important to temper all mathematical derivations with good judgment.

EFFECT OF INVENTORY CHANGE ON THE TWO METHODS

The preceding example showing the difference in format between absorption and direct costing indicated the same profit under both methods. This was due to the fact that there was no inventory change in the example used. Let us now consider some examples in which a variety of conditions is assumed.

Exhibit 12-1 shows a comparison of absorption accounting and direct costing with no inventory change; with an inventory increase; and with an inventory decrease.

Comparison of Absorption Accounting
with Direct Costing

NO INVENTORY CHANGE	ABSORPTION ACCOUNTING			DIRECT COSTING	DIFFERENCE
	Variable	Fixed	Total	Variable	
SALES			$18,000	$18,000	
Less Cost of Sales:					
Inventory-Beginning	-	-	-	-	-
Input	9,000	7,000	16,000	9,000	-7000
Total Available	9,000	7,000	16,000	9,000	-7000
Inventory-Ending (deduct)	-	-	-	-	-
Cost of Sales	9,000	7,000	16,000	9,000	-7000
Profit before period cost			2,000	9,000	+7000
Period cost (deduct)				7,000	+7000
Profit after period cost			2,000	2,000	
INVENTORY INCREASE					
SALES			$25,000	$25,000	
Less Cost of Sales:					
Inventory-Beginning	-	-	-	-	-
Input	18,000	7,000	25,000	18,000	-7000
Total Available	18,000	7,000	25,000	18,000	-7000
Inventory-Ending (deduct)	6,000	4,000	10,000	6,000	-4000
Cost of Sales	12,000	3,000	15,000	12,000	-3000
Profit before period cost			10,000	13,000	+3000
Period cost (deduct)				7,000	-7000
Profit after period cost			10,000	6,000	-4000
INVENTORY DECREASE					
SALES			$12,000	$12,000	
Less Cost of Sales:					
Inventory-Beginning	6,000	4,000	10,000	6,000	-4000
Input	3,000	7,000	10,000	3,000	-7000
Total Available	9,000	11,000	20,000	9,000	-11000
Inventory-Ending (deduct)	3,000	2,000	5,000	3,000	-2000
Cost of Sales	6,000	9,000	15,000	6,000	-9000
Profit before period cost			-3,000	6,000	+9000
Profit cost (deduct)				7,000	+7000
Profit after period cost			-3,000	-1,000	+2000
TOTAL-THREE PERIODS					
SALES			$55,000	$55,000	
Less Cost of Sales:					
Inventory-Beginning	-	-	-	-	-
Input	30,000	21,000	51,000	30,000	-21000
Total Available	30,000	21,000	51,000	30,000	-21000
Less Ending Inventory	3,000	2,000	5,000	3,000	-2000
Cost of Sales	27,000	19,000	46,000	27,000	-19000
Profit before period cost			9,000	28,000	+19000
Period cost (deduct)				21,000	+21000
Net Profit			9,000	7,000	-2000

Exhibit 12-1

The composite results for the three periods are also shown. It shows the sales, the cost of sales calculations, profit before application of period cost to the direct costing column, and the results after deduction of period costs. The absorption accounting figures are broken down into variable and fixed elements so comparisons can be made with the direct costing method. Note that the variable column under absorption accounting is exactly the same as under direct costing. Note also in the second illustration (inventory increase) that although the $7,000 input of fixed costs is the same as the period cost appearing in the direct costing column, $4,000 of the $7,000 remains in the ending inventory, leaving only $3,000 of the $7,000 to be charged to expense. The difference of $4,000 represents the difference between the profit of $10,000 under absorption accounting and $6,000 under direct costing.

The next illustration shows the results of an inventory decrease. Although the input of fixed costs is again $7,000 under absorption accounting, the same amount as the period cost to be taken against profit and loss under direct costing, there is an inventory decrease which releases $2,000 additional fixed costs into cost of sales. This $2,000 is the reconciling difference between the $3,000 loss under absorption accounting and the $1,000 loss under direct costing.

PRODUCT LINE PROFITABILITY

The management of an organization which is broken down by product line requires that operating results be broken down similarly. When the manufacturing process is such that a single plant-wide overhead rate is sufficient to do an effective costing of the product, no problem is presented by the direct costing format requiring a product line breakdown of period cost because the allocation can be made proportionate to the distribution of the base (direct labor, machine hours, or other method used to apply overhead to the product).

However, when a single plant-wide overhead rate is not applicable–and more companies will find this to be the case than not–a problem of allocation is presented when absorption accounting is converted to direct costing. Under absorption costing, the allocation of overhead to product line becomes automatic through the absorption process which takes departmental overhead rates into account. To attempt to allocate the total period cost under direct costing in one across-the-board computation could yield erroneous results.

Exhibit 12-2 illustrates an income statement broken down by product line under the direct costing system. Note that the overhead to be allocated amounts to $195,000. Of this, $22,000 is allocated to product line A, the smallest of the three. The profit for this product amounts to $6,000. If the $195,000 had been allocated differently so that ½ of 1%, more or less, had been allocated to product line A, the profit would have been approximately $1,000 more or $1,000 less–a substantial difference in this product line because it would increase the profit percentage to 7% or drop it to 5%. The effect would not be as great on products B and C because a ½ of 1% error in allocation to a large product line would not have as large an impact on the final profit percentage since the dollar volume of sales is four to five times as great.

It is important to bear in mind that changing to a direct costing system will mean that equitable means must be found to allocate large period costs to product lines,

Product Line Operating Statement

	TOTAL	PRODUCT A	PRODUCT B	PRODUCT C
SALES	$1,000,000	$100,000	$410,000	$490,000
Variable Costs				
Material	170,000	20,000	60,000	90,000
Direct Labor	118,000	8,000	40,000	70,000
Overhead	142,000	12,000	55,000	75,000
Commissions	60,000	6,000	24,000	30,000
Total Variable Cost	490,000	46,000	179,000	265,000
Variable Costs as a % of Sales	49%	46%	44%	54%
Fixed Costs				
Directly Assignable	105,000	15,000	52,000	38,000
Allocated Overhead	195,000	22,000	82,000	91,000
Administration	75,000	6,000	29,000	40,000
Selling	62,000	5,000	17,000	40,000
Total Fixed Costs	437,000	48,000	180,000	209,000
Profit Before Taxes	73,000	6,000	51,000	16,000
Profit as a % of Sales	7.3%	6.0%	12.4%	3.3%

Exhibit 12-2

unless management is willing to ignore full costing by product line–in most cases an unlikely circumstance. Also of importance is the margin of error which becomes more critical with the small product lines where a slight margin of error can often make the difference between loss or profit. This is not peculiar to direct costing but is a characteristic of all cost systems.

EVALUATION OF INDIVIDUAL PRODUCT TYPE PROFITABILITY

Under normal conditions, if product A sells at $300 per unit, and product B sells at $350, the sales department might be inclined to push product B, other things being equal. Under the direct costing concept a breakdown of the costs of these two products might show the following:

	Product A	Product B
SALES PRICE	$300.00	$350.00
Variable Costs		
Material	89.70	129.85
Direct Labor	20.70	37.80
Variable Overhead	25.50	34.30
Total Variable Cost	135.90	201.95

Balance left for fixed cost	$164.10	$148.05

Variable Costs as a % of Sales

SALES PRICE	100.0%	100.0%
Variable Costs		
Material	29.9	37.1
Direct Labor	6.9	10.8
Variable Overhead	8.5	9.8
Total Variable Cost	45.3%	57.7%
Balance left for fixed cost	54.7%	42.3%

The breakdown of the dollar content of variable costs in products A and B indicates that variable costs for the former amount to $135.90, leaving $164.10 to cover fixed costs. Product B, on the other hand, has a variable cost content of $201.95, leaving only $148.05 for fixed costs. It is usually more convenient to convert the dollars to percentages of sales price in making this type of analysis in order that all products will be compared with a single common denominator–percentage of the sales dollar.

Comparing products A and B on this basis we find that product B's variable costs are 57.7% of the sales price, leaving 42.3% to cover fixed costs (and profit). Product A, on the other hand, has a variable percentage of 45.3, leaving 54.7% to cover fixed costs. Thus, even though product B has the higher selling price of the two, product A is the more profitable, dollar for dollar.

Use of percentages will facilitate easy comparisons of the relative profitability of all items in the line simultaneously. An abbreviated example is shown below:

PRODUCT	Sales Price	Index of Profitability
A	$300.00	54.7%
AA	339.75	49.1
B	350.00	42.3
BB	450.00	48.2
BBB	475.50	46.6
C	255.65	49.9
D	198.00	39.5
E	100.00	48.5
EE	125.30	43.0
F	175.50	52.0
G	180.90	41.1

In appraising the relative profitability of a number of products, this single index will rate all products in the line quickly on a common basis. Thus, product D, with an index of profitability of 39.5, is highlighted as the least profitable of the line while product A, referred to previously, is the most profitable with an index of 54.7.

HOW ERRONEOUS OVERHEAD APPLICATION
CAN DISTORT PRODUCT COSTS

Many discussions on the subject of direct costing include procedures for developing product costs, but do not mention the pitfalls which can result in erroneous information.

Under standard costs it took a number of years for managers to become aware of the pitfalls of the single plant-wide overhead rate. As a result, departmental (cost center) overhead rates came more and more into use as a means of giving proper weighting to the variations in overhead cost of the various manufacturing operations. While direct costing reduces the margin of error in application of overhead by excluding fixed costs from consideration, the problem is still real because variable overhead rates will vary from one manufacturing process to another. Illustrative of this are three companies whose variable overhead rates are shown below. These range from a $6,000,000-a-year manufacturer of small components to a $50,000,000-a-year appliance manufacturer.

Company No. 1 would fall under the classification of light manufacturing. While its variable overhead rates do not fluctuate very widely from one department to another (considering the wide margin of error which is characterisitic of overhead rate determination), the range is 39% to 66%. In this company, as in most others, all products do not use the manufacturing facilities in the same proportions. Furnace Processing, which has the highest rate of the group, is bypassed entirely by some of the products, therefore use of the average 46% rate would overstate the cost of these products and would understate the products which use Furnace Processing facilities.

Company No. 2, likewise, has variations from department to department but the variations are far greater—ranging from 54% to 213%. Here again the time spent in each department by the various products in the line varies depending upon the amount of press shop work, amount of plating required, machine shop and screw machine parts, and assembly labor. Use of the average plant rate of 105% would penalize some of the products and understate the cost of others.

Company No. 3, smaller than Company No. 2, shows more stability in its variable rates than the larger company. In spite of the greater stability, the highest rate is twice as great as the lowest. In its radio line, some of the radios use a metal cabinet which requires more time in the Sheet Metal Shop and Plating than a radio using a plastic cabinet which is purchased as material. Since the Sheet Metal Shop and Plating are the two highest rates in the entire group, use of the average rate of 65% would penalize the radios using plastic cabinets and would undercost the ones using metal.

COMPANY NO. 1

Variable Overhead Rates of a
Small Components Manufacturer

Parts Stamping	41%
Coil Winding	46
Furnace Processing	66

Assembly	39
Test	42
Average	46%

COMPANY NO. 2

Variable Overhead Rates of an Appliance Manufacturer

Metal Press Shop	213%
Machine Shop	110
Screw Machines	143
Plating	135
Assembly	67
Inspection	54
Average	105%

COMPANY NO. 3

Variable Overhead Rates of a Radio Manufacturer

Sheet Metal Shop	78%
Machine Shop	71
Plating	107
Assembly	64
Inspection	53
Average	65%

Note: Department names are those actually used by the three companies. "Metal Press Shop" in Company No. 2 is the same as "Sheet Metal Shop" in Company No. 3. "Test" in Company No. 1 is quite similar to "Inspection" in Company No. 2 and Company No. 3.

The foregoing examples highlight the importance of taking into account the differences in the manufacturing operations. Let us consider the example of two products calculated two ways to demonstrate the effect on the index of profitability. The two manufacturing departments used are Metal Press Shop with an overhead rate of 500% broken down as follows: 200% variable and 300% fixed. The other department is Assembly with an overhead rate of 100% made up of 50% variable and 50% fixed. The average variable plant-wide rate is 133%. Using the average plant-wide rate the analysis is as follows:

	Product A	Product B
Selling Price	$180.00	$215.00
Variable Costs		
Material	15.00	15.00
Direct Labor	45.00	45.00

Overhead @ 133%	60.00	60.00
Total Variable	$120.00	$120.00
% Variable	67%	56%
Index of Profitability	33%	44%

If we allow for the different overhead rates in Metal Shop and Assembly the results would be as follows:

	Product A	*Product B*
Selling Price	$180.00	$215.00
Variable Costs		
Material	15.00	15.00
Direct Labor—Assembly	30.00	10.00
Direct Labor—Heavy Press Section	15.00	35.00
Overhead—Assembly @ 50%	15.00	5.00
Overhead—Heavy Press @ 200%	30.00	70.00
Total Variable	$105.00	$135.00
% Variable	58%	63%
Index of Profitability	42%	37%

In the example using the average plant-wide rate of 133%, product B appears to be the more profitable of the two. This is quite obvious without making the calculations, because variable costs are the same but the selling price for product B is $35 greater. In most instances this does not become evident until the calculations are made. In the second illustration using individual overhead rates for Assembly and for Heavy Presses, the costs come out to $105 and $135 respectively with the index of profitability indicating that product A is the more profitable of the two. In actual practice, this would indicate that the cost of making product B is too great, because the product using the heavier facilities should be the more profitable. The index of profitability would give management a clue as to which products require work to be done. Use of an average rate would never accomplish this.

DIRECT COSTING FOR EVALUATION OF "PLUS" BUSINESS AT REDUCED PRICES

Because direct costing makes it possible to quickly analyze profitability of additional sales volume without the distorting effect of inventory changes on costs, some companies use the reasoning which was given the author by one business man who said:

> I now recoup all my fixed costs in the sales which I'm currently booking. If I know what my direct costs are, I can set prices about 20% higher than my direct costs and come up with a lot of profitable-plus business without expanding my facilities one iota. I make a well-advertised brand name product, which I could sell in bulk to a private brand distributor at substantially lower prices.

In an interview with the official of another company, the conversation on the subject of marginal income pricing took this turn, when the interviewee said:

> We studied the possibilities of taking on a new product line on several occasions. With direct costing, we determine what our additional income will be because of the additional volume. We then match this with the additional outlay of capital and other costs required to get into the business. If the additional outlay doesn't eat up too much of the additional profit we go into the business.

While the use of direct costing is an invaluable tool in determining how much prices can be reduced in order to obtain new business, this tool must be used with discretion. Obviously, during a period of declining sales volume it would be altogether too easy to book a substantial volume of business at reduced prices because the current business is presumably absorbing the full fixed cost complement. But what will happen if the "plus" business becomes predominant? Normal cost controls do not set up red flags to highlight this problem except when profits begin to erode. It would be well, in the interest of guarding against this possibility, to code sales which are taken on a reduced price basis and to continually compare these sales with the volume of regular type business in order to highlight an imbalanced condition. While proponents of direct costing are quick to point out the price-cutting advantages of the system, they are not sufficiently vocal on the dangers of unconsciously overdoing a good thing.

DISSEMINATION OF SALES PRICE INFORMATION

Some managements make it a practice to withhold sales price information from groups other than sales and accounting under the theory that sales prices are of no concern to the others. While in theory this policy may seem plausible, it should be borne in mind that other groups, such as manufacturing and engineering, can make substantial contributions to management profitability if they are "part of the team."

In one company, a factory maintenance man learned quite by accident that one product in the line had a very low selling price, but had to be kept in the catalog in order to round out the line. He had observed that the manufacturing operation which involved soldering some pins which projected out of a plastic shell was of the "Rube Goldberg" variety, involving a series of levered and catapulting mechanisms to dip the product into the solder pot, and then by spring action to throw the unit against a canvas backdrop to shake off the excess solder. Frequently, the plastic shell was splattered with the solder and rework was necessary to make the piece acceptable for shipment. The maintenance man modified an obsolete drill press so it could first be used to lower the piece into the solder pot to the right depth, automatically; then it was raised and the drill press head rotated the product and shook off the excess solder with no splattering on the part itself—with a substantial saving of labor cost.

In another company, the highly competitive nature of consumer entertainment products, such as radio and television, was brought home to a group of engineers when selling prices were compared with cost to emphasize the need for greater simplicity of design. One engineer in the group commented that he had not realized the low price at which television sets were sold to the dealers (distributors) because he had always made his comparisons with the prices he paid when he had purchased his set at the store. As a result, several cost savings were achieved during that model year without sacrificing quality.

These savings might not have otherwise been achieved because the general viewpoint of this group was, "Cut down on the number of brackets? Why? You'll only save 10 cents." When advised of the narrow profit margin and the fact that the cost and potential saving was not 10 cents, but 10 cents multiplied by 500,000 sets, or $50,000, attitudes changed quickly.

Cost consciousness becomes more real when key employees become aware of the narrow profit margins between manufacturing costs and factory selling prices. Managers in industry might well reconsider their policies regarding the revelation of selling price information within their organizations.

CONVERTING FROM ABSORPTION TO DIRECT COSTING

The hopes of many direct costing proponents that direct costing would be accepted by the IRS and SEC were dashed when the Federal Register, on September 19, 1973, declared that Internal Revenue regulations would require the use of a "full absorption" method of inventory costing for all taxpayers engaged in manufacturing or production operations. This need not be considered a deterrent because many companies are carrying their inventories at full cost and are identifying the variable and fixed segments separately. The fixed portion is adjusted each accounting period and the adjustment added to or deducted from the direct costing profit to arrive at the results which would have been obtained from absorption costing. Some multiplant companies carry the fixed portion of the inventory on the corporate books to permit the plants to operate on a "pure" direct costing basis. Inasmuch as installation of a direct costing system means "keeping two sets of books," it might be easier for those planning to convert to direct costing to stay with their present systems and develop differentials to be used in adjusting the income statements to a direct costing basis.

Exhibit 12-3 illustrates a method which can be used in conjunction with the absorption costing system to arrive at direct costing results on a statistical basis. The month's transactions would be processed in the normal manner using absorption or full costs. Upon closing the books for the month, a memo set of ledger sheets similar to the section marked "Differential Between Absorption Accounting and Direct Costing" would be prepared. Only the fixed cost portion of the transactions would be posted to the differential accounts. These would be posted as contra-entries to reduce the absorption accounts to the variable costs only. A credit to the inventory account and a debit to cost of sales under absorption accounting would be reduced to a direct costing basis through a debit to the inventory differential account and credit to the cost of sales in the amount of the period cost. Using period 2 in the exhibit as an illustration, the inventory (under absorption costing) is relieved of $15,000 with a debit to cost of sales in the same amount. The differential inventory account is debited for $3,000 which reduces the inventory relief to $12,000 under direct costing. Cost of Sales is likewise credited for $3,000. Exhibit 12-3 (continued) shows the direct cost ledger accounts for reconciliation purposes only.

Absorption Accounting

	Input Variable	Input Fixed	Inventory			C/S	Sales	P&L after Period Cost of $7,000/Mo.
1.	9000	7000	-0- *	16000		16000	18000	2000
2.	18000	7000	-0- *	25000		15000	25000	10000
3.	3000	7000	10000 *	10000	15000	15000	12000	3000
	30000	21000	5000 *			46000	55000	3000 / 12000

Differential Between Absorption Accounting and Direct Costing

	Input Variable	Input Fixed	Inventory			C/S
1.		7000	7000	-0- *		7000
2.		7000	7000	-0- *		3000
3.		7000	7000	9000	4000 *	9000
		21000	2000 *			19000

Direct Costing

	Input Variable	Input Fixed	Inventory		C/S	Sales	P&L after Period Cost of $7,000/Mo.
1.	9000		-0- *	9000	9000	18000	2000
2.	18000		-0- *	18000	12000	25000	6000
3.	3000		6000 *	3000	6000	12000	1000
	30000		3000 *		27000	55000	1000 / 8000

* Inventory Balances

Exhibit 12-3

AN ALTERNATIVE METHOD OF DIRECT COSTING

An alternative method of achieving direct costing results without the requirement of adjusting inventories is to compare variable and fixed manufacturing costs with the equivalent sales value of production. Inasmuch as the sales value of production represents the potential sales of what was produced, adjustment for period costs in inventory is not a factor and can be ignored. In instances where the sales value of production cannot be conveniently calculated, the illustrations below demonstrate how it can be determined. Beginning with the income statement, the first step is to convert cost of sales to the current month's manufacturing cost. This is done by adjusting the cost of sales by the inventory increase or decrease.

INCOME STATEMENT
($000 Omitted)

Net Sales	$461
Less Cost of Sales	389
Gross Profit	$ 72
Cost of Sales (from above)	$389
Less inventory decrease	32
Manufacturing Cost	$357

The next step is to adjust the net sales by the inventory decrease to arrive at sales value of production:

Net Sales	$461
Less inventory decrease	32
Sales Value of Production	$429

Subtracting the current month's manufacturing cost from the sales value of production, we find that gross profit is the same as calculated previously:

Sales Value of Production	$429
Less Manufacturing Cost	357
Gross Profit	$ 72

If a breakdown of the manufacturing cost by the variable and fixed cost is made, we can then develop a direct costing presentation without being concerned with fixed costs remaining in inventory:

SALES VALUE OF PRODUCTION		$429
Less Variable Costs		
Material	$182	
Direct Labor	35	
Indirect Labor	21	
Maintenance	10	

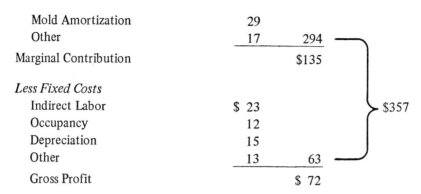

Mold Amortization	29	
Other	17	294
Marginal Contribution		$135
Less Fixed Costs		
Indirect Labor	$ 23	
Occupancy	12	
Depreciation	15	
Other	13	63
Gross Profit		$ 72

A deficiency of this method is the adjustment of the sales figure by an inventory change valued at cost. If the change is large, then the sales value of production can be overstated or understated to the extent of the potential markup in the inventory change. This can be overcome, however, by applying a markup. If the inventory fluctuations are not great, there should be relatively little distortion.

Also, in some manufacturing operations it is entirely possible that the current month's production may have an entirely different cost to sales ratio than the current month's sales. In such instances it would be more desirable to extend the transfers to finished goods by the selling price to arrive at sales value of production and then to add or subtract the work-in-process inventory change.

CONCLUSIONS

Because of tax department and other considerations, most companies embarking on a direct costing installation require that the fixed cost segment of inventory be retained on the books and adjusted each period. Abandonment of the absorption system, which makes this valuation automatically as the product moves through the manufacturing process, requires another method to be used. The substitute computation is frequently arbitrary and does not weight for differences in departmental contribution. As a result, changes in product mix are not accounted for correctly in the fixed cost adjustment. In addition to distorted balance sheet valuations, this approach makes it difficult in planning to forecast the fixed portion of inventory on a logical basis.

It would be far more desirable to retain the absorption flow of costs and then to adjust to direct costing by "backing out" the fixed costs in the manner discussed in this chapter. This would retain consistency in the method used for valuing inventories and would not introduce arbitrary methods of making overall adjustments to large pools of fixed costs in inventory. All the benefits of direct costing would then be incorporated in the financial statements while the basic books of account, which are of no interest to the operating managers, would remain unaffected.

Direct costing is usually applied to sales and cost of sales. Serious consideration should also be given to application of this concept to sales value of production and manufacturing costs. Since factory expenditures in making the product account for as much as 60% to 80% of the sales dollar, and, since this month's manufacturing cost will become next month's cost of sales, it would be highly beneficial to measure, currently, this large element on a direct costing basis. The factory manager would then have valuable information on breakeven levels; he would know the profit volume relationships on a current basis; and he would have a financial statement directly correlated with conditions under his control. While the benefits of direct costing are self-evident, the application of these techniques, as with all new systems, must be carefully evaluated before departing from previously established methods.

In utilizing direct costs for pricing remember that application of a factor to direct costs in order to arrive at a sales price assumes that material, labor, and variable overhead are an equitable basis for recovery of fixed costs. And if the factor used is the same for all products being priced, the assumption is automatically made that the ratio of material, labor, and overhead is constant for all products so priced–a highly unlikely circumstance.

Reconstruction of the profit and loss results by product line on a full costing basis through the arbitrary allocation of fixed costs can be deceptive, if departmental effort expended on each product line is not taken into account. Here again, be wary of the overall split of a large amount of period cost on an arbitrary basis.

The lessons learned through years of experience with other systems must not be discarded without first making certain that the answers provided by the new system are soundly developed and that they meet the test of good business judgment.

> Although it is not legal to use direct costing for external reporting, there are many benefits in using it for internal analysis.

13

The Accounting System
and Cost Control

A good accounting system does not guarantee good cost controls.

The mere existence of a good accounting system is not an automatic guarantee that management will have good cost controls. The accounting system, as such, is historical—it summarizes what happened several weeks ago on an after-the-fact basis.

This does not give the operating management timely facts on which it can act, because excess material usage, scrap, high labor and overhead costs are not being shown on a day-to-day and week-to-week basis so that corrective action can be taken as soon as an unfavorable trend becomes apparent.

Too often the accounting system, which admittedly has an important mission in reporting the financial condition of the business to the owners, results in a paperwork routine which fully occupies too many financial groups to the extent that the more pertinent day-to-day controls are never properly implemented. While the financial executive's responsibilities in making up payrolls, billing customers, paying suppliers, monitoring inventories, controlling capital acquisitions, preparing budgets, and summarizing expenditures is not to be dismissed lightly, he must, in spite of these demands, find a way to implement timely cost controls. He need not personally oversee every facet of the implementation, nor should he jealously guard the prerogatives of the accounting group. He should enlist the aid of other members in the organization: production control in preparing information needed for measurement of material utilization; the quality group for reporting of scrap; the industrial engineering group for labor efficiency reports. Most companies have substantial amounts of good basic information already available, which needs only to be correlated, recast into a meaningful and actionable report.

By the nature of his position, the financial executive is looked upon by his fellow managers as the logical one to act as catalyst in the assembly, interpretation, and distribution of this information. This chapter will discuss the types of analysis which should be made and the various reports that are necessary in order to properly control costs.

CONTROL OF MATERIAL COST

Material is probably the most difficult element of manufacturing cost to account for. Actual usage is not known in many instances until an inventory is taken. Taking inventories can be expensive and time consuming. This undoubtedly is one of the reasons accountability is lacking on a more frequent basis. It is not sufficient to report material (and labor) efficiencies once a month or after the completion of a job. Management must have this information on a more timely and more frequent basis.

Although material accountability presents some real problems, the case for control is not hopeless. It will be found that although many items of material need to be accounted for, a small number of items will usually make up a large percentage of the total. Even if an inventory is required in order to properly report material usage on a more frequent basis, the inventory need only cover the few items. This is the selective control technique.

HOW ONE COMPANY USES THE SELECTIVE CONTROL TECHNIQUE FOR MATERIAL CONTROL

One company effected substantially better material control through use of this technique. An analysis showed that 87 different material items were used in normal production and that 14 of these accounted for 52% of the value. Although fuller than 52% coverage would have been desirable (27 items were required for 85% coverage), it was felt in the interest of economy and speed that only 14 items would be controlled at the outset. Arrangements were made with the factory to take an inventory of the 14 key items each Friday shortly before close of work. The stockroom would also furnish the financial group with figures showing the number of the items issued and returned to stock. These were furnished daily along with the number of units that were produced and accepted by the stockroom. Receipt of these figures on a daily basis permitted cursory checks to be made to detect unusually low or unusually high activity, a circumstance that resulted in the financial group becoming more production oriented through questions which arose and which required answers by production personnel. Daily receipt of production and issue figures facilitated the accumulation of the figures during the week so the final day's production and issues needed only to be added to the prior four days' totals. As soon as the inventory information was available, each item was summarized and the material utilization percentage determined, as illustrated in Exhibit 13-1.

The beginning inventory is always the same as the preceding week's ending inventory—unless an error is found. Issues to the floor are added to the beginning

Weekly Material Utilization Report

(figures are in units)

w/e_____

Part #	Beginning Inventory	Issues to Floor	Returns	Ending Inventory	Material Usage	Production	Utiliz. %
135812	98,156			2,926	95,230	82,812	87%
138819	98,000	18,045		26,000	90,045	82,812	92
144404	5,400	96,750		10,750	91,400	82,812	90
211362	3,500	63,500			67,000	51,891	77
223414	860	252,695	3,010	8,624	241,921	252,190	104
201134	8,000	378,510	6,000	3,080	377,430	252,170	67
199966	15,530	133,000		7,224	141,306	101,527	72
211633	14,217	33,400		26,307	21,310	19,683	92
198986	8,820	69,000	11,000		66,820	24,066	36
253007	1,550	35,650	21,130	3,000	13,070	5,689	44
244031	3,640	10,500	2,860	3,920	7,360	5,689	77
22306	2,000	8,150		1,000	9,150	5,689	62
23364	15,754	88,540	6,653	12,507	85,134	65,482	77
19966	5,370	104,275	6,900	19,800	82,945	65,482	79

Exhibit 13-1

inventory to determine the total amount of material available. This figure is reduced by returns to stock, which sometimes were high because they represented rejects due to poor workmanship by a preceding department. The adjusted amount is then reduced by the ending inventory to arrive at the amount of material usage. This, divided into the output or production, results in a material utilization percentage.

Part 198986 is illustrative of the use which may be put to this type of control. The beginning inventory amounts to 8,820 units; 69,000 units were issued to cover the next two weeks' production requirements. The 11,000 returns to stock represented defective parts which were returned to stock. The entire amount of material available, less returns, was used in the production of 24,066 finished parts—a material utilization of only 36%. Investigation into this low percentage revealed that the quality of the parts which were issued from stock was generally poor. Only 11,000 were returned to stock, although more should have been returned, because of a rush order which had to be filled for a customer requiring immediate delivery. As a result of poorly fitting parts, over 66,000 had to be used to make 24,000 finished units. The financial group, as a result of this experience, began to watch for large returns to stock as a clue to repetition of this type of low utilization. To prevent similar problems in the future, rush production of parts such as 198986 was minimized by maintaining a min-max inventory in stock sufficient to take care of two or three weeks' production requirements. When issues would be made to the floor in the future, there was greater assurance that the parts would not be defective because adequate lead times were provided all departments to eliminate waste due to haste. Through inspection of the utilization figures, trends were carefully watched to determine what could be done to improve utilization. This report also provided a weekly analysis of inventory of the 14 dominant items. If an inventory remained too high and was untouched for four weeks in a row, questions were asked, and frequently it was possible to obtain orders to reduce the inventory to tolerable limits. This eliminated later obsolescence and consequent writeoffs.

Maintaining this type of report in units rather than in dollars eliminates a great deal of work in dollarizing the figures. Since the 14 items represent over half the value of all materials used, there was no need to incur additional cost to reconfirm this fact each week by time-consuming extensions of price by quantity.

INVENTORY-TAKING NOT ALWAYS A PREREQUISITE TO MATERIAL CONTROL

It is not always necessary to account for inventory changes to obtain effective control. When the flow of the product and its components can be monitored so "unaccounted-for disappearance" is not an important factor, an analysis of spoilage provides adequate control. This type of control is usually more economical than the weekly material utilization report. It is also more timely because spoilage information can be provided hourly if need be.

One of the companies whose material cost control procedures were studied prepared a daily spoilage report which showed the number of each unit rejected (minor items omitted). If the defect could be reworked, the spoilage quantity was adjusted and the rework cost noted. This report was issued each morning for the preceding day, with a short statement explaining major causes of an unusually high spoilage rate.

The information appearing on the daily report is summarized on a weekly basis by type of unit and the defect causing the rejection. Dollar values are then assigned and a listing is made in order of dollar magnitude of spoilage, with the highest cost items appearing at the top of the list. A specimen copy of this report is shown in Exhibit 13-2.

The part number rejected is shown as well as the final product in which the part appears. The week's scheduled production is shown in order that a relationship might be made as to the magnitude of rejects. While a "Percent Rejects to Week's Scheduled Production" might be useful for this purpose, it was decided that every additional column adds to the cost of the report and to the preparation time. The next to the last column shows the reject code while the last column shows the dollar cost of the rejects. The total week's rejects of $2,477.26 is annualized to emphasize the magnitude of spoilage over a year's time. The prior week's annualized total is also shown for comparative purposes.

The report is closed out at the close of business on Tuesday and issued Wednesday morning. In a weekly meeting held on Wednesday shortly after distribution of the report, the quality assurance group and production foremen discuss the causes of spoilage and suggest remedies. Primary emphasis would be placed on the first three items, which account for 70% of the rejects. If time permits, the fourth item, which

Weekly Spoilage Report
(dollar value of rejects)

w/e_____

Part #	Used on Product No.	Week's Scheduled Production	No. of Rejects	Type of Defect	Total Cost
603	78396	300	19	116	$ 625.38
301	69842	150	9	43	531.52
673	39461	75	8	52	503.61
498	21312	890	150	14	342.16
306	14398	250	14	16	221.03
403	31982	600	32	6	114.32
106	21699	300	25	55	98.14
198	4443	250	8	62	41.10
					$2,477.26

This week's annualized total $123,863.00
Prior week's annualized total $114,132.75

Exhibit 13-2

accounts for another 10%, would be discussed. When appropriate, other parties such as the purchasing agent or material control supervisor are called in. The purchasing agent might be called in on a disucssion of quality of parts or other materials being purchased while the material control supervisor might be called in on a discussion dealing with defects due to rough handling of parts or improper storage. Actual participation by these parties has a more salutary effect than a telephoned complaint delivered in haste and received in haste. The purpose of the mid-week meeting is to permit action to be taken in the same week as the decisions and recommendations are made. The results are carefully reviewed in the following week's meeting to determine if the problems have been corrected.

Another company which assembles components that, once assembled, cannot be taken apart for repair, summarizes weekly spoilage in units on a cumulative basis. The figures correspond with the sequence of operations, and are illustrated in Exhibit 13-3. At assembly operation 1, 100 units were started but one was rejected, with the result showing 99.0% good. Operation 2 shows 99 starts with one rejected. Operation 3, with 98 starts because two had already been rejected, resulted in three rejects or 96.9% good units. Operations 4 and 5 follow the same pattern. The cumulative "% good" shows the cumulative effect of losses all along the line. While this figure is readily apparent from looking at the column headed "Good Units" and relating this to 100 starts at operation 1, it is not always possible in actual practice to determine this figure in this manner. The reason is that all units started in each operation are not always completely processed and forwarded to the next operation in the same week. The illustration following would be more typical.

239

Assembly Operations	No. of Starts	Good Units	% Good to Starts	Cum. % Good	Rejects
1	145	145	100.0%	100.0%	—
2	140	134	95.7	95.7	6
3	42	41	97.6	93.4	1
4	41	36	87.8	82.0	5

The cumulative % good would be calculated as follows:

100.0% in operation 1 multiplied by 95.7% in operation 2 = 95.7%
95.7% in operation 2 multiplied by 97.6% in operation 3 = 93.4%
93.4% in operation 3 multiplied by 87.8% in operation 4 = 82.0%

The significance of the cumulative percentage of rejects is that it highlights the total impact of accumulated spoilage. It appraises the overall effect of the rejects rather than looking at only a segment at a time. Referring again to Exhibit 13-3, it should be little consolation to management to see that operations 1, 2, and 3 are running better than 90% when only 65% of all units started are good.

This type of control highlights such losses without requiring time-consuming cost calculations. While application of costs to the units would better equate for relative values, it is questionable that the additional information obtained would justify the cost and possible delay in issuance of the report.

Weekly Spoilage Report
(units scrapped)
w/e_____

Assembly Operations	No. of Starts	Good Units	% Good to Starts	Cum. % Good	Rejects
1	100	99	99.0%	99.0%	1
2	99	98	99.0	98.0	1
3	98	95	96.9	95.0	3
4	95	75	78.9	74.9	20
5	75	65	86.7	65.0	10

Exhibit 13-3

MATERIAL CONTROL IN MACHINE-PACED OPERATIONS

When a manufacturing process is paced by automatic equipment, and machine hours rather than direct labor become the index of productivity, material control can be simplified by tying in productivity with the running time of the machines. Illustrative of this are the comparative weights of finished product per machine hour.

PRODUCTION PER MACHINE HOUR

Part #_____   Department _____

W/E	Number of Machine Hours	Pounds of Finished Production Per Machine Hour
2/7	250	13.02
2/14	310	13.40
2/21	249	12.55
2/28	361	12.70
3/7	279	12.52
3/14	214	10.22

The part is a large volume item which requires several punch presses. The weight of the finished parts is divided by the aggregate of the machine hours of all the presses running the part to arrive at "pounds of production per machine hour." While this index does not take directly into account the spoiled material and parts that have been rejected, the "pounds of production per machine hour" will automatically account for this. The reason is that if the raw material is defective or if the quality of the part is questionable, roving inspectors will require stoppage of the presses for checking parts and making adjustments. These delays are counted as running time. Therefore, when production falls because of such delays, machine hours continue to mount up. The result will be low yield per machine hour. The week of 3/14 is illustrative of such a situation. Note that production has dropped to 10.22 pounds per machine hour—the lowest for the six weeks shown. This report covers a relatively inexpensive part made of steel. A part made of bronze or copper would show the pounds of production per machine hour for each individual press running that part so that material usage caused by a particular press with a defective die or other defect would be quickly highlighted. While this type of report is not scientific by any means, it is basic in its simplicity, and an economical report for those industries producing certain types of products of low unit value.

In some machine operations, such as plastics molding, this type of control would not be as effective because the value of the finished product is substantially greater. The metal part referred to previously might sell for a maximum of $.05 each and weight of the finished product would be indicative of the material used.

In a plastics operation, when the product is represented by such items as trays, containers, cabinets, and other formed parts, the greater value and bulk warrant use of a more sophisticated type of reporting. In addition to the greater unit cost and bulk, output is not as closely correlated with machine hours because an attendant stops and starts the press each time it completes the cycle in order to remove the finished part. (This is not true in all cases because many small plastic items are frequently formed on fully automatic presses.) To obtain more effective material control in this case, a report similar to Exhibit 13-4 is recommended.

Material Utilization Report
Plastic Molding

| Press Type | Hours Running Time | Total Net Production | Total Theo. Production | % Eff. | Powder Consumption | | % Utiliz. |
					Actual # Powder Used	Theo. # Powder Used	
Rotary	7,343	13,705,000	14,761,094	93%	221,690	203,891	92%
741 Stokes	5,585	4,421,683	4,695,061	94%	82,900	73,795	89%
800 Stokes	3,392	845,455	951,848	89%	11,040	7,445	67%
200 Stokes	1,492	801,347	808,097	99%	3,410	2,223	65%

Exhibit 13-4

The total theoretical production of 14,761,094 shown under "Rotary" indicates the number of units which should have been produced with a running time of 7,343 hours. The actual production of 13,705,000 is divided by the theoretical production to show the percentage efficiency of 93%.

The theoretical amount of powder which should have been consumed to make 13,705,000 units is shown to be 203,891 pounds. Since 221,690 pounds were actually used, the percentage utilization is 92%. Obtaining figures on actual usage of material might entail taking into consideration changes in floor inventories, unless records are kept on the actual amount of powder put into the press hoppers.

CONTROL OF DIRECT LABOR

As modern industry becomes more and more competitive and automation increases, direct labor becomes smaller and smaller in relation to material and overhead. Frequently, direct labor is less than 10% of manufacturing cost while material and overhead will comprise 90%. Yet, surprisingly, labor receives substantially more attention than the other two larger elements. Standards are developed for direct labor for each operation by element; measurements are made for each detailed operation comparing the "standard time allowed" with the actual, and daily reports issued. Exhibit 13-5 represents an extract of a typical direct labor performance report for a machine shop.

In the company studied, this report is prepared on mechanical equipment and is distributed daily to each foreman. Although it is prepared on a daily basis, it cannot be distributed the following day but the day after that. To make distribution on the very next day would require the machine accounting section to operate on the second shift—a cost which the management of the company would prefer to avoid.

A survey was made of the foremen receiving the reports to determine to what use the information shown was being put. The comments were as follows:

Daily Direct Labor Performance Report

Dept.	Machine Shop					Date	June 17
Operator	Part #	Operation	Quantity	Standard Hours/pc.	Actual Hrs. on Std.	Std. Hrs. Earned	% Eff.
2701	516220	52	28	.0209	2.10	.59	
	502075	26	10	.0714	1.40	.71	
					3.50	1.30	37%
1432	67105	31	125	.0392	5.20	4.90	
	75160	52	23	.0553	1.40	1.27	
	75160	58	23	.0588	1.40	1.35	
					8.00	7.52	94%
2190	502071	99	20	.0714	1.38	1.43	104%
3426	80957	39	44	.1053	5.85	4.63	79%
5387	61499	51	35	.0424	3.50	1.48	
	61499	51	75	.0424	3.50	3.18	
	61499	51	15	.0424	1.00	.64	
					8.00	5.30	66%
3305	75158	120	38	.1540	5.50	5.85	
	502971	190	5	.6667	2.50	3.33	
					8.00	9.18	115%
				Total Departmental Efficiency			86.8%

Exhibit 13-5

Comment No. 1. I receive the report two days late. What good is it for me to approach an employee who was inefficient two days ago and ask him why he didn't do the job in less time? I've got to do this while he's still on the job. Find a way for me to monitor the efficiency of 125 people on an hour-to-hour basis and I can do something about it, but don't ask me to review what 125 people did two days ago.

Comment No. 2. Yes, I use the report. It's good for my department because the operations don't change too much. I look it over to see if I have operators who are consistently inefficient. Then I talk to them. One time, however, I found an operator who was always over 100% efficiency. I checked out of curiosity and found he wasn't reporting his production correctly. This made me wonder if any others were doing the same. It would be expensive for me to find out.

Comment No. 3. I stopped looking at these reports. Many of the standards are so out of date that the figures don't mean anything. Look at this one: how could an operator perform at 275%? It's obvious that something's wrong. I'm not complaining. I know it costs money to keep revising all those standards. What I say is, let's cut out some of this kind of paperwork and save money. There must be cheaper ways of doing this job.

Comment No. 4. No, I don't like the report. I tried to use it but found that my people were fudging production figures. Here's one case right here. I know this bird doesn't do 95% efficiency. He's clever, though. If you checked back you'd find that his charges to "off standard" are very high. He charges time to standard only when the job looks easy. Sure, I know I have to sign off on his time cards and make sure they're right, but I also have to get out the production or we won't have any customers.

Although several others interviewed conceded that the report was an excellent one, the general impression gained was that it was seldom referred to, because so many standards were going out of date faster than they could be revised; because the report was late; and because the mass of detail it contained could not be digested and used on a timely basis. A like survey made in another company using a similar report disclosed surprisingly similar results.

In pursuing the reporting of labor efficiency further and discussing it with the individuals interviewed, there was general agreement that corrective steps to make this daily report useful would be too expensive. One of the group suggested:

The accounting department uses standards for its cost system. Even if these are frozen for six months, why don't they price up production counts taken from the move tickets and give us a weekly summary showing the number produced, the standard allowed cost, and the actual direct labor cost? This would tell us on a weekly basis what the monthly variance report tells us at the end of each month. This way we'll know week by week how we'll stand on the monthly report, and we can take the necessary action.

In response to a question asked this same individual, "How can you do something about it when you don't know which operator was inefficient?", he replied:

I know which of my operators are efficient and which are inefficient without paperwork six inches high to tell me. I also know which parts are giving me trouble and I'm constantly trying to correct this. All I'm asking is cut out all this paperwork, free up the industrial engineers so they can get out on the floor and clean up the methods. That's what industrial engineers are for—to help the factory with its problems, not create more. Is this asking for too much?

Exhibit 13-6 shows a weekly labor efficiency report based on the use of accounting standards. The production figures shown on the report as "Quantity" were taken from inspection tickets. The quantity of each unit was extended by the standard labor hour allowance. A total standard allowance was developed for each department and this was compared with the total actual labor hours incurred.

Because the daily labor efficiency reports for this time period had indicated an efficiency of 86.8%, as compared to 63% on the new format, an analysis was made to segregate the items making up the difference. The analysis showed that total actual hours paid for included the following:

Hours on Standard	2,259.89
Repair or Rework	100.54
Off Standard	280.84
Downtime	227.45
Set-up	264.13
Total Hours Paid For	3,132.85

	Part No.	Quantity	Std. Hours Per Piece	Std. Hours Earned
	51622	100	.0209	2.0900
	50275	65	.0714	.4641
	67105	70	.0392	2.7440
	502071	100	.0714	7.1400

Weekly Labor Efficiency Report

Department _____   w/e _____

	Part No.	Quantity	Std. Hours Per Piece	Std. Hours Earned
	80957	80	.1053	8.4240
	75158	150	.1540	23.1000
				1961.7500
		Actual hours paid for		3132.8500
		departmental efficiency		63%

Exhibit 13-6

The 86.8% efficiency on the daily format had been arrived at by dividing hours on standard into standard hours earned of 1,961.75. While this percentage is technically correct, because a comparison is being made of efficiency while standard work is being performed, it can be misleading from an overall cost control point of view because the hours devoted to standard work include only about two-thirds of the total hours paid for. For good cost control, management must be able to see the entire picture readily. Efficiency while on standard would come close to 100% if enough time is classified as off-standard. Frequently, departmental foremen will, on their own prerogative, classify work as off-standard if they do not agree with the standard allowance that has been set. Relating the efficiency to the grand total of all hours paid for shows the total picture without such distortions.

A control, to be effective, must have the unqualified acceptance of those for whom it is intended. Unless this acceptance exists the control might as well not be used. It would be far better to have a simple index of productivity that is acceptable than a system which is almost perfect but unacceptable.

OVERHEAD RATES AS A MEANS FOR CONTROL

Because overhead is the most elusive of the three elements of cost, it is discussed more fully in other chapters. At this point it might be appropriate to discuss a common misconception that overhead rates can be used to determine the efficiency of a manufacturing operation. Since the overhead rate is based on the interaction of two variables (amount of overhead and amount of direct labor), it cannot be used for this type of measurement. The following examples will illustrate this point:

Example 1. For the first example let us take a company whose annual direct labor cost is $1,500,000 and overhead, $1,200,000. The overhead rate is $1,200,000 ÷ $1,500,000 or 80%.

Example 2. In this case, assume that through better layout and methods, the direct labor cost is reduced to $1,200,000 and overhead remains unchanged. In this instance, the overhead rate becomes 100% ($1,200,000 ÷ $1,200,000). However, even though the overhead rate increased by 20 percentage points, the total cost has been reduced by $300,000.

Example 3. The manufacturing process has been automated so that many of the assembly operations are performed by automatic devices. With such an installation, labor cost has been cut to $400,000, but overhead, because of a larger capital investment, has increased to $1,600,000. This would result in an overhead rate of 400% ($1,600,000 ÷ 400,000). However, in spite of this large increase in the rate, the total labor and overhead cost has been reduced by $700,000 from the figures shown in Example 1.

The results are summarized below:

	Example 1	*Example 2*	*Example 3*
Labor	$1,500,000	$1,200,000	$ 400,000
Overhead	1,200,00	1,200,000	1,600,000
Total	$2,700,000	$2,400,000	$2,000,000
Overhead Rate	80%	100%	400%

Unfortunately, because of the tendency of customers and procurement agencies to look at overhead rates as an indicator of cost, some companies "gimmick" their accounting systems to make the rate appear low even though they may be highly efficient producers. This practice frequently results in internal confusion and loss of accounting control. Continued insistence on low overhead rates may well result in generally higher costs because of the spread of accounting "gimmicks" and the resultant loss of control.

EFFECT OF SMALL ORDERS ON COSTS

Manufacturing people quite generally complain of the effect of small orders on costs. The complaint is based on the fact that it is necessary to spend a certain amount of time in preparing for a run. The preparation time is usually the same for a run of 100, for example, as it is for 10,000. A small run usually does not allow sufficient time for buildup of momentum to overcome the period of learning required for an operator to get into stride.

WHAT ONE COMPANY LEARNED
ABOUT THE SIZE OF ITS ORDERS

Because of complaints of the production people in one company that short runs were resulting in lowered efficiencies, an analysis of orders received over a two-month period was made. The total number of orders received was 298. These were broken down by product line as follows:

	Total orders	Large orders	Small orders	Small orders % of total
Product line A	18	15	3	17%
Product line B	12	6	6	50
Product line C	29	10	19	66
Product line D	132	41	91	69
Product line E	22	9	13	59
Product line F	19	13	6	32
Product line G	41	13	28	68
Product line H	25	15	10	40
Total	298	122	176	59%

The tabulation indicated that 59% of the orders were in the category of small orders amounting to less than $300. While $300 was considered as the breakpoint between large orders and small orders, this figure would vary by company and by the nature of the product. Further analysis of the 298 orders showed that large orders did not necessarily mean large shipments, although the entire order could be fabricated at one time. This is illustrated in the analysis of the number of shipments for the large orders and small orders.

Large orders (over $300)	No. of orders	No. of shipments	Ratio of shipments to orders
Product line A	15	28	
Product line B	6	9	
Product line C	10	18	
Product line D	41	76	
Product line E	9	13	
Product line F	13	21	
Product line G	13	23	
Product line H	15	35	
Total	122	223	1.8

Small orders (under $300)	No. of orders	No. of shipments	Ratio of shipments to orders
Product line A	3	4	
Product line B	6	7	
Product line C	19	20	
Product line D	91	107	
Product line E	13	13	

	No. of orders	No. of shipments	Ratio of shipments to orders
Product line F	6	6	
Product line G	28	30	
Product line H	10	11	
Total	176	198	1.1

All orders	No. of orders	No. of shipments	Ratio of shipments to orders
Product line A	18	32	
Product line B	12	16	
Product line C	29	38	
Product line D	132	183	
Product line E	22	26	
Product line F	19	27	
Product line G	41	53	
Product line H	25	46	
Total	298	421	1.4

Note that under the large order category 122 orders were shipped in 223 installments, a ratio of 1.8 shipments per order, which meant additional handling, storage, packaging, and paperwork. The ratio for small orders is 1.1, and the ratio for all orders is 1.4.

Because the larger orders had this large number of shipments per order, which had the effect of almost doubling the number of shipments, a further analysis was indicated. One order for 20,000 units with a selling price of approximately $60 per 1000 was broken down into releases as follows:

	Units	Sales Value
1/20	1,200	$ 75
2/3	3,500	220
2/10	5,000	314
2/17	6,000	377
2/24	3,000	188
3/1	1,300	82
	20,000	$1,256

A second order for 40,000 units selling for approximately $10 per 1000 was broken down into authorized releases as follows:

	Units	Sales Value
12/20	4,000	$ 38
1/3	9,000	86
1/10	9,000	87

1/17	9,000	86
1/24	9,000	87
	40,000	$384

Another order, this time under $300, was broken down as follows:

	Units	Sales Value
1/3	5,000	$22
1/10	800	3
1/17	800	3
1/24	800	3
1/31	4,900	21
2/28	800	3
3/7	800	3
3/14	200	1
	14,100	$59

The worst offenders were found to be two sister divisions within the same company. Although customers outside the company, who accounted for about half of the sales, ordered on a release basis, the size of the releases was substantially larger than releases authorized by the other divisions within the company. It was quite obvious that selling within the company was not profitable, particularly in view of the fact that interdivisional transfer prices were lower than prices charged to customers outside the company. The action taken in this case was to request that the ordering divisions stock the low unit cost parts on a modified min-max basis—ordering only when the inventory reached an order point which provided a sufficient backlog for the selling division to process economically. The savings from this study increased profits by 14%. Undoubtedly, a similar study in most companies would bear fruit.

COST REDUCTION THROUGH BETTER UTILIZATION OF EQUIPMENT

In an interview with James F. Gormeley, senior consultant on the Manufacturing Services Staff of the Raytheon Company, he emphasized the importance of optimum utilization of equipment. He expressed the view that since depreciation is not an out-of-pocket cost, efforts to reduce it are usually limited to accounting exercises which may be based more on tax considerations than "cost" considerations. He recommended reducing depreciation (and equipment rental) expenses to a cost-per-hour basis, to obtain an effective measurement of utilization.

Taking $30,000 as the cost of a large press, and assuming a 10-year depreciation, the tax basis of this cost would be $3,000 per year on a straight line depreciation scale. In reducing this cost to an hourly cost basis, certain assumptions must be made:

1. 200 working days per year
2. 6 working hours per day (machine working hours)

The hourly rate for the machine is then computed as follows:

$$\text{Machine cost per hour} = \frac{\$30{,}000}{(10 \text{ years}) (200 \text{ days}) (6 \text{ hours})} = \$2.50 \text{ per hr.}$$

A $2.50 hourly rate appears to be a minor element of cost since it is approximately the same as the direct labor cost per hour. However, at the time the purchase was justified, let us assume that a payback of two years was assumed. Then, the machine cost per hour becomes:

$$\text{Machine cost per hour} = \frac{\$30{,}000}{(2 \text{ years}) (200 \text{ days}) (6 \text{ hours})} = \$12.50 \text{ per hr.}$$

Now the hourly machine cost is substantially more expensive than direct labor. A relatively small improvement in utilization of the equipment will result in greater gains than if the direct labor were eliminated entirely. It becomes apparent that one method for reducing the machine cost per hour is to increase the number of "working days" per year. A 50-working-day-load would increase the cost to $50 per hour whereas a 250-working-day-load would reduce the rate to $10 per hour. This difference will not be an out-of-pocket saving but will certainly place a relative importance on a previously neglected aspect of machine loading efficiency.

Cost per hour can be decreased by increasing the number of hours which the machine is used. The table shown below makes a comparison of the hourly machine cost under six situations:

	One Shift Per Day	Two Shifts Per Day
50 days per year	$50.00	$25.00
200 days per year	$12.50	$ 6.25
250 days per year	$10.00	$ 5.00

While the accounting system does not normally develop this type of information on a routine basis, the financial group can, by this approach, make its management aware of potential cost reduction possibilities.

In embarking on a program of better machine utilization it is better not to attempt to evaluate every piece of equipment in the plant. It is better to start with the equipment having a significant investment and working down to the equipment representing a smaller investment. The hourly machine rates should be based on reasonable payback periods, actual working days of use, and actual working hours.

Machine utilization can be improved through elimination of the causes of downtime and other delays; increasing machine speeds wherever practical to do so; installing automatic devices to permit machines to operate when the operator is called away; disposal of excess capacity; discontinuance of manufacture of products requiring single purpose, lightly loaded equipment; purchasing outside capacity for lightly loaded equipment; and consolidating loads on lightly loaded equipment.

GOOD COST CONTROL REQUIRES FAMILIARITY WITH THE MANUFACTURING OPERATION

The answers to excessive costs and losses in profits cannot be determined entirely from the books of account. To resort to accounting information for such answers will prove fruitless in many instances unless accounting information is accompanied by a familiarity with the manufacturing operation. This was demonstrated in the case of one plastics molding company which found in the first quarter that $453,000 in sales resulted in a $15,000 loss. Sales for the same period in the preceding year had been $498,000 with profits of $118,000. The only information of significance available in the accounting records was that mold costs were substantially higher in the current year and that rework costs were excessive. This explanation fell far short of bringing to light the full picture.

Review of the manufacturing operations revealed that there were two separate plants located approximately 50 miles apart. The molding plant's production usually required some assembly work such as stamping of numbers and letters, fastening of spring clips, or combining molded parts with other assemblies. This assembly work, as well as the numbering and lettering, was performed at the second plant because the labor costs were lower in that area. In the period in which the profit had eroded, the same procedures were being followed but the type of product had changed somewhat. The major part of the production was molding of Lucite clock lenses at the molding plant and forwarding them to the lower labor cost plant for the stamping of the numerals. Because Lucite scratches very easily with the slightest pressure, it was necessary to wrap each lens in soft paper and then to cell pack to avoid friction in transportation. At the assembly plant it was necessary to unpack, stamp the numbers, and then repack the lenses for shipment to the customer.

The clock lenses were molded in a two-at-a-time mold. Because it is impossible to make two molds exactly the same, there was a slight difference in the curvature of the two molds. As a result, when the numerals were stamped on the face of the lens, the printing was light on some of the lenses where the curvature was different. The reason for this was not immediately known, but after a period of investigation the differences in mold curvature were determined to be the cause. This had resulted in thousands of costly rejects which had to be sorted by mold of origin and then cleaned and restamped. All this handling resulted in substantial rejects which had to be thrown away.

In view of the foregoing, it was quite obvious why profits had eroded. As a result of this finding, the stamping operations for the clock lens were transferred to the molding plant, even though the labor rates were higher. Now, as the lenses came off the press, they were routed directly to either of two stamping machines—each designed for the individual curvature of each lens. Upon completion of the stamping operation, the product was packaged for the first and only time and shipped directly to the customer.

Rejections and rework dropped substantially and the profit picture improved markedly. As a result of this experience, a closer look was taken at some of the other operations being transferred to the assembly plant to determine whether the lower labor rate was advantageous in all cases.

This example serves to illustrate the importance of familiarizing oneself with the manufacturing operations if cost reduction goals are to be achieved. Some individuals in management who are aware that they should know the manufacturing operation better, bemoan the fact that they are too busy and do not have the time. In many cases it is really not lack of time but frustration at not knowing where to start in the quest of this knowledge. Inasmuch as factory operations usually begin at an earlier hour than office activities, the individual who claims to be too busy would do well to arrive earlier and take a walk through the factory each morning—following the normal flow of work through production. A brief stop at each major department foreman's desk inquiring as to the most troublesome production problem will be most fruitful. The individual taking such a tour could perceive what raw materials were being received into the store rooms and whether large quantities of material were being rejected. A review of the shipping area would show which products were being readied for shipment. Following the production through the factory would provide information as to which departments were active and which were slow. Work-in-process stores areas would reveal the current line of products being produced. Analysis of the items at rework areas and scrap collection points would give a clue to problems in manufacture. Questions asked of the production people would be most revealing and would elicit the respect of the factory for such an individual who will take the trouble to inquire. *Effective cost control cannot be achieved in any other way.*

> Good cost controls cannot be developed and monitored from behind a desk—they require close collaboration with operating personnel and proximity to operating problems.

14

What Cost System Is Best

for Your Purposes?

> The cost system, to be effective, must reflect differences in product cost. When the product is highly customized a job cost system is mandatory.

Many accounting practitioners, accustomed to using standard costs and variances, tend to denegrate job costing. Some point up the advantages of management by exception available through use of predetermined standards and they relegate job costing to the days of the one-man management type of operation. Undeniably, standard process costing for standardized products (and standard direct costing) have many advantages that provide management with valuable analytical data.

Job costing is generally categorized as the cost system to use when customized products are involved. There is no question as to the correctness of this association. The problem is that customized products are frequently not treated as such. A good modern-day example is nuclear components used for constructing nuclear energy plants. When these are manufactured in the same facilities as the non-nuclear components of the same configuration and size, there is a tendency on the part of the accounting department to pattern the cost system to suit the dominant product. This means that if a standard cost system is used, the customized product will be improperly costed because of the use of predetermined costs that assume standard methods of manufacturing for each product.

Using nuclear components as an example, the balance of this chapter will explain why any customized product built in small quantities to very demanding specifications cannot be properly costed through use of predetermined standards—a characteristic of standard process costing.

WHY NUCLEAR COMPONENT COSTING IS DIFFERENT

Early components used for nuclear applications were built to the same specifications as those used for commercial purposes. Use of predetermined standards for both did not matter inasmuch as each was made in the same manner and to the same specifications.

Because of strong public fear of nuclear disaster the Atomic Energy Commission pressed all manufacturers of nuclear components to come up with specifications that would guard against any remote possibility of accidents. This pressure ultimately resulted in an expansion of the ASME (American Society of Mechanical Engineers) Code.

Manufacturers have found that the Code's requirements have not resulted in greater standardization, as some had expected; individual customers have established even stricter requirements than those called for in the Code. In effect, each nuclear component is a custom job. As one engineering executive of a company put it: "The Code sets minimum quality levels but this does not result in standardized manufacturing procedures because each customer modifies to suit his own needs. As a result, each manufacturer has become a specialty house."

IMPACT OF TIGHTER SPECIFICATIONS ON COSTS

The advent of these stricter requirements has naturally had a great impact on the amount of inspection, quality assurance, engineering, contract administration, and rework. Additionally, the manufacturing cycle is greatly lengthened because of the many interruptions for inspection and the need for rework to meet Code and customer requirements. Yet the manufacturers of these components are mainly commercial concerns, the bulk of whose products require no such care in manufacture. Nuclear versions of these components posed all the problems associated with manufacturing to extremely close tolerances, whereas the manufacturers were accustomed to dealing with relatively loose tolerances. This problem situation is spreading to more and more manufacturers as more and more emphasis is put on nuclear energy

Inspection. The cost of inspection for nuclear components is more than double that required for commercial types. There can be as many as 900 inspection, hold, verification and approval points as illustrated in Exhibit 14-1 for one of the nuclear products. This exhibit summarizes the requirements of a large customer of one of the nuclear component manufacturing companies.

Manufacturing interruption. The impact of increased inspection, not only by the manufacturer's personnel, but also by the customer representatives and third party inspectors, results in production delays and consequently a much longer manufacturing cycle during which costs keep increasing and investment is tied up.

Quality Assurance. In the manufacture of commercial type components the quality function does not go much beyond the inspection stage. With the more

	MANU-FACTURER	CUSTOMER	CODE	TOTAL
Review of Procedures/				
Drawings	100	55		155
Purchase Orders	15			15
Certifications (Chemical and Physical Characteristics)				
Body	35	35	35	105
Bonnet	35	35	35	105
Disc	25	25	25	75
Seats	15	15		30
Bushing	10	10		20
Bolting	15	15	15	45
Other	30	30		60
	165	165	110	440
Data Book	1	1	1	3
Inspection at Vendor				
Body	8	8		16
Bonnet	8	8		16
Disc	16	16		32
Seats	16	16		32
Bolting	5	5		10
Other	2	2		4
	55	55		110
Inspection in Process				
Body	22	21	16	59
Bonnet	17	16	11	44
Disc	9	8	4	21
Seats	7	6		13
Bushing	4	3		7
Other	30	1	1	32
	89	55	32	176
GRAND TOTAL	425	331	143	899

NOTES:
    1) Utility has option to review, witness, verify and approve any of the
       above categories.
    2) Figures do not include waivers or rejected material notices.

Exhibit 14-1

demanding requirement for Code adherence in making nuclear components, the quality assurance function must relate to the total controlled manufacturing system. To do this, Quality Assurance must take responsibility for:

- audit and control of suppliers to assure conformance to code and contract requirements.
- internal training of inspection personnel.

- audit and control of internal departments for conformance to code and contract requirements.
- control of internal quality standards.
- development and monitoring of programs for calibration of measuring equipment.
- control of quality documentation.

The opinion expressed by several manufacturers is that the net effect on cost of assuring conformance can more than triple the cost of the quality function.

Engineering. Engineering must also expand its role. It must go far beyond the relatively simple requirements of commercial type components. In commercial types the customer can order by a simple designation such as catalog number. But when a nuclear version is being ordered, the customer must provide a design specification along with his order for each different type. Accordingly, for each and every contract, engineering must:

- design the end product according to the design specifications that were furnished.
- certify that the design meets code and contract requirements.
- spell out specifications for purchase of material by customer order.
- make detail drawings for the shop based on customer design specifications and write instructions.
- write test procedures.
- coordinate customer requirements with manufacturing procedures.

According to industry engineers, engineering costs in a nuclear product (component) can be expected to be double or triple the cost of the commercial version.

Contract Administration. In any product in which manufacturing procedures are spelled out in great detail and documentation for each step is required, a close liaison must be maintained between the manufacturer and the customer. This liaison goes much further than the conventional customer service function. It is called contract administration and has the following requirements:

- act as contact with the customer—providing the necessary liaison on all matters relating to the contract.
- monitor status of the job and prepare progress reports.
- review all correspondence relating to the contract.
- furnish customer with any information required by him.
- monitor witness inspection dates.
- close out orders and finalize documentation.

Rework. in a commercial type, rework would normally be considered as overhead. In many cases, the parts would be scrapped rather than investing additional labor and overhead in salvage. In nuclear production, rework is an unavoidable cost and should be considered as direct rather than overhead.

Mixed Production. Companies manufacturing the commercial type product in the same facility that is used for making nuclear products can expect to find costs of the commercial type increasing. This is due to the normal tendency to upgrade lower graded products when two disparate types are being manufactured.

The foregoing are some of the factors that will greatly impact the need for more definitive costs—particularly when commercial and nuclear types are being made in the same facility. Costs that have traditionally been classified as indirect must now be considered as direct. The "traditional" definition of what is direct and what is indirect must be abandoned in favor of a definition that will recognize costs that are identifiable and supportable as direct charges to each contract. What these costs are and how they should be measured will be the subject of the sections that follow.

IDENTIFYING COSTS DIRECTLY WITH THE CONTRACT

It has been traditional in some valve manufacturing companies to consider as overhead such items as packing, gaskets, bolting, welding material, purchased services, incoming freight, shipping preparation, engineering/drafting, rework and other costs. In light of the more demanding requirements in nuclear work, these costs have increased greatly in magnitude. They can also vary quite radically from one contract to another. Because of such variations, inclusion of these costs in the overhead rate could result in allocations to contracts that are quite different from reality. The following examples are illustrative of this.

One executive had strong feelings against treating purchased services as an overhead expense. He felt that purchased services, particularly as they related to foundry castings, should be considered as material cost. His comment was:

> Material costs are appreciably higher due primarily to the software or documentation that must be provided for the nuclear class material. Not only is more non-destructive testing required, but also the documentation to substantiate it is extensive. A foundry, for example, must provide heat treatment procedures of how castings will be processed; charts of the temperature and time of heat treatment are required; calibration records of the temperature-recording equipment must be furnished; complete radiographic procedures, qualifications and film packages are called for and other procedures or certifications of additional nondestructive testing, such as magnetic, particle or ultra-sonic testing, are required.

Another executive who observed that the cost of a nuclear product (component) can be as much as four times that of the same type for commercial applications made the following comment:[1]

> A large difference occurs during final assembly, test, inspection, and preparation for shipment. We found that over thirty additional hours were spent in completing the nuclear valves. The extra time went into such items as additional particle tests inspection of finished surfaces for a customer's inspector, additional time required by the Q.C.

[1]Depending upon the type, a nuclear component can cost two to ten times as much as its commercial counterpart.

Department to prepare a "Record Package" for the customer, special cleaning, packaging and preparation for shipment, and more complex test and inspection requirements. Many of these extras are in cost areas that may be concealed in a general overhead account, but when they are identified and studied, they show a substantial number of extra hours which we feel should be charged directly against a nuclear order.

A discussion of the various costs that should be identified more specifically follows:

Supply Type Items. In most accounting systems items of relatively small value are expensed at time of purchase and charged into an overhead account. An allowance is provided for these items through application of the overhead rate.

This is an acceptable expedient when items like a nut cost only five cents each, gasket material only a few cents per sheet, and welding material so little that it can be practically ignored. Since the aggregate cost of "supply type" expenses like the foregoing can amount to as much as $1,500 for a nuclear valve, it is highly desirable that such items be considered to be direct material and charged directly to the product on which used.

Incoming Freight. In some companies, incoming freight is treated as an overhead expense. When manufacturers were, by and large, making castings in their own foundries, incoming freight was not as substantial an item as it is now when many companies purchase their castings from outside foundries. If these higher costs are included in overhead as in the past, and allocated to the various products on the basis of an overhead rate applied to direct labor, the amount charged to individual items could be greatly distorted. This distortion occurs because the labor content in a valve does not correctly reflect the material content. Note in Exhibit 14-2 that the line representing material cost in the various sizes is quite different in slope than the line representing labor cost.[2]

A more accurate approach would be to identify the amount of incoming freight actually incurred for each casting and to add this amount to the cost of the casting as material.

Rework. The requirement for non-destructive examinations means that certain additional operations will need to be performed when defects are found. These are:

- gouging
- welding
- grinding
- hand dressing
- x-ray (if defects still present, cycle starts again)
- heat treat
- remachining
- inspection

---

[2]The plottings in Exhibit 14-2 are made to a semi-logarithmic scale. A line on such a scale reflects percentage, rather than absolute dollar changes.

COST COMPARISON

LABOR/OVERHEAD CONTENT VERSUS BASE MATERIAL FOR THE

600# CS PRESSURE SEAL VALVES

COST PER UNIT

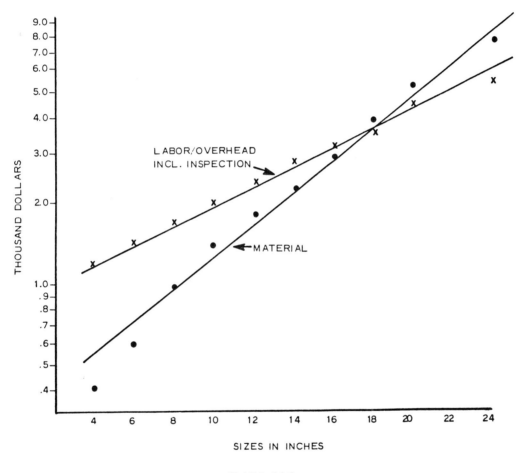

Exhibit 14-2

Companies that include rework as part of overhead are allocating such costs to the various valves on the basis of the amount of direct labor required to make the valve. Obviously, when the rework operations can be specifically identified with the valve on which they are being performed, it would be more accurate to have the individuals doing the work charge their time to the specific component and charge it as direct labor.

Special Tooling, Fixtures, and Patterns. The cost of these items could have a wide range. Special tooling could cost as much as $18,000 and patterns and fixtures could cost as much as $5,000. Since these items are usually made for a specific item the cost should, like material, be charged directly to that item rather than spreading such costs through an overhead rate. It is conceivable that fixtures, tooling and patterns could be used for a subsequent order. The method of amortizing such costs against orders is a separate matter, the treatment of which depends upon the negotiations made with the customer.

Shipping Costs. Traditionally, some companies consider shipping to be part of the selling group of expenses, rather than identifying them as part of the manufacturing cost. Before the advent of the nuclear types, the commercial versions could be loaded on trucks with little or no protective packing so that shipping cost was merely a handling expense.

This is no longer the case with nuclear components, for example, which must be crated to protect the weld end and the operating mechanisms. The crating and bagging of a large nuclear component could amount to as much as $2,500. The operations required to prepare the product for shipment should be identified as direct labor and charged to the specific order.

Engineering/Drafting. The concept of product engineering has been expanded greatly with the introduction of nuclear products. The function now includes design, writing instructions to the shop and the purchasing department, preparing detail drawings, writing test procedures and coordinating with the customer. Engineering/drafting effort can start as much as a year before the shop begins to build the product.

Because of the foregoing factors, and in the interest of matching costs with revenues, engineering—as well as other related items—must be charged as direct costs when incurred. Application of such costs through a manufacturing overhead rate (or a G & A rate) rather than a direct charge, will not yield correct product costs. Take the case of a customer ordering two or more nuclear components of the same type while another customer orders the same number but each of a different type. Application of this cost through an overhead rate would overstate the cost of engineering/drafting to the first customer and understate the second.

The proper way of charging this function to the product is to identify the charges as direct costs to the specific product. Engineering/drafting, then, would become direct labor to which the engineering overhead rate would be applied. The same principal would apply to Quality Assurance.

If there are individuals in a company working on both commercial and nuclear components who find it impractical to charge their time to specific products, a nuclear material buyer, for example, it may be preferable to develop a nuclear overhead rate applied to nuclear direct labor.

Contracts Administration. Contract administration is a liaison function in which the administrator or project manager acts as a coordinator between the customer and the company. He must review all correspondence, monitor the status of the job, advise the customer of witness inspection dates, close out the orders and finalize the documentation.

The effort required for each contract is not likely to vary with the amount of shop labor required to make the product, so this expense should not be allocated through an overhead rate; it should be considered as a direct charge supported by time charges.

Those nuclear component manufacturing companies that do not have a Contracts Administration group must perform the function nonetheless. Undoubtedly the work is being performed by several individuals in such departments as production control, purchasing, accounting or some other service department. If so, then the cost of the function is most likely being included in the product through application of the overhead or G & A rate—causing distortions. The Contracts Administration function, whether a separate department or not, must recognize the amount of cost incurred against each contract and must be so charged to assure proper costing.

WHICH COST SYSTEM IS CORRECT?

There is no pat answer to this question. The accounting system must adapt to the state of technology. When a product is new, unit volume small, and changes frequent, a job cost system is the most appropriate—it provides the means for identifying each cost as it relates to the specific job.

Standard Versus Custom Engineered Valves. As certain products became standardized in past years, those companies that specialized in these types quite correctly adopted a standard cost system of accounting. Standard costs were predetermined; these became the cost of production and the inventory values from which variances were calculated.

Predetermined Standard Costs Versus Job Costing. However, when the complexity and proliferation of specifications expand, as they did for nuclear plant requirements—the various components can no longer be considered to be standard. Each one can be quite different in its specifications—each customer buying the same component can have different requirements for it. Also, purchases are low in terms of units purchased. Since the nuclear component is generally not a standardized product, then standard costs cannot be used by costing—a job costing system accumulating actual costs is mandatory. It is entirely possible that as nuclear plant production becomes standardized, nuclear components too will achieve a greater degree of standardization at some future time.[3]

Companies making standard type components who then add some nuclear components to their line are in the most vulnerable position when it comes to proper costing; they are not likely to change their cost system to accommodate the few nuclear items that have just been added to the line. Such costs as engineering, quality assurance, and contract administration, which are substantially larger for nuclear

---

[3] See Engineering News Record dated July 26, 1973, page 11, entitled: "Utility Group Orders Six Identical Nuclear Units."

products, are likely to be included in the overhead rate and allocated on the basis of direct labor or in the general and administrative rate.

Thus, if nuclear items make up only 10% of the business, the additional costs applicable to this 10% will be spread over all products. The excess costs charged to the commercial types will probably not be noticed, but the cost of the nuclear will appear to be substantially lower than the true cost. Because the undercosted nuclear components will appear to be highly profitable, management will be encouraged to bring in more such business. As the proportion of nuclear business increases, the costing inadequacies of the standard cost system will become evident as the overcosted commercial types indicate lower and lower profitability. This situation bears out the observation made by one executive who states:

> We continued to use standard costs to value our castings after we sold out our standard line. When non-destructive examinations became a larger and larger factor on nuclear castings, our variances from standard became correspondingly larger. The variances identified the excess cost all right, but they didn't tell us what product the variances should be charged to. We considered building the non-destructive examination costs into the standards since we recognized this was part of the material cost, but gave up the idea because of the infinite number of standards we would have had to keep in file.
>
> After this experience, we gave up on standard costing of nuclear products and went to job costing.

Another company executive had this to say:

> A custom engineered product produced in a manufacturing system designed for standardized volume production creates costing problems which need far more attention than management generally gives.

Format for Accumulating Job Costs. The conventional job order cost system used by many companies accumulates three categories of cost. These are:

Material
Direct Labor
Overhead (usually applied on direct labor)

Under this conventional format, such costs as engineering/drafting, quality assurance and rework would be included in overhead. Since overhead is usually applied to products through a departmental overhead rate based on direct labor, these costs are distributed in proportion to the amount of labor contained in the various products.

When custom engineered products such as nuclear components are made in the same facilities as standard products, use of this conventional format will result in the spreading of too much overhead to the standard products, which properly belongs with the custom engineered items.

More and more companies dealing in government contract work have added an additional category called "Direct Charges" to identify such costs as special tooling or special equipment purchased for a specific job. This does not, however, provide for specific direct charging of such costs as engineering/drafting and quality assurance if these are left in the overhead category.

A more appropriate format would be one that recognizes as direct cost items like the following:

Engineering/drafting
Quality Assurance
Rework

An example of such a format in use by a company making both nuclear and high specification non-nuclear products is shown below:

	BREAKDOWN OF HOURS			BREAKDOWN OF DOLLARS		
	Budgeted Hours	Actual Hours To Date	Estimated Hours to Complete	Budgeted Dollars	Actual Dollars To Date	Estimated Dollars to Complete
Labor and Overhead	1,655	—	1,655	$ 27,608	$ —	$ 27,608
Rework	279	—	279	4,655	—	4,655
Material	—	—	—	110,190	—	110,190
Engineering	264	214	50	1,588	3,110	—
Drafting	250	293	—	1,504	2,819	—
Direct Charges	—	—	—	12,875	23,108	—
TOTAL	2,448	507	1,984	$158,420	$29,037	$142,453

Estimate to Complete. The budgeted hours and budgeted dollars are synonymous with "estimated," the budget being based on the original estimate used to establish the selling price. The estimated hours and estimated dollars to complete are represented by the difference between the actual accumulated hours and dollars and the cumulative budgeted hours and dollars.

In the event that a customer requests a change after negotiations have been completed, the new estimated hours and dollars would be added (or subtracted) to arrive at an updated estimate. Performance against this latest estimate is an important measure and should be monitored closely. It is not enough to simply compare actual costs with the estimate because mere incurrence of costs does not assure accomplishment. What is needed is an estimate of the hours and dollars required to complete the job.

This "estimate to complete" should be added to the costs incurred to date. The resulting total should then be compared with the estimate to determine whether the job will be completed within budget or if there will be an overrun.

This should be a monthly procedure. On critical jobs it may be necessary to do this weekly.

Labor and Overhead. Although many companies prefer to record direct labor separately from overhead, this company prefers to combine these two elements of cost. Either approach is acceptable. Inspection is included as direct labor and overhead is applied in the same manner as it is for all other direct labor operations. Overhead rates are established separately for the machining, welding and assembly and test operations.

Rework. Rework, which in a standard product would normally be considered as an overhead item, is properly recorded as a direct cost chargeable with overhead directly to the specific job.

Material. This includes not only the cost of castings, operators, bolting and welding material; it also includes the incoming freight and cost of upgrading.

Engineering and Drafting. These two categories of cost go hand in hand since drafting supports the engineering. The illustrative job cost format shown previously indicates a fair sized expenditure for engineering and drafting even before any actual production has begun. This is a realistic expectation and it points up that this type of expenditure is incurred before any labor operations have been performed. This also points up the fallacy of including engineering/drafting in the overhead rate since there would then be no such cost charged against the job until labor operations have been performed on the product. In the event of a customer cancellation in the early stages of a job, there would be no data to support these early charges.

This company includes its quality assurance costs in the engineering category. The engineering/drafting and quality assurance costs include overhead of these functions as well as the directly identifiable charges.

Direct Charges. These include such items of cost as tooling, patterns and other special equipment, as well as contracts administration.

REASONS FOR DEFICIENT COST ESTIMATES

The importance of good product costing for custom engineered products cannot be overemphasized. Some of the reasons for deficient cost estimates are:

- arbitrary costing through use of predetermined standards
- failure to take into account cost escalation factors
- requests for changes
- hasty estimating

Arbitrary Costing. Standardized products can be costed at predetermined standards with a reasonable degree of accuracy. Customer engineered items such as nuclear components cannot be costed through use of predetermined standards because of the many variations and differences in customer requirements that make it impractical to establish individual standards for all the possible combinations. Nor does the answer lie in "guesstimated token adders" that are used to adjust a predetermined standard to arrive at an actual cost. (If adders are used, there must be assurance that the costs they represent will be fully absorbed.) Consequently, custom engineered products must be costed through a system that will identify the actual costs, as well as the budget, for each job (see "Format for accumulating job costs" in preceding section). Availability of the actual costs, correctly compiled, will provide a basis for monitoring performance as well as providing feedback on the correctness of the estimates.

Cost Escalation on Future Commitments. Cost estimates that may be correct at the time they are prepared could become very inaccurate if escalation factors are not taken into account to provide for cost increases with the passage of time. This is important when one considers how many commitments are made for delivery a year or more hence—during which inflationary cost factors continue with unrelenting pressure.

Requests for Changes. Requests for changes are frequently accepted from the customer with insufficient consideration of the impact of such a change in terms of additional out-of-pocket costs or the extended time during which inventory investment is tied up. Requests for changes should be handled in the same manner followed in making all cost estimates. The amount of additional cost required to comply with the change should be known to management as soon after receipt of the request as possible.

Hasty Estimating. There is no better way to assure faulty cost estimates than to make them in haste to meet an unreasonable deadline. One way to assure better utilization of a limited time allowance (though every effort should be made to obtain a reasonable amount of time) is for extra copies of the customer's order to be made available for purposes of obtaining, simultaneously, the various segments of information that are required in putting together an estimate. Availability of reliable history on past jobs can also be very helpful in cutting time requirements for making cost estimates.

VERIFICATION OF PRODUCT COST ESTIMATES—BUILDING THE HISTORY

A cost system provides the basis for regular accumulation of costs. In the accumulation process the system must correctly reflect actual product costs that can be used to verify the correctness of the cost estimates. These can be summarized in two basic reports illustrated in Exhibit 14-3:

• Unit costs of orders shipped
• Cost history record

These reports include the following data:

Unit Costs of Orders Shipped. This is a unit cost breakdown by individual nuclear valves that have been sold during the period. The various elements of material, labor and overhead cost, tooling and non-manufacturing direct charges are shown on a per unit basis. Each of these costs is compared with the original estimate that was made at

COST HISTORY RECORD
ALTERNATIVE I

UNIT COSTS OF ORDERS SHIPPED

ORDER NO.	QUAN.	TOTAL MATERIAL COST						TOOLING AND PATTERNS	TOTAL LABOR AND OVERHEAD				TOTAL MFG. COST	SELLING PRICE	GROSS PROFIT %	NON-MFG. DIRECT CHARGES
		BODY	BONNET	DISC.	OPERATOR	OTHER	TOTAL		MACHINING	WELDING	ASSEMBLY AND TEST	TOTAL				
4" 300# S.S.																
ACTUAL 22113-11	2	$327	$268	$54	$966	$235	$1,850	$24	$617	$318	$299	$1,234	$3,108	$5,044	38.4%	$410
ESTIMATE	2	620	460	35	834	213	2,162	—	721	350	371	1,442	3,604	5,044	28.5	580
12" 900# Ca. St.																
ACTUAL 26126-12	1	3,123	991	165	3,904	1,341	9,524	2,140	3,174	1,597	1,578	6,349	18,013	16,602	(8.5)	1,040
ESTIMATE	1	2,138	874	126	2,004	1,027	6,169	2,515	2,056	1,019	1,037	4,112	12,796	16,602	22.9	796
20" 150# Ca. St.																
ACTUAL 23957-15	2	1,288	154	229	—	376	2,047	15	682	362	320	1,364	3,426	5,910	42.0	804
ESTIMATE	5	1,015	148	297	—	260	1,720	—	607	365	342	1,314	3,034	5,910	48.7	760
30" 150# Ca. St.																
ACTUAL 24628-16	2	2,943	349	441	—	688	4,421	—	1,474	716	757	2,947	7,368	20,200	63.5	1,149
ESTIMATE	2	4,984	300	501	—	861	6,646	5,028	2,215	1,097	1,119	4,431	16,105	20,200	20.3	1,296

COST HISTORY RECORD
UNIT COST

PRODUCT ___20" 150# GATE VALVE___

SHOP ORDER #	QUAN.	MATERIAL COST						HOURS					TOTAL MFG. COST	SALES PRICE	GROSS PROFIT	NON-MFG. DIRECT CHARGES
		BODY	BONNET	DISC.	OPERATOR	OTHER	TOTAL MATERIAL	UPGRADE	MACHINE SHOP	WELD	ASSEMBLY	TOTAL HOURS				
21428-16	3	$1,285	$163	$246	—	$346	$2,040	3	57	14	21	95	$3,521	$5,910	$2,389	$1,519
21585-17	2	1,273	162	241	—	345	2,021	4	58	12	18	92	3,502	5,910	2,408	1,307
23561-14	2	1,311	189	220	—	298	2,018	5	71	29	22	127	3,982	5,910	1,928	1,275
23957-15	5	1,288	154	229	—	376	2,047	4	63	16	21	104	3,426	5,910	2,484	804

Exhibit 14-3

the time the item was quoted to the customer. A comparison is also made of the total manufacturing cost with the selling price. This report also provides clues as to where further analysis is required. Illustrative of this is the 12″ 900# Carbon Steel valve for which the actual cost of the body was $3,123 while the original estimate called for $2,138. The difference of $985 in excess costs is explained as follows:

	Estimate	Actual	Excess Costs
Body weight	1450 #	1810 #	
Cost of body	$1,888	$2,444	$556
Heat charts	–	15	15
Charpy tests	–	45	45
Film	200	455	255
Rough machine	50	164	114
Total	$2,138	$3,123	$985

The estimate, which was incorrectly made, assumed that an elliptically shaped body would be used. Since a round shape was called for, more pounds of material were required. These were purchased at a higher cost per pound than was estimated. In addition, certain other costs listed above were not recognized or were understated.

Companies that fail to compare actual costs with the original estimate are missing an important step in the process of management control.

Cost History Record. This is also a unit cost analysis which embodies most of the elements shown above. There are two differences, however.

- This history record recasts the actual valve costs to show the cost history of all similar items on a single document.
- In place of the labor and overhead costs which are shown on the "Unit Costs of Orders Shipped," this record shows the labor hours in the various departments. Hours are preferable in making comparisons of jobs at different periods of time because they eliminate the inflationary effects of wage increases.

The cost history record illustrated in Exhibit 14-3 summarizes the elements of cost on a single sheet for an entire valve.

There is also an alternative method that breaks down the elements for each of the major parts making up a valve. For example, the material, labor and overhead are broken down for each of the major parts such as body, bonnet and disc. This is illustrated in Exhibit 14-4.

Either method provides the kind of information required to verify the accuracy of estimates. In addition to this verification, there are other advantages.

1. Future estimating will be improved.

COST HISTORY RECORD
ALTERNATIVE 2

SUMMARY — DESCRIPTION: 2" GATE VALVE

MO	YEAR	ORDER NO.	CUSTOMER	STANDARD	ACTUAL	UNITS SOLD PRICE
9	7X	27327-18	JC P EL		49,600 00	56,718.00
9	7X	27327-19			51,241 80	56,718.00
10	7X	26499-31			44,369 67	56,718.00
12	7X	29320-32			50,394 92	56,718.00
12	7X	29320-33			51,271 31	56,718.00

COST HISTORY RECORD — ALL OTHER

DATE	ORDER NO.	QUAN.	QUAN. MADE	ALLOY	MATERIAL	DIRECT LABOR	BURDEN	TOTAL COST
						152	1,142 62	9,434 23

COST HISTORY RECORD — STEMS

DATE	ORDER NO.	QUAN.	QUAN. MADE	ALLOY	MATERIAL	DIRECT LABOR	BURDEN	TOTAL COST
				CB	302 80	150 83	504 37	958 00

COST HISTORY RECORD — DISCS

DATE	ORDER NO.	QUAN.	QUAN. MADE	ALLOY	MATERIAL	DIRECT LABOR	BURDEN	TOTAL COST
9-7X	27327-18		1	CP	2,354 16	656 03	2,133 10	5,143 29
9-7X	27327-19		1	CP	2,324 75	345 75	1,138 61	3,808 41

COST HISTORY RECORD — BONNETS

DATE	ORDER NO.	QUAN.	QUAN. MADE	ALLOY	MATERIAL	DIRECT LABOR	BURDEN	TOTAL COST
9-7X	27327-18		1	CP	6,255 06	391 74	1,235 20	7,882 00
9-7X	27327-19		1	CP	6,262 43	446 53	1,418 73	8,127 69
								7,538 08

COST HISTORY RECORD — BODY ASSEMBLIES

DATE	ORDER NO.	QUAN.	QUAN. MADE	ALLOY	MATERIAL	DIRECT LABOR	BURDEN	TOTAL COST
9-7X	27327-18		1	CP	22,702 97	853 79	2,625 72	26,182 48
9-7X	27327-19		1	CP	22,721 04	1,018 53	3,045 35	26,784 92
10-7X	28499-31		1	CP	21,991 74	1,562 40	5,374 07	28,928 21
12-7X	29320-32		1	CP	22,001 64	1,616 66	5,639 88	29,258 18
12-7X	29320-33		1	CP	24,918 06	821 59	2,827 44	28,567 09

268

Exhibit 14-4

2. These records develop history which will provide a useful basis for making estimates as well as developing standards for the future. Once these standards have been developed, they can be used as a measure of performance as the valve progresses through the operations.
3. Visibility is given to the profitability of different jobs. Profitability trends as well as cost trends will be more clearly evident.

SUMMARY

Costs such as engineering, quality and rework, which are normally part of overhead and applied through an overhead rate based on direct labor, cannot be allocated in the conventional manner when nuclear components are being made. Costs of this type that are substantially greater for nuclear components must be excluded from the overhead rate and applied to the jobs on a "direct charge" basis in much the same manner as material is identified by job. Companies with sophisticated systems in which predetermined standards are used are particularly vulnerable to cost distortion.

When improper accounting procedures are being followed there is every likelihood that these deficiencies will be carried over into the estimating process. For this reason, the following basic guidelines should be followed:

1. The cost system must provide for direct charging of major costs that are identifiable with a job.
2. When "adders" are used to adjust for differences among jobs because direct charging is impractical, these adders must be tested to assure that the costs they represent will be recovered in the normal volume of business.
3. Estimates must provide for inflationary factors during periods of rising prices. The time phasing of such escalation must be explicitly stated and firmly enforced.
4. The cost impact of all engineering changes must be estimated in the same manner as if a new job were being estimated.
5. The cost system must go "full circle" to provide feedback through a comparison of actual costs with the original cost estimate used for quoting the job.

The tighter specifications called for in nuclear components, the rigid documentation requirements and the multiplicity of different specifications for the same product ordered by different companies add up to substantially higher costs for nuclear components than for their commercial counterparts. The adequacy of a cost system is not measured by its degree of sophistication but by its ability to identify these product cost differences and to relate them to the cost estimate.

In customized work, cost estimating is an important prerequisite to establishing a selling price. After the job has been accepted, it is equally important that comparisons be made of actual costs with the estimates.

15

Sharpening Cost Responsibilities

> Close intermingling of costs for an entire product division makes it difficult for either the sales manager or manufacturing manager to accept responsibility for the financial results.

Many companies reaching post-war peaks of expansion found that they had expanded beyond their ability to finance their varied activities. Managements, realizing that a policy of retrenchment and close controls must be adopted, took a critical look at the conventional forms in which budgetary controls and income statements were being used. Many found that the close intermingling of costs for an entire product division made it difficult for either the sales manager or manufacturing manager willingly to accept responsibility for the financial results. In the event of a poor showing, each could blame the other and neither could be pinned down.

This chapter describes how financial responsibility and control can be pinpointed, how the income statement can reflect these responsibilities, and how budgets can be established for use in forecasting and control.

MAPPING OUT THE NEW ORGANIZATION

Under a functional responsibility, there is a complete separation of the manufacturing, sales, and engineering functions. This permits a top manufacturing man to head up all manufacturing within a homogeneous group of products. It likewise permits a strong sales personality, who might be devoid of manufacturing know-how, to spark the selling effort without being concerned directly with the problems of manufacturing or engineering the product. Such an arrangement would also permit the research and development group to spread its know-how over all products and thus relieve the manufacturing staff of all engineering problems except those pertaining directly to production.

Under this arrangement, the manufacturing manager would base his production schedules on sales forecasts received from the sales division. Manufacturing would sell to Sales at an agreed-on price which, besides covering the cost of material, labor and overhead, must also include in its overhead charge an amount to cover interest on investment. This is a monthly percentage of the total cost of fixed assets and inventories used in manufacturing, based on the current prime rate. Finished goods would not be included in the base as they would become the property of the sales division immediately upon completion.

The sales division would be broken down by product managers—one for each group of products requiring a similar type of effort. Transfers from Manufacturing become finished goods in the sales division and cost of sales on the Sales income statement as they are sold. The sales division's income statement picks up the usual deductions and allowances, selling expenses, advertising, commissions, and freight. In addition, it is charged for the development engineering based on engineering development orders. Finally, interest on investment is provided for. Here, as in manufacturing, the rate charged is the current prime rate each month for receivables and finished inventories. Interest on investment is a means of distributing the corporate office costs. The advantage of this method is that it places an incentive on reduction of inventories. The corporate office, in turn, must hold its costs below the aggregate of interest charges made to all the divisions.

THE INCOME STATEMENT

In preparing the operating statement at month-end, the manufacturing and sales operating costs are placed side by side in order to show the combined results for each product. Thus the income statement will show a profit which reflects the volume of orders released to the manufacturing group. If this volume is greater or less than that needed for complete absorption of the fixed costs of manufacturing, the profit will be increased or decreased accordingly, through allocation of over- and under-absorbed overhead. This emphasizes the sales division's responsibility to keep the factory loaded. The method of distributing the over- or under-absorbed overhead is demonstrated below:

	Labor in Production Schedule	Labor Incurred	Difference	Difference X fixed Ovhd. Rate
Product A	$ 300,000	$300,000	–0–	–0–
Product B	300,000	100,000	(200,000)	(150,000)
Product C	100,000	50,000	(50,000)	(37,500)
Product D	100,000	150,000	50,000	37,500
Product E	200,000	200,000	–0–	–0–
	$1,000,000	$800,000	(200,000)	(150,000)

THE ANNUAL BUDGET

Initially, in preparing the budget for the coming year, each division prepares annual figures only. Working with annual amounts reduces the work substantially and cuts down the time required for preparation. The budget should be reviewed carefully to determine whether the return on investment in inventories and fixed assets is within satisfactory limits. The divisional budgets are consolidated on an overall company basis to determine whether the total company plan for the new year meets with management's approval.

SALES ESTIMATES—THE STARTING POINT

Each product manager collects from his staff a realistic estimate of the sales which can be anticipated for the subsequent year. The pressure for realism is self-generated because the sales group realizes that an over-optimistic forecast bears the penalty of a corresponding amount of under-absorbed overhead. On the other hand, too conservative an estimate will cause the overhead rates used in transfer prices to be too high, resulting in an inaccurate cost-of-sales ratio during the coming year.

Each product manager's sales estimate made up for the total year is then broken down by months on the product's normal seasonal pattern adjusted for known factors.

THE MANUFACTURING DIVISION BUDGET

As soon as sales estimates are approved, they are forwarded to the manufacturing division. The production control and methods departments evaluate the sales figures in terms of material and labor needed to produce each product. With these two elements of cost determined, overhead requirements are then calculated. In calculating overhead, individual budgets are prepared for each of the centers, i.e., production control, purchasing, accounting, assembly, quality control, etc. These are consolidated for a total manufacturing budget and overhead rates are then determined.

THE SALES DIVISION BUDGET

Having established its annual sales level forecast by products, and knowing the cost of transfers made to it by manufacturing, the sales division calculates various other costs and deductions (appearing on the income statement in Figure 15-1). Engineering expense is estimated jointly by the sales division and the research and development division after evaluation of the plans for the coming year.

FORECASTING AND CONTROL

The figures in *Exhibit 15-2* are the basis for forecasting overhead costs for various annual and monthly levels of activity. These are prepared in columnar form similar to that of *Exhibits 15-3 and 15-4.*

PRODUCT G

PROFIT-AND-LOSS STATEMENT

	Manufacturing Division	Sales Division	Interdiv. Elimination	Combined Result
Gross Sales	$	$200,000	$	$200,000
Less Returns		6,000.		6,000
Net Sales	150,000	194,000	150,000	194,000

	Manufacturing Division	Sales Division	Interdiv. Elimination	Combined Result
Cost of Sales				
Material	74,000	76,000	74,000	76,000
Labor	30,000	32,000	30,000	32,000
Overhead	36,000	37,000	36,000	37,000
Total Cost of Sales	140,000	145,000	140,000	145,000
Overhead Incurred	36,000			36,000
Overhead Absorbed	30,000			30,000
(Over) or Under-absorbed	6,000			6,000
Distribution Costs				
Selling Expenses		15,000		15,000
Advertising Expenses		1,000		1,000
Commissions Paid Out		2,000		2,000
Freight Out		500		500
Total Distribution Costs		18,500		18,500
Engineering Expense		12,000		12,000
Division Profit or Loss	4,000	18,500	10,000	12,500
Interest on Investment	5,000	8,000		13,000
Company Profit or Loss	(1,000)	10,500	10,000	(500)

Exhibit 15-1

Exhibit 15-3 (annual basis) gives management the overhead costs for nine levels of activity ranging from $2,100,000 to $4,500,000 in direct labor annually. This is a wide range, but it dramatizes the impact of volume on costs in a manner similar to that of a breakeven chart (which would start at zero activity and cover a much wider range).

Exhibit 15-4 has been prepared in a similar manner except that the figures cover a four-week period. In comparing the actual overhead costs for the month with the allowable costs shown for the applicable direct labor level, management has a simple and readily understandable basis for control.

Division: Equipment Manufacturing
Department: Department A

	Total Annual Cost	Fixed	Variable	Var. % of D. L.*
Salaries and Overtime	$271,597	$175,677	$ 95,920	2.667
Disability Payments	920	600	320	.009
Taxes—Payroll	8,510	5,550	2,960	.082
Insurance—Compensation	506	330	176	.005
Employee Benefits	3,588	2,340	1,248	.035
Supplies from Stores	200	200	—	—
Other Purchased Supplies	500	500	—	—
Office Supplies	7,500	7,500	—	—
Postage	50	50	—	—
Photos and Prints	1,500	1,500	—	—
Freight-In	68,000		68,000	1.890
Dues Subscriptions	150	150	—	—
Purchased Services	150	150	—	—
Insurance—Other	1,000	1,000	—	—
Travel	18,200	—	18,200	.506
Telephone	30,000	—	30,000	.834
Total Overhead Expenses	412,371	195,547	216,824	6.028
Work Order Charges	500	500	—	—
Allocated Credits	(56,915)	(56,915)	—	—
Total After Debits and Credits	$355,956	$139,132	$216,824	6.028

* Total Direct Labor Used As a Base = $3,597,000.

Exhibit 15-2

CONTROL OF MATERIAL AND DIRECT LABOR

Material and direct labor are controlled in the factory by comparing actual cost with standard costs. In addition to this conventional method, the sales division, through its interest in transfer prices, utilizes a secondary control by analyzing the material and labor in the cost of transfers to them. Each product's income statement actually applies to a homogeneous group of products. It follows that the percentage relationship of material and labor in the cost of sales to sales is watched closely. The significance of material and labor as direct costs in the product, and the effect on the

DEPARTMENT A BUDGET
ANNUAL BASIS

Direct Labor Levels

	$2,100,000	$2,400,000	$2,700,000	$3,000,000	$3,300,000	$3,600,000	$3,900,000	$4,200,000	$4,500,000
Salaries and Overtime	231,684	239,685	247,686	255,687 *	263,688	271,689	279,690	287,691	295,692
Disability Payments	789	816	843	870	897	924	951	978	1,005
Taxes—Payroll	7,272	7,518	7,764	8,010	8,256	8,502	8,748	8,994	9,240
Insurance—Compensation	435	450	465	480	495	510	525	540	555
Employee Benefits	3,075	3,180	3,285	3,390	3,495	3,600	3,705	3,810	3,915
Supplies from Stores	200	200	200	200	200	200	200	200	200
Other Purchased Supplies	500	500	500	500	500	500	500	500	500
Office Supplies	7,500	7,500	7,500	7,500	7,500	7,500	7,500	7,500	7,500
Postage	50	50	50	50	50	50	50	50	50
Photos and Prints	1,500	1,500	1,500	1,500	1,500	1,500	1,500	1,500	1,500
Freight-In	39,690	45,360	51,030	56,700	62,370	68,040	73,710	79,380	85,050
Dues Subscriptions	150	150	150	150	150	150	150	150	150
Purchased Services	150	150	150	150	150	150	150	150	150
Insurance—Other	1,000	1,000	1,000	1,000	1,000	1,000	1,000	1,000	1,000
Travel	10,626	12,144	13,662	15,180	16,698	18,216	19,734	21,252	22,770
Telephone	17,514	20,016	22,518	25,020	27,522	30,024	32,526	35,028	37,530
Total O/H Expenses	322,135	340,219	358,303	376,387	394,471	412,555	430,639	448,723	466,807
Work Order Charges	500	500	500	500	500	500	500	500	500
Allocated Credits	(56,915)	(56,915)	(56,915)	(56,915)	(56,915)	(56,915)	(56,915)	(56,915)	(56,915)
Total After Debits and Credits	$ 265,720	$ 283,804	$ 301,888	$ 319,972	$ 338,056	$ 356,140	$ 374,224	$ 392,308	$ 410,392
Overhead Rate	12.7%	11.8%	11.2%	10.7%	10.2%	9.9%	9.6%	9.3%	9.1%

*Calculation Per Formula in Exhibit 15-2
$3,000,000 × 2.667% (Variable) + $175,677 (Fixed) = $255,687

Exhibit 15-3

DEPARTMENT A BUDGET
AT VARIOUS DIRECT LABOR LEVELS
FOUR-WEEK PERIOD

Direct Labor Levels

	$200,000	$225,000	$250,000	$275,000	$300,000	$325,000	$350,000	$375,000	$400,000	$425,000	$450,000	$475,000
Salaries and Overtime	19,388	20,055	20,722	21,389	22,056 *	22,722	23,389	24,055	24,721	25,388	26,054	26,721
Disability Payments	65	68	71	73	75	77	80	82	84	86	89	91
Taxes—Payroll	608	628	649	669	690	710	731	751	772	792	813	833
Insurance—Compensation	36	37	38	39	40	41	43	44	45	46	48	49
Employee Benefits	257	265	274	283	291	301	309	318	327	335	344	353
Supplies from Stores	16	16	16	16	16	16	16	16	16	16	16	16
Other Purchased Supplies	40	40	40	40	40	40	40	40	40	40	40	40
Office Supplies	600	600	600	600	600	600	600	600	600	600	600	600
Postage	4	4	4	4	4	4	4	4	4	4	4	4
Photos and Prints	120	120	120	120	120	120	120	120	120	120	120	120
Freight—In	3,780	4,253	4,725	5,198	5,670	6,143	6,615	7,088	7,560	8,033	8,505	8,976
Dues Subscriptions	12	12	12	12	12	12	12	12	12	12	12	12
Purchased Services	12	12	12	12	12	12	12	12	12	12	12	12
Insurance—Other	80	80	80	80	80	80	80	80	80	80	80	80
Travel	1,012	1,139	1,265	1,392	1,518	1,645	1,771	1,898	2,024	2,151	2,277	2,404
Telephone	1,568	1,877	2,085	2,294	2,502	2,711	2,919	3,128	3,336	3,545	3,753	3,962
Total O/H Expenses	27,699	29,206	30,713	32,221	33,726	35,234	36,741	38,248	39,753	41,260	42,767	44,273
Work Order Charges	40	40	40	40	40	40	40	40	40	40	40	40
Allocated Credits	(4,552)	(4,552)	(4,552)	(4,552)	(4,552)	(4,552)	(4,552)	(4,552)	(4,552)	(4,552)	(4,552)	(4,552)
Total After Debits and Credits	$ 23,187	$ 24,694	$ 26,201	$ 27,709	$ 29,214	$ 30,722	$ 32,229	$ 33,736	$ 35,241	$ 36,748	$ 38,255	$ 39,761

*Calculation Per Formula in Exhibit 15-2
$300,000 × 2.667% (Variable) + 4/50 of $175,677 (Fixed) = $22,056

Exhibit 15-4

profit for which each product manager is responsible, raise questions which should result in cost-saving changes in design. This is particularly significant because the sales division frequently initiates requests for changes in design. The sales group, being fully aware of customer desires, works closely with the engineering group.

THE SALES DIVISION—SEPARATING FIXED AND VARIABLE COSTS

Fixed and variable costs in the sales division are separated in a manner similar to that followed in manufacturing—the major difference being that the level of activity is based on sales rather than direct labor. Cost of sales, discounts, royalties, freight out, commissions, service expense, and interest on investment are considered completely variable. Most of the remaining cost is considered fixed. Where certain costs such as advertising, for example, are partly variable and partly fixed, the formula takes both into account.

Exhibit 15-5 shows the total annual cost for all items which appear in the income statement. As in manufacturing, it also lists the fixed costs, the variable costs and the variable as a percentage of total sales for the year. The breakeven sales volume is shown on the last line of this exhibit.

Exhibit 15-6 shows the income statement for levels of sales at intervals of $500,000 ranging from $11.5 million per year to $16 million. It illustrates through a columnar profit-and-loss spread the effect of volume on profits.

Exhibit 15-7 also shows the profit-and-loss spread for the various volumes of sales on a four-week-period basis. Thus, as each month's profit-and-loss results become available, the product manager will consult the appropriate sales level column in *Exhibit 15-7* and compare the allowable costs with the actual.

DETERMINATION OF THE OVERHEAD RATE

With the fixed and variable formula now determined, we are ready for the final step in development of the budget—the determination of the overhead rate to be used in valuing inventories and preparing cost estimates for bidding.

The first step is to determine the level of activity at which the overhead rate will be calculated. To see how the proper level of activity upon which to base an overhead rate is determined, let us assume that the investment in inventories (exclusive of valuation reserves) and the original cost of manufacturing fixed assets is as follows:

Inventories	$12,000,000
Mfg. Fixed Assets	3,000,000
Total	$15,000,000

This type of investment is considered controllable because inventories are directly determined by the factory and sales departments. At the same time, the manufacturing fixed assets are controllable, in the sense that the better the utilization of equipment, the lower the investment.

	Total	Fixed	Variable	Variable % of Sales
Gross Sales	$15,377,000	$ —	$ —	—
Less Discounts	74,000	—	74,000	.48%
Less Royalties	176,000	—	176,000	1.14
Less Allowances	89,000	—	89,000	.58
Net Sales	15,038,000	—	—	—
Cost of Sales	11,735,000	—	11,735,000	76.31
Gross Operating Profit	3,303,000	—	—	—
Selling Expense	980,000	980,000	—	—
Service Expense	220,000	—	220,000	1.43
Warehouse Expense	144,000	144,000	—	—
Advertising	881,000	496,576	384,425	2.50
Commissions	52,000	—	52,000	.34
Bad Debts	74,000	—	74,000	.48
Engineering and Product Design	212,000	212,000	—	—
Total Expense	2,563,000	1,832,575	730,425	4.75
Division Profit or Loss	740,000	—	—	—
Interest on Investment	264,000	264,000	—	—
Company Profit or Loss	476,000	—	—	—
Total Cost	$14,901,000	$2,096,575	$12,804,425	83.26%

Breakeven Sales = $2,096,575 divided by (100.00% — 83.26%) = $12,524,000

Exhibit 15-5

Exhibit 15-8 illustrates how the controllable investment is converted to equivalent annual sales at various levels—the sales levels being determined by the number of turns of investment from 2.2 to 3.0 turns per year. The range stops at 3.0 turns because it was assumed that additional fixed assets would be needed to go beyond this point. Using the first column as an example, if $15 million in investment is turned over 2.2 times, the resulting annual sales figure is $33 million. Direct labor, which is the base for calculating the overhead rate, is taken to be 10 per cent of sales—the same mix of sales being assumed at all levels. Fixed costs were determined elsewhere to be $1,850,000 per year while variable costs were determined to be 70 percent of direct labor.

With the variable portion of the overhead rate determined to be 70 percent, the next step is to calculate the fixed portion. (This rate is calculated separately because it

PRODUCT E BUDGET

AT VARIOUS SALES LEVELS

ANNUAL BASIS

	$11,500,000	$12,000,000	$12,500,000	$13,000,000	$13,500,000	$14,000,000	$14,500,000	$15,000,000	$15,500,000	$16,000,000
Gross Sales	$11,500,000	$12,000,000	$12,500,000	$13,000,000	$13,500,000	$14,000,000	$14,500,000	$15,000,000	$15,500,000	$16,000,000
Less Discounts	55,200	57,600	60,000	62,400	64,700	67,100	69,500	71,900	74,400	76,800
Less Royalties	131,500	137,300	142,900	148,700	154,400	160,200	165,900	171,600	177,300	183,000
Less Allowances	66,300	69,100	72,100	74,900	77,900	80,700	82,600	86,500	89,300	92,200
Net Sales	11,247,000	11,736,000	12,225,000	12,714,000	13,203,000	13,692,000	14,182,000	14,670,000	15,159,000	15,648,000
Cost of Sales	8,775,650	9,157,200	9,538,750	9,920,300	10,301,850	10,683,400	11,064,950	11,446,400	11,827,950	12,209,500
Gross Operating Profit	2,471,350	2,578,800	2,686,250	2,793,700	2,901,150	3,008,600	3,117,050	3,223,600	3,331,050	3,438,500
Selling Expense	980,000	980,000	980,000	980,000	980,000	980,000	980,000	980,000	980,000	980,000
Service Expense	164,500	171,600	178,700	185,900	193,000	200,200	207,350	214,500	221,650	228,800
Warehouse Expense	144,000	144,000	144,000	144,000	144,000	144,000	144,000	144,000	144,000	144,000
Advertising	784,076	796,576 *	809,076	821,576	834,076	846,576	859,076	871,576	884,076	896,576
Commissions	38,870	40,560	42,250	43,940	45,630	47,320	49,010	50,700	52,390	54,080
Freight-Out (Not Applicable)										
Bad Debts	55,200	57,600	60,000	62,400	64,800	67,200	69,600	72,000	74,400	76,800
Engineering and Product Design	212,000	212,000	212,000	212,000	212,000	212,000	212,000	212,000	212,000	212,000
Total Expense	2,378,646	2,402,336	2,426,026	2,449,816	2,473,506	2,497,296	2,521,036	2,544,776	2,568,516	2,592,256
Division Profit or Loss	92,704	176,464	260,224	343,884	427,644	511,304	596,014	678,824	762,534	846,244
Interest on Investment	264,000	264,000	264,000	264,000	264,000	264,000	264,000	264,000	264,000	264,000
Company Profit or Loss	$ (171,294)	$ (87,536)	$ (3,776)	$ 79,884	$ 163,644	$ 247,304	$ 332,014	$ 414,824	$ 498,534	$ 582,244

*Calculation Per Formula in Exhibit 15-5

$12,000,000 × 2.50% (Variable) Plus $496,576 (Fixed) = $796,576

Exhibit 15-6

PRODUCT E BUDGET
AT VARIOUS SALES LEVELS
FOUR-WEEK PERIOD

	$600,000	$800,000	$1,000,000	$1,200,000	$1,400,000	$1,600,000	$1,800,000	$2,000,000	$2,200,000	$2,400,000
Gross Sales	$600,000	$800,000	$1,000,000	$1,200,000	$1,400,000	$1,600,000	$1,800,000	$2,000,000	$2,200,000	$2,400,000
Less Discounts	2,300	3,840	4,800	5,760	6,720	7,680	8,640	9,600	10,560	11,520
Less Royalties	6,340	9,120	11,400	13,680	15,960	18,240	20,520	22,800	25,080	27,360
Less Allowances	3,480	4,640	5,800	6,960	8,120	9,280	10,440	11,600	12,760	13,920
Net Sales	586,800	782,400	978,000	1,173,600	1,369,200	1,564,800	1,760,400	1,956,000	2,151,600	2,347,200
Cost of Sales	457,860	610,480	763,100	915,720	1,068,340	1,220,960	1,373,580	1,526,200	1,678,820	1,831,440
Gross Operating Profit	128,940	171,920	214,900	257,880	300,860	343,840	386,820	429,800	472,780	515,760
Selling Expense	78,600	78,600	78,600	78,600	78,600	78,600	78,600	78,600	78,600	78,600
Service Expense	6,840	9,120	11,400	13,680	15,960	18,240	20,520	22,800	25,080	27,360
Warehouse Expense	11,520	11,520	11,520	11,520	11,520	11,520	11,520	11,520	11,520	11,520
Advertising	54,724	59,724 *	64,724	69,724	74,724	79,724	84,724	89,724	94,724	99,724
Commissions	2,028	2,704	3,380	4,056	4,732	5,408	6,084	6,760	7,436	8,112
Bad Debts	2,886	3,848	4,810	5,772	6,734	7,696	8,658	9,620	10,582	11,544
Engineering and Product Design	16,980	16,980	16,980	16,980	16,980	16,980	16,980	16,980	16,980	16,980
Total Expense	175,578	182,496	191,414	200,332	209,250	218,168	227,086	236,004	244,922	253,840
Division Profit or Loss	(44,638)	(10,576)	23,486	57,548	91,610	125,672	159,734	193,796	227,858	261,920
Interest on Investment	21,120	21,120	21,120	21,120	21,120	21,120	21,120	21,120	21,120	21,120
Company Profit or Loss	$(65,758)	$(31,696)	$ 2,366	$ 36,428	$ 70,490	$104,552	$138,614	$172,676	$206,738	$240,800

*Calculation Per Formula in Exhibit 15-5

$800,000 × 2.50% (Variable) Plus 4/50 of $496,576 = $59,724

Exhibit 15-7

281

CALCULATIONS OF OVERHEAD RATES AT SEVERAL LEVELS OF ACTIVITY

Investment Turns Per Year	2.2	2.4	2.6	2.8	3.0
Sales Volume Based on Above	$33,000,000	$36,000,000	$39,000,000	$42,000,000	$45,000,000
Labor Content—10%	3,300,000	3,600,000	3,900,000	4,200,000	4,500,000
Overhead Cost					
Fixed Cost	1,850,000	1,850,000	1,850,000	1,850,000	1,850,000
Variable Cost	2,310,000	2,520,000	2,730,000	2,940,000	3,150,000
Total	4,160,000	4,370,000	4,580,000	4,790,000	5,000,000
Overhead Rate					
Fixed	56%	51%	47%	44%	41%
Variable	70	70	70	70	70
Total	126%	121%	117%	114%	111%

Exhibit 15-8

is used to spread over- and under-absorbed overhead to the various products.) The fixed overhead rate is calculated by dividing the direct labor for each level into the fixed cost of $1,850,000. In the example, *Exhibit 15-8*, the overhead rate ranges from 111 percent to 126 percent. The controller of one company that adopted this system found that the particular product under review was earning a profit on sales of 9 percent, which was considered to be satisfactory. Anything over this amount would invite competition. As a result, the markup factor in pricing was frozen at a point which would realize 9 percent profit on sales, with a volume of sales set at a level which would result in a return on investment of 25 percent.

The determination of the necessary sales volume is simply a matter of mathematics, since 25 percent divided by 9 percent equals 2.8. This means that the investment of $15 million must be turned 2.8 times per year, requiring a sales volume of $42 million.

CONCLUSIONS

Budgeting for the year in total and presenting the annualized budget to management for its approval will substantially cut the time required for preparation.

The preparation of separate income statements for manufacturing and for sales has the effect of setting up each group as if it were in business for itself. Where excess manufacturing costs previously were buried in cost-of-sales figures in a composite statement, the sales group can now scrutinize the transfer prices readily. In the past, the sales department might have been tempted to sell merely to increase volume, without regard to the profitability of the items or size of the resulting production run. Now it would make certain that the items that are sold will have sufficient margin to realize an adequate return. Likewise, the sales department realizes that the factory must be kept loaded with optimum production runs in order to keep transfer prices competitive.

The manufacturing manager would also become conscious of performance because he realizes that his results will be clearly spelled out in a separate statement. It is true that standards and variances from standard accomplish the same type of control and constitute an important analysis function in the controller's department. But being responsible for results on an income statement which is scrutinized not only by the officers of the company but by the board of directors as well, creates an aura of responsibility not readily attainable through reporting by conventional methods.

The procedures outlined here can be applied to almost any corporate structure manufacturing and selling a commercial product. Many companies have sales organizations which cross product lines—thus diffusing the profit-and-loss responsibility to an even greater extent than when a sales organization exists for each individual product.

The keystone to success of any type of control is management follow-up. Inasmuch as the income statement is a key focal point of any management control, the extent to which responsibility can be assigned for profit-and-loss results will determine the measure of control exercised over each major segment of the organization.

> Without profit responsibility the sales department might be tempted to sell merely to increase volume, without regard to the profitability of the items sold or the size of the resulting production runs.

16

Highlighting Critical Financial Data Reporting Through Proper Use of Graphs

Graphs are highly useful in converting masses of numerical data into pictorial presentations. However, improperly prepared graphs can be deceptive.

Because of the magnitude of statistical information presented to management each day, it frequently becomes difficult to discern meaningful trends from pure numbers alone. This is where use of graphs comes into play. By converting figures into a pictorial presentation, it is possible to more readily see trends at a glance. The addition of each bit of new information immediately places it in its proper perspective in relation to the data of preceding periods.

However, like any statistical device, graphs must be carefully prepared in order to avoid distortions and unintentional deceptions. This chapter will discuss the common errors that are made in the preparation of graphs and it will describe several types which can be used for more effective management control.

HOW GRAPHS CAN BE DECEPTIVE

Distortions occur most frequently through incorrect use of scales. This also includes the use of natural scale paper when semi-log paper should be used. Exhibit 16-1, which compares the backlog for research and development contracts with production contracts, is illustrative of the *incorrect use of scales*.

Since research and development work usually leads to production work, the graph showing the sharp upward trend of reasearch would indicate that one need not be too

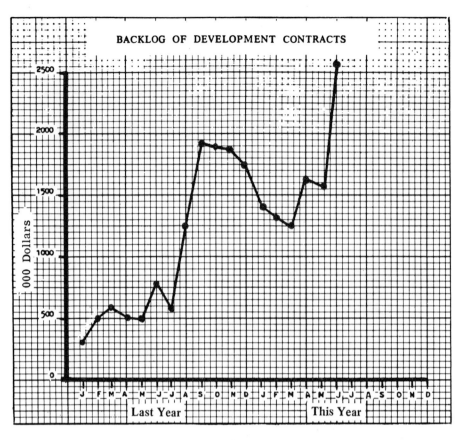

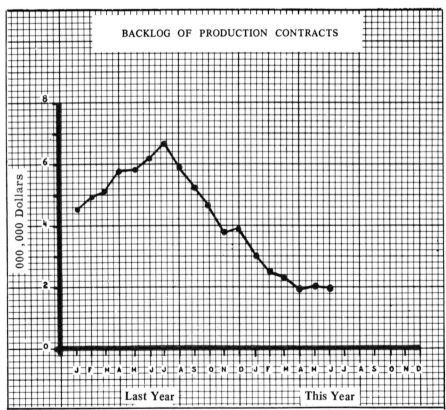

Exhibit 16-1

concerned about the current downtrend of production orders. However, in reviewing Exhibit 16-2, which combines the research effort and production on a single common scale, the relationship is quite different.

Here one sees that the downtrending production contracts actually are a much more substantial portion of the total business effort and that research and development contracts, though trending upward sharply, are not as dominant in the picture as would be indicated by the separately drawn graphs. It is important, when comparing two series of data, to look at them in their proper relationship to each other.

Exhibits 16-3 and 16-4, which compare sales with selling expenses, depict a case where two items of quite different magnitudes can be better presented on semi-logarithmic paper. Note that these items plotted on natural scale paper indicate that selling expenses are moving upward imperceptibly while sales are moving upward in a sharp uptrend. By studying this graph one would not become too concerned. However, in plotting these data on semi-log paper, as in Exhibit 16-4, it becomes apparent that selling expenses are rising at a much faster rate than sales.

Semi-log paper is designed to show relative changes rather than absolute changes. This is accomplished through use of a scale which decreases in size in such fashion that the distance between 2 and 3 is the same as 20 and 30, 200 and 300, 2,000,000 and 3,000,000. This type of scale is also useful when looking at a series of figures which increases or decreases sharply. Exhibit 16-5, which depicts the trend of the stock market in the 1920's is a good example. Note that the line for 50 industrials moves from an area of 140 to approximately 370. A 10% increase when the stock is 140 results in a movement of 14 points. When the stock is at 370, a 10% increase would mean a movement of 37 points. On natural scale paper, therefore, a 10% increase at 370 would show up as being more than twice as great as a 10% increase at the 140 level. Semi-log paper would show the same increase at both 140 and 370.

IMPROPER SELECTION OF SCALES

A well-known newspaper, seeking to get across to its readers the message that the bond market was being hurt by inflation, published the four graphs shown across the upper half of Exhibit 16-6.

The horizontal scales show each of the first five years in total and the sixth year by months. The vertical scales show the interest rates which range from 3.5% to 12%. The graphs were intended to show the comparative interest rates of the various offerings.

In scanning these graphs, one would conclude that the interest on utility bonds is the highest of the four, with treasury bills next and federal funds third.

Upon closer examination of the scales, it becomes evident that federal funds are at 12%, making them the highest; utility bonds at 9.5% are second. This is quite a different picture.

The message intended by the graphs that were published in this newspaper does not come across correctly because of improper selection of scales. When redrawn properly, as shown in the lower half of the exhibit, on scales that are consistent for all four graphs, it becomes evident that interest on federal funds is the highest, utility bonds second, conventional mortgages third and treasury bills fourth.

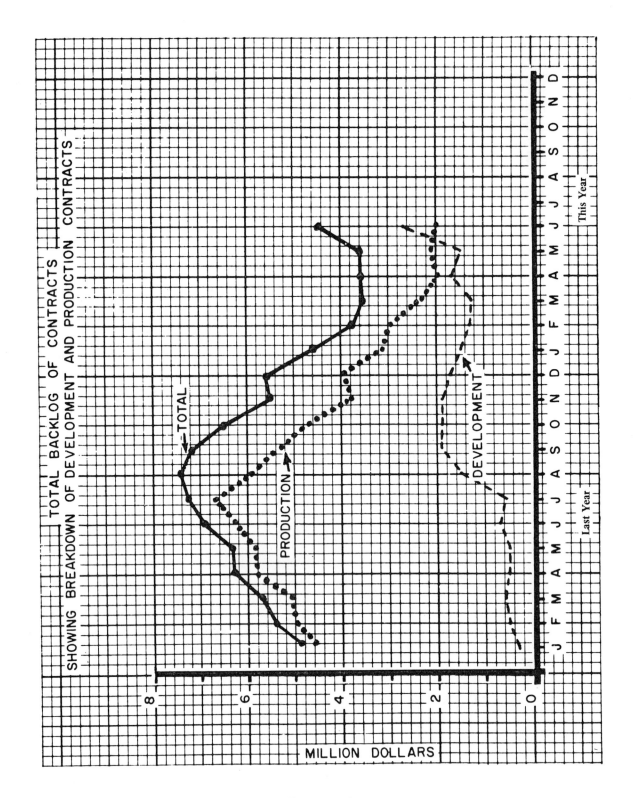

Exhibit 16-2

288

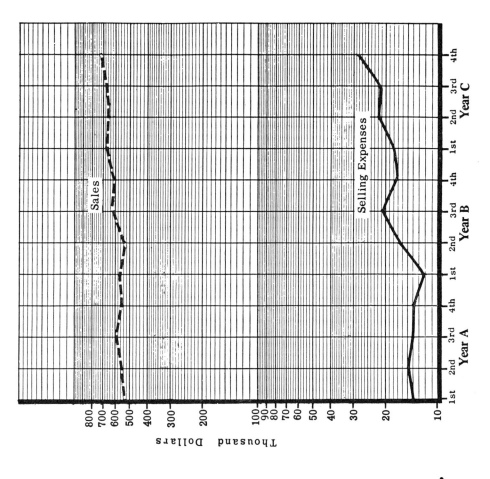

COMPARISON OF SALES WITH SELLING EXPENSES

(Semi-log Scale)

Exhibit 16-4

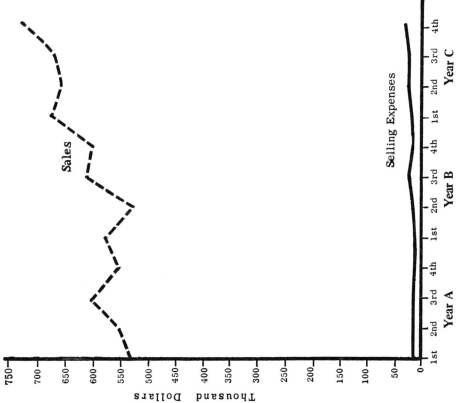

COMPARISON OF SALES WITH SELLING EXPENSES

(Natural Scale)

Exhibit 16-3

Stock Market in the 1920's

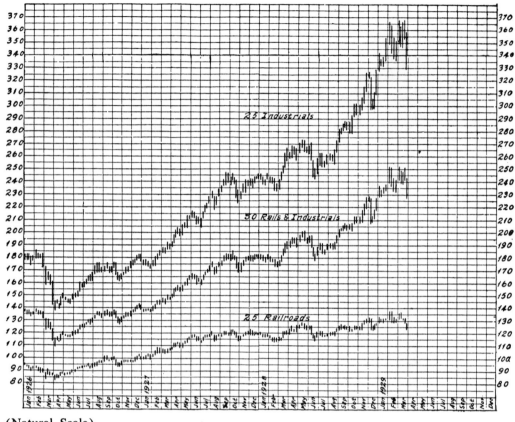

(Natural Scale)

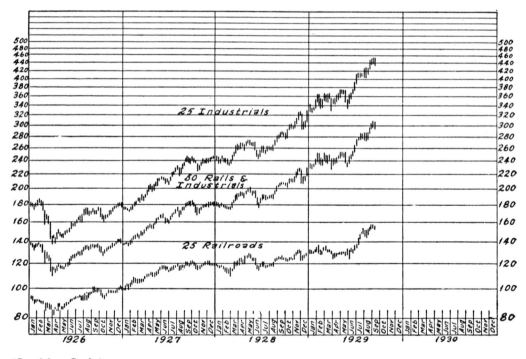

(Semi-log Scale)

Reprinted by permission of *Forbes, Magazine of Business & Finance*

Exhibit 16-5

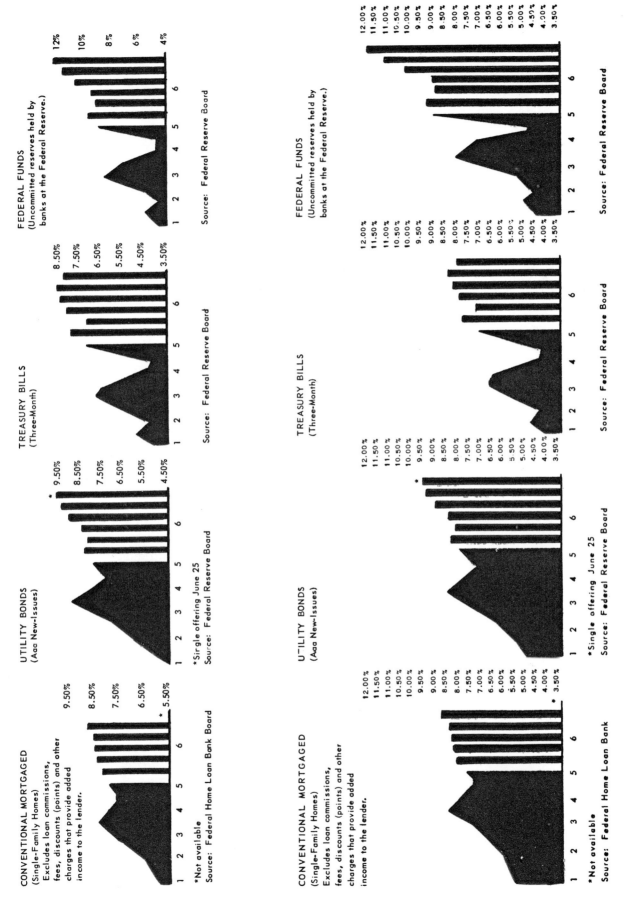

Exhibit 16-6

Pictorial means of presenting data are intended to make it easier for the reader to make fast comparisons. If scales are not properly drawn, the reader can be misled. It would be better not to present material graphically if the proper effort is not taken to present the information in proper perspective.

WATCHING THE TREND OF ORDERS AND BACKLOG

With competition as fierce as it is, modern industry must constantly have its finger on the pulse of customer requirements. A clue to these requirements is available through a study of the trend of new orders. The company which can move quickly and ship these orders promptly is the company which will be remembered by the customer when subsequent new orders are placed. Utilization of this technique for customer good will is equivalent to having an invisible sales force. Many companies prepare a daily or weekly report showing the new orders received, shipments, and the resulting backlog. The backlog is a residue figure which can be used for an indicator as to whether incoming orders are on the increase or decrease. Exhibit 16-7 illustrates such a report. A new week is added to the preceding weeks so that prior reports need not be filed or consulted. Exhibit 16-8 plots the figures contained in Exhibit 16-7 to show pictorially the trend of new orders as reflected in the backlog. The graph could be used to the exclusion of the statistical report where the emphasis is on watching trends. Natural scales are used because absolute values are important in measuring new orders, shipments and the resulting backlog balance.

INVENTORY CONTROL

The acquisition of capital equipment is usually controlled at time of purchase through justification of the expenditure. Once purchased, there is little control which can be exercised except through proper maintenance and optimum utilization. Inventories, on the other hand, are a perishable commodity, subject to rapid obsolescence because of advances being made in many industries. Exhibit 16-9 shows how inventories can be monitored through comparison with budgeted allowances. Sales are also included in the graph with a forecasted amount. If sales should fall below their forecasted volume or increase above the forecast, use of semi-log paper will facilitate comparison of rate of increase or decrease with rate of increase or decrease of sales.

MANUFACTURING COSTS AND PRODUCTIVITY

Exhibit 16-10 demonstrates how unit costs can be monitored through graphic presentation of key figures. The top portion of the exhibit shows the number of units produced per day while the middle section shows the percentage of the units which were scrapped. Bench scrap indicates parts and partial units which were scrapped while the larger scrap figure indicates finished units scrapped. The lower portion shows the breakdown of the actual material, labor and overhead per unit. Note the correlation between volume of production, scrap, and cost per unit. As volume drops, the percentage of scrap moves up and the cost per unit increases. The reverse is also true.

ORDER INTAKE VERSUS SHIPMENTS AND BACKLOG

Weeks	New Orders	Shipments	Backlog
1	$26,310	$11,415	$120,065
2	15,960	16,205	119,820
3	12,100	12,402	119,518
4	12,350	12,075	119,793
5	21,100	10,779	130,714
6	13,965	11,905	132,774
7	17,014	9,642	140,146
8	22,212	18,060	144,298
9	16,126	13,782	146,642
10	17,130	18,392	145,380
11	21,324	23,062	143,642
12	19,134	26,436	136,340
13	16,031	37,345	115,026
14	11,213	13,619	112,620
15	11,962	19,947	104,635
16	13,402	14,696	103,341
17	12,111	13,390	102,062
18	10,320	12,165	100,217
19	10,721	20,736	90,202
20	11,420	23,580	78,042
21	11,306	15,046	74,302
22	11,904	13,225	72,981
23	13,416	17,731	68,666
24	13,333	15,738	66,261
25	12,620	14,781	64,100
26	11,220	12,270	63,050
27	11,350	12,300	62,100
28	11,441	11,561	61,980
29	16,688	15,643	63,025
30	15,843	14,878	63,990
31	14,400	14,328	64,062
32	13,926	15,946	62,042
33	14,667	13,062	63,647
34	16,660	16,591	63,716
35	18,899	18,417	64,198
36	25,554	14,360	75,392
37	20,002	18,349	77,045
38	18,309	14,738	80,616
39	14,445	14,023	81,038
40	13,212	12,053	82,197
41	13,196	12,057	83,336
42	11,778	16,198	78,916
43	11,662	10,470	80,108
44	15,925	18,261	77,772
45	20,669	27,403	71,038
46	12,210	13,031	70,217
47	13,312	18,030	65,499
48	14,121	18,503	61,117
49	14,365	17,426	58,061
50	20,259	30,103	48,217

Exhibit 16-7

The month of January (this year) represents a period in which two plants manufacturing a similar product were merged under the same roof. Note how the percentage of scrap has increased from a low of 12% in January to a high of over 28% in June (this year). The month of July (this year) shows a substantial improvement wherein scrap was reduced to 17%.

ORDER INTAKE VERSUS SHIPMENTS AND BACKLOG

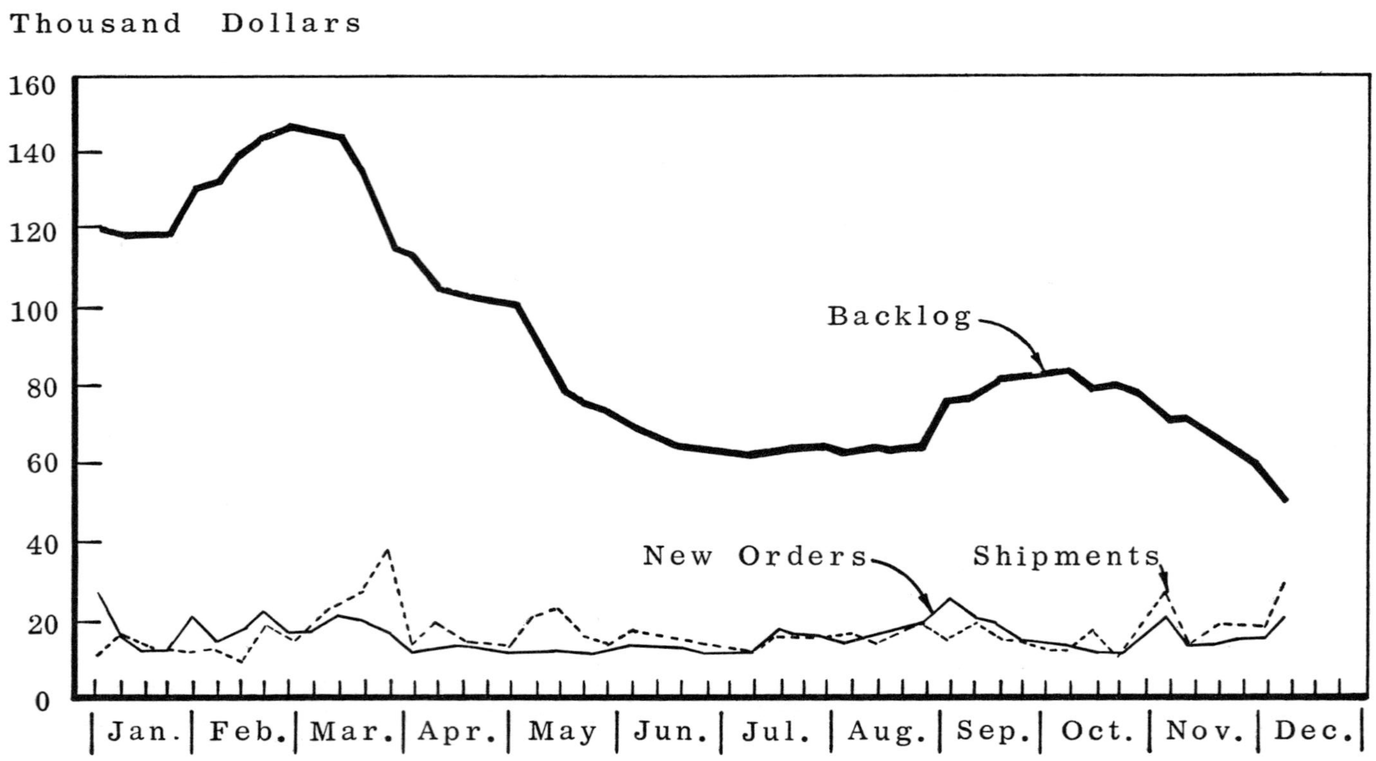

Thousand Dollars

Exhibit 16-8

294

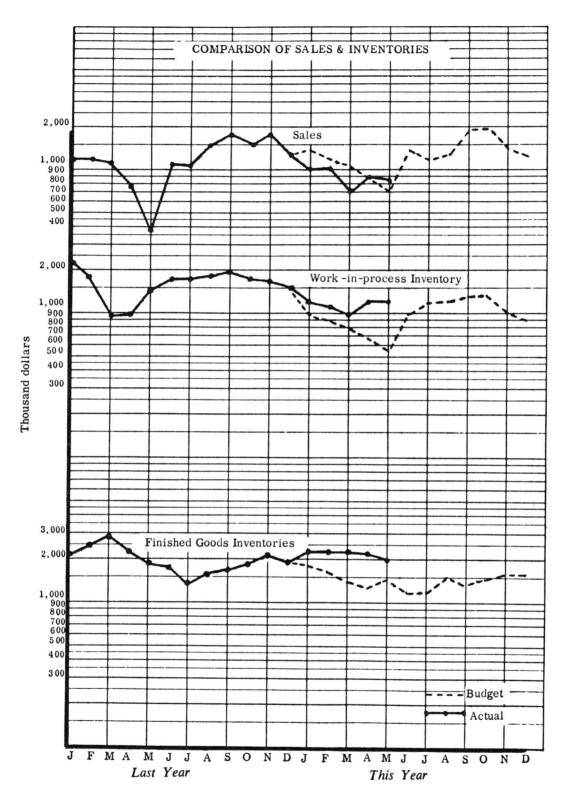

COMPARISON OF SALES & INVENTORIES

Sales

Work-in-process Inventory

Finished Goods Inventories

- - - - Budget

Actual

J F M A M J J A S O N D J F M A M J J A S O N D

Last Year   *This Year*

Exhibit 16-9

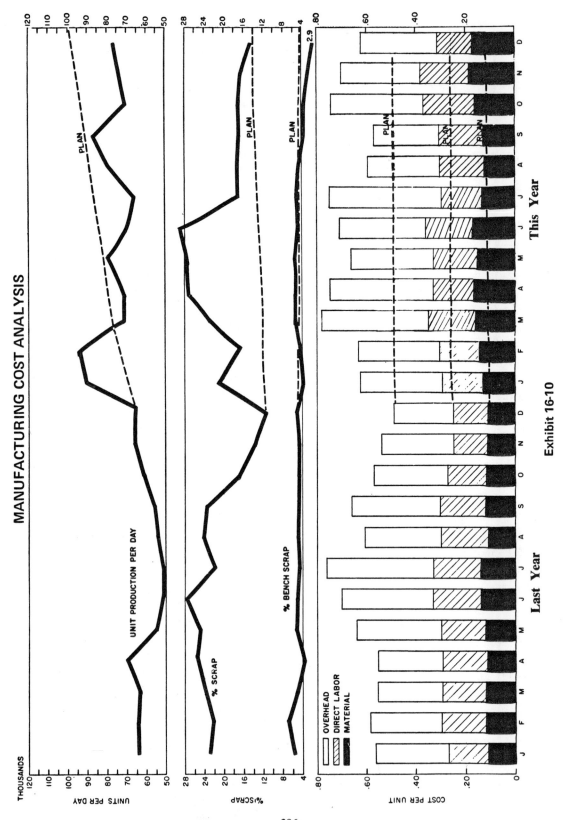

MANUFACTURING COST ANALYSIS

Exhibit 16-10

296

Cost per unit is still high in that month, however, because production per day is low. Note in the months of August and September (this year), when volume of production increased, that unit costs dropped to the lowest amount for the year. When volume dropped again in the following month, unit costs increased. By studying such relationships as portrayed in this graph over a period of time, one can make observations and form relationships which will be useful in predicting future trends—information which is not readily discernible in raw statistics. The dotted lines labeled "plan" indicate the planned goals for the end of the year.

Exhibit 16-11 shows the production per day in the upper portion. This is the same series of figures as used in the top part of Exhibit 16-10. The middle section shows the production per day per direct labor employee and per total employee. These two lines serve as a rough measure of productivity. The bar charts in the lower third show the relative numbers of direct labor employees, indirect labor employees in production departments and indirect labor employees in service departments (referred to as overhead labor). Note how the latter group has been reduced since the consolidation of the two plants in January of this year.

Note the tendency for productivity per employee to decline with a reduction in volume. Since the productivity per direct labor employee has fallen off more sharply than productivity per total employee during the first seven months of this year, this could indicate that the direct labor was not under as complete control as the indirect.

Frequently one will find that formal measures of productivity are lacking when most needed—as in instances when a new product has been added or after consolidation of two activities. During this transitional period, management cannot sit and wait for the development of precise measures—it needs some rough measure to use as a guide during the interim period. Exhibits 16-10 and 16-11 are intended to serve this purpose.

USE OF GRAPHS TO DRAMATIZE NEED FOR ACTION

Management personnel, being human, are not always alert to rapid changes in events. Sometimes an unfavorable situation must be dramatized in order to receive action. Exhibit 16-12 illustrates an actual situation where the trend of productivity has turned downward. This graph was forwarded to the plant management, but no effective action appeared to be taken. As the downward trend in productivity continued, Exhibit 16-13 was prepared. This contains the productivity data in Exhibit 16-12 plotted together with the productivity date of another plant which had in the preceding year dropped into a bad loss position. The issuance of this graph, which showed parallel trends and which indicated likelihood of a loss situation being duplicated in Plant 1, resulted in prompt action.

CONCLUSION

The need for some means of presenting to management a digest of pertinent information is obvious. Graphic methods play an important part in fulfilling this need.

PRODUCTIVITY ANALYSIS

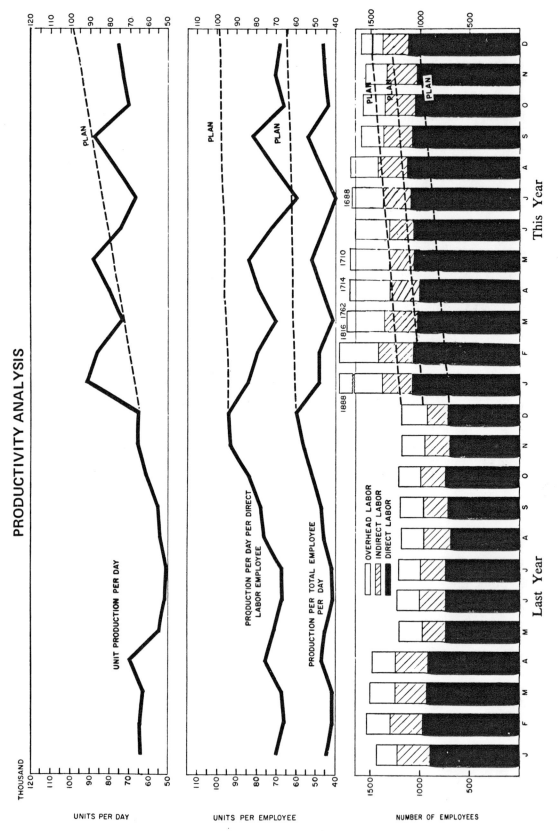

Exhibit 16-11

PLANT I

PRODUCTION
PER DIRECT LABOR HOUR

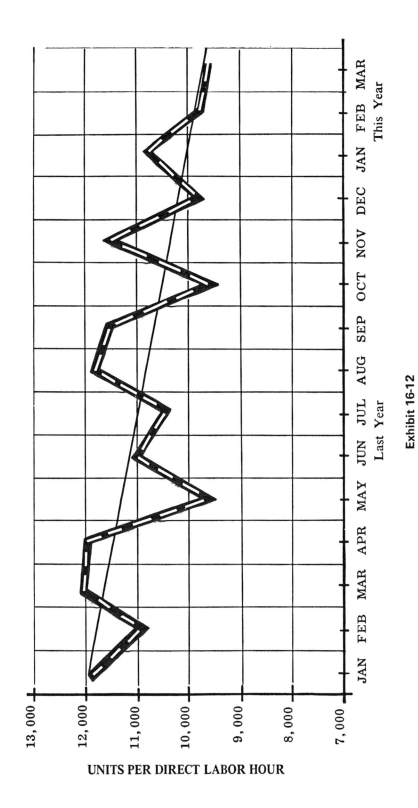

Exhibit 16-12

PRODUCTION PER DIRECT LABOR HOUR

FOR PLANT 1 AND PLANT 2

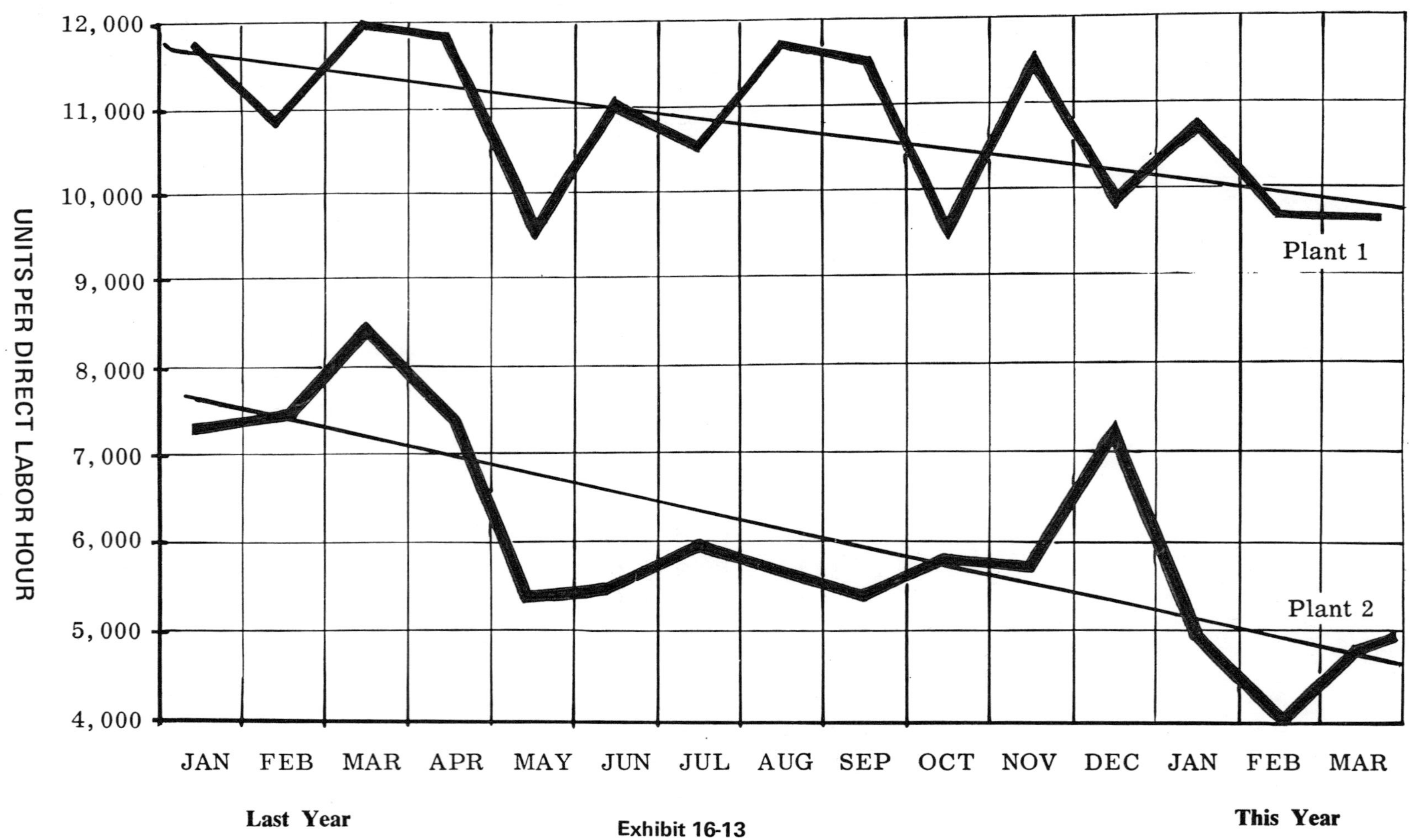

Plant 1

Plant 2

12,000
11,000
10,000
9,000
8,000
7,000
6,000
5,000
4,000

UNITS PER DIRECT LABOR HOUR

JAN FEB MAR APR MAY JUN JUL AUG SEP OCT NOV DEC JAN FEB MAR

Last Year

This Year

Exhibit 16-13

In the use of graphs it is essential that proper scales and the correct type of graph paper be used to avoid deceptive conclusions. Yet, in spite of the importance of correct presentation of data, many managers will rely on clerks who are unskilled in the techniques to make graphic presentations for their review. The use of lettering guides and colored tape frequently lends a touch of professionalism to data which is basically misleading. In the preparation of graphs:

1. Don't try to to compare too many items at one time on a single graph. Use several simple ones rather than a single complex presentation.
2. The graph should tell the story at a glance. If it takes effort and extended study to interpret the message, then the graph has not been properly prepared.
3. Use graphs if you want to dramatize your message. An unfavorable slope downward can appear to be insignificant or it can be made to look like a dangerous downward trend. Choice of scales will make the difference. Exaggerate a bit if you must, in order to get attention, but don't distort the facts.
4. When presenting graphic analyses, don't burden the managers with too many. Select the ones needing immediate attention.

A graph should give the message in a glance. If extended study and effort are required to make the make the analysis, the graph, in all likelihood, has not been properly prepared.

17

The Ten Commandments of
Systematic Cost Control

Based on his experience in the installation of cost controls, the author has found the following "Ten Commandments" to be a useful checklist for evaluating the effectiveness of a cost system:

1. *Control all product costs, not just a segment.* Don't get sidetracked into one favorite area to the exclusion of all others. Don't concentrate all the industrial engineering effort on controlling direct labor when labor represents only 10% of total product cost and material over 50%.

2. *Summarize the major elements of cost first.* The details are important, but restrain the temptation to show how much information is available. Recap the detail so you can show the broad picture. Then follow this up with more information in the specific areas where the need is indicated.

3. *Use graphs for more effective presentation.* Graphs are an excellent means of boiling down raw statistics for determination of trends. Here, again, emphasize the major groupings first—then get to the details as needed.

4. *Know the operation.* Don't use your accounting system like a mathematical formula to grind out answers. Get out on the firing line and investigate the facts behind these answers. Then interpret the reports for your management on the basis of your findings.

5. *Know what's in your overhead.* Find out what the dominant items are. This will not only facilitate proper allocations for determining overhead rates—it will also facilitate better control because you'll know what you're trying to control.

6. *Don't make a big project out of your flexible budget installation.* Don't waste valuable time analyzing reams of historical data and preparing scores of scatter charts. Use current information (with some reference to past history) and talk it over with the people for whom the budget is being prepared. Let them

know what you're trying to accomplish and make them party to the installation. In this way they're more likely to get behind your program and support it, and you'll come up with a far more meaningful budget.

7. *Be on the alert for incorrect overhead rates.* Make certain first that you are using the proper base. Then determine if you have the correct number of overhead recovery points throughout the process to assure that differences in the manufacturing process will be taken into account in applying overhead to the product.

8. *Use realistic rather than ideal standards in your cost system.* Accept some inefficiencies as a normal cost of doing business. If you use ideal standards with no allowances, your variances will be so large they'll lose their analytical value and the managers being measured will lose no time in discrediting the system. Most managers want a tight task to work toward, but they can't cope with the impossible.

9. *If you use direct costing, use it sensibly.* Make sure you don't get yourself trapped by incorrect pricing procedures. Be careful of lump-sum period cost allocations in developing a product line profit-and-loss statement.

10. *Don't expect the customer to pay for an inefficient operation.* Bear in mind that normal competitive pricing is based on reasonably efficient operations and optimum utilization of equipment. Develop your pricing procedures along these lines and you'll have a better chance when quoting on a new product, because you'll know better where you stand.

If these "Ten Commandments" are used as a frame of reference, they will aid immeasurably in providing realistic controls—and increased profits as a natural byproduct.

INDEX